Herbert Zoglowek,
Maria Aleksandrovich (Eds.)

Psychological and Pedagogical
Aspects of Motivation

Psychological and Pedagogical Aspects of Motivation

edited by

Herbert Zoglowek
and
Maria Aleksandrovich

LIT

Publication was prepared under the financial support of
Finnmark University College, Alta, Norway
and Pomeranian University, Słupsk, Poland

Scientific reviewer: Richard Young EdD, Professor,
Counselling Psychology

This book is printed on acid-free paper.

Bibliographic information published by the Deutsche Nationalbibliothek
The Deutsche Nationalbibliothek lists this publication in the Deutsche
Nationalbibliografie; detailed bibliographic data are available in the Internet at
http://dnb.d-nb.de.

ISBN 978-3-643-90401-0

A catalogue record for this book is available from the British Library

©LIT VERLAG GmbH & Co. KG Wien,
Zweigniederlassung Zürich 2013
Klosbachstr. 107
CH-8032 Zürich
Tel. +41 (0) 44-251 75 05
Fax +41 (0) 44-251 75 06
E-Mail: zuerich@lit-verlag.ch
http://www.lit-verlag.ch

LIT VERLAG Dr. W. Hopf
Berlin 2013
Fresnostr. 2
D-48159 Münster
Tel. +49 (0) 2 51-62 03 20
Fax +49 (0) 2 51-23 19 72
E-Mail: lit@lit-verlag.de
http://www.lit-verlag.de

Distribution:
In Germany: LIT Verlag Fresnostr. 2, D-48159 Münster
Tel. +49 (0) 2 51-620 32 22, Fax +49 (0) 2 51-922 60 99, E-mail: vertrieb@lit-verlag.de

In Austria: Medienlogistik Pichler-ÖBZ, e-mail: mlo@medien-logistik.at
In Switzerland: B + M Buch- und Medienvertrieb, e-mail: order@buch-medien.ch
In the UK: Global Book Marketing, e-mail: mo@centralbooks.com
In North America: International Specialized Book Services, e-mail: orders@isbs.com
e-books are available at www.litwebshop.de

CONTENT

Motivation is central to our experience as humans, that is, to our actions. It is predominantly concerned with the formation of the goals and intentions that are the basis for human action, that is, what we, as people, desire. We know from our own experience that we interpret human action from the perspectives of its meaning or goals and also its motivation. We assume a naïve theory that suggests little would be accomplished in life without personal motivation and the motivation that is engendered between people. Indeed, as a number of the chapters in this book suggest, the realization of a goal is indicative of the person's motivation.

The centrality of motivation in human experience is manifest by the fact that motivation is a term in common parlance. It is seen by lay people as critical to our success in careers, work, education, relationships, and other areas of life. Phenomena such as motivational speakers and motivational interviewing are commonplace. Motivation is a critical aspect of the growing global practice of coaching.

Notwithstanding the apparent centrality of motivation in human experience, it continues to challenge theorists, researchers, and practitioners. It is also a challenge for lay people in their daily lives. The puzzle of motivation, that is, what it is, how it operates, its complexity, and its relationship to other psychological constructs have generated a variety of approaches that, in effect, range across the history of modern psychology. These theories and their related research address different domains, different populations, and issues, and use a variety of research methods to arrive at their conclusions. The richness of the field of motivation theory and research is reflected in this work.

We can think of motivation as energizing action. It also drives development. We often think of it as an internal phenomenon, but need to ask ourselves to what extent is it a social phenomenon? Other questions that need to be addressed are how motivation can extend beyond separate, discrete actions to sustain longer-term projects and careers? To what extent does having goals direct our problem solving? What are the differences between motivation that energizes top-down, planned action and the motivation that generates spontaneous bottom-up action? What are the important relations between motivation and emotion, cognition and self-regulation?

The authors of the chapters of this book have addressed these questions in one way or another in a host of applied settings for different populations, using a variety of research methods. Collectively, they have argued for the importance of motivation as a construct to understand and unpack human behavior in pedagogical, recreational, sports, therapeutic, and other contexts, but most importantly, they have affirmed motivation as a critical aspect of human, goal-directed action.

Richard A. Young
University of British Columbia

INTRODUCTION

The book you are holding is a collection of articles by psychologists and pedagogues from two different countries. It is a result of a collaboration between two scientific communities from different countries, which are interested in the same field of research, i.e. motivation. We asked them to present a report on their current work, and received varied answers concerning the issue of motivation, looked at from various angles. Thus, we are now in possession of an interesting collection of works on *psychological and pedagogical aspects of motivation*. At the same time these articles also provide insight into similarities and differences, specific for given countries.

The fundamental issues regarding motivation are mostly concerned with the direction, intensity, and duration of behavior. Taking these aspects into account, the contributions of the authors for the present publication connect, in different ways, the questions of individual differences and situational constraints of the level of motivation and of subsequent performance. The importance, but also the variety of the term "motivation" is also underlined by the fact that the articles concern different subfields of psychology.

Motivation, especially achievement motivation, is a very relevant theme in **sport psychology**, for example studying people who set realistic, but challenging goals. In the book this aspect is discussed and presented in the article by *Tor Oskar Thomassen, Lars Bauger* and *Anne Marte Pensgaard*. They provide a description of the predictive ability of achievement goals and competition trait anxiety on performance levels (local, regional, national) among cross-country and biathlon athletes. As the authors conclude, the "*study found that the performance-avoidance goal was the only achievement goal significantly predicting performance level among young cross-country skiers and biathlon athletes*". Another special aspect of achievement motivation, i.e. risk seeking, is presented in the article by *Piotr Próchniak*. His primary aim is the description and evaluation of personal values and motives of climbers compared with people engaging in low risk sport activities. The author states that "*climbers are people with a strong set of values, who listen to others but make the ultimate decision themselves. Moreover, climbers will never act against their most important values, regardless of other people's actions or opinions*". With a philosophical starting point, the article by *Dagmar Dahl* centers upon another interesting topic. She is looking for, analyzing and discussing the connections between religious belief as motivational basis or a motivational "kick" for sports performance. The main conclusion which the author reaches is that "*Sport and Religion are not closed systems. There might be differences in the personal experiences of motivation where aspects like identity, gender, culture and relationship can play important parts*".

Basic aspects of motivational theory are presented in **educational psychology.** Here we speak among others about intrinsic and extrinsic motivation and its finer aspects, such as how seeking information about a task can depend on whether the task is motivated by approach goals or avoidance goals. Such aspects are considered, in a philosophical and empirical way, in the article by *Herbert Zoglowek*. He presents a comprehensive overview of the understanding of the Norwegian phenomenon of friluftsliv. The presentation of the author's own research on motives for friluftsliv are interpreted and incorporated in the discussion about a special pedagogical approach to explain friluftsliv. As conclusion, the author used Erich Fromm's philosophical-psychological fundamental concept of biophilia and add "*...the pedagogical approach towards the education of character provides the idea of a didactic concept of friluftsliv, which, in turn, shows the pedagogical importance and possibilities of friluftsliv for learning and development*". Many will claim that the most important motivational factor in education is the teacher. This assertion is emphasized in the article by *Ewa Murawska*. The author presents an optimistic view and analysis of the components of teachers' professional success and concludes with the following afterthought: "*Satisfying experiences such as this one enable me to state with absolutely certainty: It is worth being a teacher! Only that and no less than that*".

Cognitive psychology is one more subfield strongly connected to motivation theories. According to motivation theory, the perception one has of oneself and one's perceived abilities has an important effect on task motivation. Such cognitive aspects of motivation have been discussed by *Slawomir Pasikowski* in his article, where he considers and evaluates the relationship of readiness to resist with creativity. The general conclusion which arises from the study is *"that resistance and creativity are not determined by birth order alone, but rather by a combination of this variable with others such as gender. Sometimes gender turns out to be much more important in predicting resistance and creativity"*. A similar approach is presented by *Emilia Kardaś*. However, her interests lie in the field of psychology of the elderly. In her article she presents and discusses the results of research on volitional control and styles of coping with stress in old age and comes to the conclusion: *"successful ageing depends on the acceptance of one's own age, the ability to adapt to emerging changes and personal control of one's own life."* Maria Aleksandrovich, on the other hand, is for the main part interested in dancers. She has spent a lot of time studying the dancer's milieu, and her article focuses on a special aspect of her studies: components of professional success and initiating moments for a dancing career. She concluded *"The analysis of the importance of all the variables for success in ballet showed an interesting hierarchy. In our sample, the five most important variables for professional success were Nationality, Neuroticism, Extraversion, Positive Dominate and Sub-dominate Forms of Personal Behaviour, and Conscientiousness."* Another article about *friluftsliv* is written by *Rune Waaler*. He describes two aspects of *friluftsliv* in Norwegian folk high schools. One aspect deals with the changes in the course offers over the past 10 years. The second part addresses the students' preferences for courses in these high schools over one recent school year. Both topics are based on the author's own data reported in the article. The author reaches a positive conclusion that *"...folk high schools still teach about nature experience and awaken traditional values in their students, despite the superficial impression that the entire year is centred on speed, action, developing one's skills and self realization"*.

From the subfield of **social psychology** we know that competence relevant and relating to peers plays a strong role in motivation, both in approach and avoidance goals. Oftentimes motivation for a task comes from seeking a level of proficiency, or avoiding failure. These aspects are closely studied in the article by *Irina Surina*. She describes an interesting approach to youth socialization by comparing of the socialization process of creative youths with theatrical socialization of young actors. In her conclusion, she underlines that *"the effects of the socialization process are the acquired, defined personality traits, a specific style and quality of life"*. In his second article, *Piotr Próchniak* looks at a special socialization situation in the life of young men. In his research he tries to analyze the motives of Polish policemen participating in the peacekeeping mission in the Balkan region of Kosovo. *"The results of this study indicate that policemen attained the highest scores on motives concentrated on the Self, while surprisingly (because the salary on a peacekeeping mission is higher in comparison to regular police salary), the financial motive does not dominate among the policemen"*.

Finally, motivation theory is also strongly linked to **behavioral psychology**. In fact, we believe much of the goals behind motivation can be described in terms of positive reinforcement. Such an approach is presented in a book described in the article by *Beata Pawlik*. She is studying the motivational role of animal-assisted therapy in the process of supporting children's development. The main conclusion, stemming from her research and long-term practice with children, is that *"therapy involving dogs is a valuable method of stimulating the child's overall development, especially fostering progress in emotional and social development, as well as the development of personality"*.

We wish all readers a good time reading the book and hope to motivate further engagement with this theme.

Slupsk and Alta, February 2013
Maria Aleksandrovich, Herbert Zoglowek

TOR OSKAR THOMASSEN, LARS BAUGER[1], DR. ANNE MARTE PENSGAARD[2], PHD

Finnmark University College
Department for Sports and Science
Follumsvei 31
9509 Alta, Norway
E-mail: Tor.Thomassen@hifm.no

ACHIEVEMENT MOTIVATION, ACHIEVEMENT GOALS, COMPETITION ANXIETY AND PERFORMANCE

INTRODUCTION

For a long time researchers have sought to both explain and predict behavior in achievement situations (Elliot & Conroy, 2005), and recently the achievement goal approach has emerged as an influential framework in the achievement motivation literature (Van Yperen, Elliot, & Anseel, 2009). The achievement goal framework guides our understanding of how individuals experience and respond to competence-relevant situations and is often conceptualized as the aim of competence-based actions (Elliot & Thrash, 2001). When the desire for competence is argued to be a basic construct for humans (White, 1963), both achievement motivation generally and achievement goal theory specifically should be important research domains (Elliot & Conroy, 2005). In our daily life we encounter numerous competence based situations, such as school, work, sports, hobbies and so forth, and the outcome of those situations affect how we feel about ourselves and our life. As these situations are important, the achievement contexts under investigation have predominantly been school, sports and work. In this study we wanted to see how the achievement goal and competition trait anxiety would predict the performance level of young elite cross-country skiers. Participation in cross-country competitions is normative situations which show very directly the competence of the athletes.

Previously, classical achievement motivation theories argued that the activities in achievement settings were oriented towards the attainment of success or the avoidance of failure (McClelland, Atkinson, Clark & Lowell, 1953). More recently an integrative achievement goal conceptualization has been proposed which integrates both performance and mastery and the approach and avoidance concepts (Elliot, 1995; Elliot & Harackiewicz, 1996). In this framework, in addition to motive towards success/failure, three achievement orientations are proposed: a mastery goal, a performance-approach goal and a performance-avoidance goal (Elliot & Church, 1997). The motive to achieve is posited to be a direct antecedent of both mastery goal and performance-approach goal. In Elliot and Church's (1997) trichotomous achievement goal framework, mastery goal is characterized by self-regulation toward the development of task mastery and competence, while performance-approach goal is characterized by self-regulation towards the attainment of favorable judgments of normative competence. The motive to avoid failure is regarded as a direct antecedent of performance-avoidance goal, and this goal construct is characterized as "self-regulation according to potential negative outcomes, and this avoidance orientation is posited to yield processes (e.g., anxiety and task distraction) that produce the helpless pattern of achievement outcomes" (Elliot & Church, 1997, p.218).

---

[1] Regional Competence Center for Sport and Health - North, University of Tromsø.
[2] Norwegian School of Sport Science, Oslo.

According to Elliot's (1999) review of the research on the trichotomous achievement goal framework, mastery goal concept has been linked to different positive processes and outcomes. Such as absorption in task engagement, study persistence, self-determination while studying, long-term retention of information and intrinsic motivation. Although mastery goals have been associated with some positive outcomes, they seem to be unrelated to performance outcomes (Elliot & Church, 1997). In addition, a relationship between mastery goal and intrinsic motivation has been found and seem to be mediated by task absorption (Elliot & Harackiewicz, 1996).

Links of performance goals have been documented and examined in Elliot's review (1999). Performance-avoidance goals have been associated with many negative processes and outcomes, such as poor retention of information, worry, state test anxiety, reduced competence improvements over time, lower subjective vitality, lower sport performance, self-handicapping behavior, and lower perceived sport competence (Elliot & McGregor, 1999; Elliot, Sheldon, & Church, 1997; Halvari & Kjormo, 1999; Li, 2010; Ommundsen, 2004; Skjesol & Halvari, 2005).

Performance-approach goals have been shown to be related to many positive, and a few negative, outcomes and processes. The positive outcomes include exam performance, less worry, high surface processing, self concept, self-efficacy, study persistence, lower levels of self-handicapping, sport performance, and perceived sport competence (Elliot & Church, 1997; Elliot & McGregor, 1999; Ommundsen, 2004; Skjesol & Halvari, 2005; Vansteenkiste et al., 2010). Some negative outcomes have also emerged, such as shallow processing of information, anxiety, disruptive behavior, and low retention of knowledge (Midgley, Kaplan, & Middleton, 2001). In general, Vansteekiste and colleagues (2010) argue that the adoption of performance-approach goal seem to energize individuals to put more effort into their studying and resulting in higher grades, while the focus on outperforming others do not necessarily promote the experience of learning enjoyment. With the pursuit of performance-approach being not entirely positive, some researchers have questioned for whom and under what circumstances performance-approach goals are good (Midgley et al., 2001).

As a result of the inconsistencies found for performance-approach goals, the trichotomous achievement goal framework was reworked into the 2 x 2 achievement goal model (Elliot, 1999; Elliot & Moller, 2003; Elliot & Murayama, 2008; Elliot & Thrash, 2001) which incorporates the approach-avoidance distinction for mastery goal as well as for performance goals. In this model Elliot and colleagues argued that negative effects of performance-approach goals were, for the most part, found in studies where ego-validation concerns were parts of the measure for performance-approach goals. As a result of this, ego-involvement was removed from the definition and measure of performance goals. Reviews of research conducted on 2 x 2 achievement goal model have generally found that consequences of adopting a mastery approach are overwhelmingly positive (Moller & Elliot, 2006; Roberts, Treasure, & Conroy, 2007). Roberts and colleagues (2007) found that performance-approach was the only goal that predicted superior performance, while it was also associated with task absorption, competence valuation, intrinsic motivation and less anxiety. Studies using the 2 x 2 model have yet to reveal maladaptive achievement consequences within the sport domain (Halvari, Skjesol, & Bagøien, 2011). While in the academic context the goal has been positively associated with performance in different studies, such as math performance, exam performance, WISC performance among others, but also positively associated with maladaptive help seeking strategies (Moller & Elliot, 2006). With this in mind, Moller and Elliot argued that performance-approach goals represent potential valuable but vulnerable forms of regulations. The consequences of both performance-avoidance and mastery-avoidance have been found to

12

be consequently maladaptive, with associations to test anxiety, worry, emotionality, disorganization, health center visits, and maladaptive help seeking strategies (Moller & Elliot, 2006). When it comes to sport and physical activity, performance-avoidance goals are negative linked with performance, learning indication and intrinsic motivation (Roberts et al., 2007). In sport, several studies have investigated the relationship between motive to avoid failure and sport competence. The research study by Beckmann and Kasèn (1994) among top level performers in endurance sport indicated that negative motivation and cognitive anxiety were both related to states such as worrying about the performance and its consequences, fear or avoidance of failure, and rumination about failure. These states impede performance at this level. In another study (Halvari & Thomassen, 1997), the cross-country skiers sport careers (competition level) were facilitated by a strong motive to succeed and impeded by a strong motive to avoid failure.

PURPOSE

The purpose of this study was to investigate if performance levels of cross-country skiers could be significantly predicted by variables such as motive to achieve success, motive to avoid failure, achievement goals and sport competition anxiety. As motive to achieve success is an antecedent of both mastery goal and performance-approach goal, we expect those variables to be positively correlated. With respect to motive to avoid failure, we expected it to be positively correlated to performance-avoidance goal, as motive to achieve failure is an antecedent of performance-avoidance goal. Additionally we wanted to investigate whether achievement goals could significantly predict the performance level of athletes directly. According to previous research we expected that both performance-approach and performance-avoidance goals would be significant predictors of performance levels, while mastery goals would not emerge as a significant predictor. To further explain the variance in performance levels, competition anxiety was also included in the regression model, and was expected to emerge as a significant predictor of performance levels. Since performance-avoidance goals have been linked with anxiety levels in general, it would be of interest to see how this affects our expected relationship between performance-avoidance goal and performance level. To sum up our research question was, would the independent variables achievement goals and competition anxiety, emerge as significant predictors of our dependent variable of skiers performance levels?

METHOD

Participants. The potential participants were informed about the study and were told that participation was voluntary and that all the information would be treated confidentially, after this informed consent was obtained from all participating athletes. 77 participants, 46 (59.7 %) male and 31 (40.3 %) female were recruited from ski-teams in the northern parts of Norway. Most athletes were attending sport specific high schools, age ranging from 16 to 22 years; $M = 17.11$, SD 1.8). 66 (85.7 %) of the athletes identified as cross-country skiers while 11 (14.3 %) were biathlon athletes.

MEASURES

Demographic questionnaire. The demographic questionnaire contained questions about age, gender, type of sport, geographical location, distance to prepared cross-country ski track from home and what age participants started regular systematic training.

Achievement goals. The present study used the original Achievement Goal Questionnaire (AGQ) (Elliot & Church, 1997). The scale assesses participants' mastery, performance-approach and performance-avoidance goals. It consists of 18 items, with 6 items assessing each of the three goals. We adopted a context of cross-country skiing. Example items are: "I desire to learn as much as possible through my sport" (mastery goal); "I am motivated to do better than my opponents" (performance-approach goal); and "I often think to myself: what if I perform badly in my sport" (performance-avoidance goal). In order to be consistent with the new proposed definition of performance-approach goals, items that focused on ego-involvement were removed (Halvari et al., 2011). i.e. "I want do better to show my ability to family, friends, coaches and others." With this change, the performance-approach goal subscale should concur with the definition of trying to do better than specific others or merely trying to do well in relation to a norm. Items are responded to on a seven point scale ranging from "not true at all for me" (1) to "very true for me" (7). The reason why the original AGQ was used and not the more recent 2 x 2 AGQ developed by Elliot and McGregor (2001), was related to results from two Norwegian studies (Halvari et al., 2011; Skjesol & Halvari, 2005), which yielded good indications of both reliability and validity for the original instrument.

Achievement motives. Achievement motives were assessed with the Achievement Motive Scale (AMS) (Gjesme & Nygård, 1970). The AMS has 30 items, 15 items each for assessing motive to achieve success and motive to avoid failure respectively. Example items are: "I like doing things that I am not quite certain that I can handle" (motive to achieve success) and "I dislike working with things where I am uncertain about the outcome" (motive to avoid failure). Items on both subscales are responded to using a four point scale, ranging from "not true at all" (1) to "very true" (4). Each subscale is then summed for a total score. The reliability and validity of the scale have been investigated several times by different researchers, and found to be well tuned in relation to achievement motivation theory (Halvari, 1991; 1997; Man, Nygård & Gjesme, 1994).

Sport competition anxiety. As a measure of competition anxiety trait, the Sport Competition Anxiety Test (SCAT) (Martens, 1977; Martens, Vealey & Burton, 1990) was used. The SCAT contains 15 items, 10 of which measure symptoms associated with anxiety. The remaining five items, which are not scored, are included in the inventory to reduce the likelihood of an internal response-set bias (Dunn & Dunn, 2001). Participants respond to the questions, according to how they usually feel when they are competing in their sport, on a three-point scale ranging from hardly ever (1), sometimes (2) and often (3). The scores are then summed to provide an overall measure of competition trait anxiety, and higher scores reflect a greater tendency to experience competitive anxiety. The test has shown good internal consistency when reviewed (KR-20 ranging from .95 to .97) and a high test-retest reliability (M = .77). Even though the SCAT has been used less frequently recently after other measures have been developed (i.e. the Sport Anxiety Scale), SCAT is still recognized as a valuable research tool as it continues to be used in research concerning sport anxiety (Dunn & Dunn, 2001).

Objective performance level rating. As a part of the test battery the athletes had to explicitly write down their five best results including what competition, year and placement, report points in the national cup where points are gathered in competition throughout the season and report their best placement in international, national, regional and local compe-titions. Based on this information, a coach with considerable knowledge and experience in both cross-country skiing and biathlon placed the participants into three different categories: national, regional and local performance level, with each performance level indicating whether the athlete was a contender within national, regional or local competitions respectively. In our sample, 25 (35.5 %) athletes were at the local level, 30 (39.0 %) at the regional level and 22 (28.6 %) at the national level.

RESULTS

Means, standard deviations, and correlation among the variables in the study are presented in Table 1. For all measures skewness values were between -1 and 1 and judged to be acceptable according to criteria set for use in parametric statistics (Muthén & Kaplan, 1985). Our results showed that the strongest correlation between study variables was between motive to achieve success and mastery goal. Further, motive to achieve success was negatively correlated with motive to avoid failure. The motive to avoid failure was positively correlated with performance avoidance goals and high sport competition anxiety, while it was negatively correlated with mastery goal. In addition mastery goal was positively correlated with both performance-approach and performance-avoidance goals, and negative correlated with sport competition anxiety. Performance-avoidance goals were positively correlated with sport competition anxiety.

Table 1. Means, Standard Deviation, Correlations Among Variables, and Cronbach alpha[a] (N = 77)

Variable	M	SD	1	2	3	4	5	6
1. Motive to achieve success	47.2	4.6	.70[a]					
2. Motive to avoid failure	28.2	6.9	-.30**	.89[a]				
3. Mastery goal	34.9	4.0	.48**	-.36**	.70[a]			
4. Performance approach goal	28.3	4.7	.02	-.16	.29*	.79[a]		
5. Performance avoidance goal	23.1	5.9	-.05	.31**	.26*	.33**	.66[a]	
6. Sport competition anxiety	21.6	5.0	-.09	.25*	-.23*	-.23*	.26*	.89[a]

* $p < .05$. ** $p < .01$ (two-tailed)

PREDICTION OF PERFORMANCE LEVEL

To investigate whether achievement goals and competition anxiety could significantly predict competition level among the athletes, a multinomial regression analysis was conducted and is presented in Table 2. This was the preferred method of regression as our dependent variable had more than two categories. The predictors were selected for the final model using the backward stepwise method, this method enters all hypothesized predictors first, before removing redundant predictors one by one who do not make a statistically significant contribution to the model (Field, 2009). Mastery goal, performance-approach goal and the approach x avoidance interaction where also set for inclusion in the model, but neither of the variables were deemed as significant predictors with the stepwise backward method. The fact that the mastery goal did not enter the model was not surprising and in accordance with previous research, however, we expected the performance approach goal to be a significant predictor of performance level, based on previous results. Multinomial regression revealed that both competition anxiety, χ^2 (2) = 9.73, $p < .01$, and performance avoidance goal, χ^2 (2) = 7.58, $p = .02$, were significant predictors for the participants' competition level. The model as a whole had decent effect sizes ($R^2 = .23, .25$) indicated by Nagelkerke and Cox and Snell statistics. When we further inspected the effects of the two significant predictors we observed that competition anxiety significantly predicted com-petition level between local- and national

15

competition level, while performance avoidance goal emerged as a significant predictor of competition level between regional and national competition level. The results showed that skiers on a high performance level have both significant lower competition anxiety and lower performance avoidance goal than skiers on a lower level.

Table 2. Multinomial Logistic Regression Predicting Competition Level From Competition Anxiety and Performance avoidance goal

Variable	B	SE B	Lower	Odds ratio	Upper
			\multicolumn{3}{c}{95% CI for Odds ratio}	
Competing Locally vs. Nationally					
Intercept	-6.41**	1.96			
Performance avoidance goals	.09	.06	.98	1.10	1.24
Competition anxiety	.20**	.07	1.06	1.22	1.41
Competing regionally vs. Nationally					
Intercept	-3.87*	1.66			
Performance avoidance goals	.14**	.06	1.04	1.16	1.29
Competition anxiety	.05	.06	.92	1.05	1.19

Note. $N = 77$. CI = confidence interval. $R^2 = .23$ (Cox & Snell), .25 (Nagelkerke). Model $\chi^2(4) = 19.59, p < .001$. * $p < .05$, ** p $< .01$.

DISCUSSION

This study intended to further examine the relationship between motivational aspects, anxiety and sport performance level. We found that motive to achieve success was positively related to mastery goal. This supported the theory of achievement goals, where motive to achieve success is posited to be a direct antecedent of mastery goal (Elliot & Church, 1997). In addition to predicting mastery goal, motive to achieve success is also posited to be an antecedent of performance-approach goal. This relationship did not emerge in our study, where the two variables were non-related. Although others have found the same lack of relationship (Thomassen & Halvari, 2007), this finding is somewhat surprising as motive to achieve success is defined as a disposition towards expectations of positive affects and attainment of positive achievement outcomes in general (McClelland et al., 1953) and performance-approach is characterized by self-regulation directed towards attainment of favorable judgments of normative competence (Elliot & Church, 1997). The performance approach were, however, conceptualized as a more complex form of regulation, where it can serve both motive to achieve success and motive to avoid failure. Surprisingly then, we did not find a significant relationship between motive to avoid failure and performance-approach either. Therefore, our result does not support any of the proposed antecedents of performance-approach. The motive to avoid failure, on the other hand, was in our study positively related to performance-avoidance goal, and supported the evidence (Elliot & Church, 1997) that it is an antecedent of performance-avoidance.

When we viewed achievement goals in relation to competition trait anxiety, we observed that both mastery and performance-approach goals were negatively related to competition trait anxiety while performance-avoidance goal was positively related. In regard to mastery goal, this adds to the positive outcomes related to this construct in the literature. The fact

16

that performance-approach in our study were negatively associated with competition anxiety, seems contradictory to previous studies where it was positively associated with anxiety (Midgley et al., 2001). However, this could be very well explained by the updated definition of the construct (Elliot, 1999; Elliot & Moller, 2003; Elliot & Murayama, 2008) which removes ego-involvement as an inherent component of performance-approach goals and thus the former association to perceived anxiety.

ACHIEVEMENT GOALS AND SPORT PERFORMANCE

As performance goals have been linked with different performance outcomes we wanted to investigate whether the variables could significantly predict performance level in sport. We also suspected competition anxiety to be a significant predictor of performance level although how anxiety affects performance is a complex issue and no definite conclusions have been made (Weinberg & Gould, 2011). We argue that in our case, where the outcome measure was an overall judgment of performance and not just based on one specific competition, an elevated competition trait anxiety would lead to lower performance level.

In our logistic regression only two factors were significant predictors of our performance categories: performance-avoidance goal and competition anxiety. The last predictor to be removed before the final model was performance-approach goal, and it was not even close to contributing significantly (with a p value of .60.) This is in contrast to some studies that have shown that performance-approach seems to be associated with the level of sport performance (Halvari & Kjormo, 1999; Roberts et al., 2007). Further, our result show that competition anxiety significantly predicted whether the athletes competed at the local or national level. More specifically, athletes at the local club level, reported higher levels of competitive anxiety than national level athletes. Even though the same tendency was observed with performance-avoidance goal, it was non-significant. In contrast, performance-avoidance goal significantly predicted whether the athletes competed at the regional or national level, while the degree of competition anxiety did not. This indicates that the more performance-avoidance goal oriented the athletes were, the more likely they were to compete at the regional level. With these results in mind, it seems that competition anxiety is more detrimental for performance at the lower competitive levels than on the national level, and that performance-avoidance is more detrimental for performance at a high level than at a low level. Although it is difficult to point to any causal direction of these results we may speculate that athletes at the higher level are likely to have had more competition experience and could have learned to view anxiety as a catalyst for performance, while at the lower levels the same anxiety could be viewed as an inhibitor (Jones, 1995). Regarding the role of the performance-avoidance goal, it seems to play a more critical role at higher competition levels than for lower competition levels, while this may not be the case for the lower competition levels. This seems reasonable, since at higher competition levels there could be a greater focus on placement and ranking, and self-regulation towards avoiding negative outcomes becomes a stronger performance inhibitor.

LIMITATIONS

Firstly, our measure of competitive trait anxiety has previously been shown to have some psychometric challenges, in that some studies have failed to support the unidimensional structure of the instrument. In respect to the scale structure Karterolis (1997) found a two-factor model, with an eight-item somatic factor and a two-item cognitive factor, produced slightly better goodness-of-fit indices compared with a one-item solution with a confirmatory factor analysis. The two factor solution also emerged with better fit indices in Dunn and Dunn (2001) maximum likelihood confirmatory factor analysis. They concluded however, in accordance with Smith, Smoll and Wiechman (1998), that it would be inappropriate to create a separate subscale when only two items loaded on the cognitive factor. A viable option for the measurement of competition trait anxiety could be "Sport Anxiety Scale" (Smith, Smoll, & Schutz, 1990). It is however important to note that this newer competitive trait scale also has some psychometric problems, as Dunn, Dunn, Wilson and Syrotuik (2000) identified, regarding two items in the scale supposedly measuring concentration disruption. Thus the choice of instrument to measure trait anxiety in sport remains a challenge.

Secondly, we did not investigate possible mediator effects of achievement goals in relation to performance level, and it is possible that both mastery goal and performance-approach goal affects sport performance through variables not measured in this study.

Thirdly, this study did not use the newest achievement goal framework, that is, the 2 x 2 achievement model (Elliot, 1999). Although the performance goals in our study were in accordance with this new model, it may be more appropriate to use the new measure in future studies. This instrument also captures the approach-avoidance distinction for mastery goal as well as for performance goals, which may be useful.

Lastly, all data was based on self-report which has been criticized as participants can misunderstand questions, avoid using the extremes or might seek to gain researchers approval rather than reveal true information. This might be most prevalent in our performance variable, since this was an expert's judgment of the best performances the athletes stated in the questionnaire. It is possible that both participants and the expert could be biased in their judgment and reporting of performance.

CONCLUSION

This study found that performance-avoidance goal was the only achievement goal significantly predicting performance level among young cross-country skiers and biathlon athletes. In addition competition trait anxiety was a significant predictor of performance levels in the same model. Performance-avoidance was a significant predictor of performance level when comparing regional and national level, while competition anxiety was a significant predictor when comparing local with national performance level. Future studies should incorporate the newest theories and measures of achievement goal theory and competition anxiety to further understand how these factors affect objective performance indicators.

REFERENCES

Beckmann, J. & Kasèn, M. (1994). Action and state orientation and the performance of top athletes. In J. Kuhl & J. Beckmann (Eds.), Volition and personality. Action versus state orientation (pp. 439-452). Seattle: Hogrefe & Hober.

Dunn, J. G. H. & Dunn, J. C. (2001). Relationships among the Sport Competition Anxiety Test, the Sport Anxiety Scale, and the Collegiate Hockey Worry Scale. *Journal of Applied Sport Psychology, 13*(4), 411-429. doi: 10.1080/104132001753226274

Dunn, J. G. H., Dunn, J. C., Wilson, P. M. & Syrotuik, D. G. (2000). Reexamining the factorial composition and factor structure of the Sport Anxiety Scale *Journal of Sport & Exercise Psychology, 22*(2), 183-193.

Elliot, A. J. (1995). Approach and avoidance achievement goals: An intrinsic motivation analysis. *Dissertation Abstracts International: Section B: The Sciences and Engineering, 55*(7-B), 3061.

Elliot, A. J. (1999). Approach and avoidance motivation and achievement goals. *Educational Psychologist, 34*(3), 169-189.

Elliot, A. J. & Church, M. A. (1997). A hierarchical model of approach and avoidance achievement motivation. *Journal of Personality and Social Psychology, 72*(1), 218-232.

Elliot, A. J. & Conroy, D. E. (2005). Beyond the dichotomous model of achievement goals in sport and exercise psychology. *Sport and Exercise Psychology Review, 1*, 17-25.

Elliot, A. J. & Harackiewicz, J. M. (1996). Approach and avoidance achievement goals and intrinsic motivation: A mediational analysis. *Journal of Personality and Social Psychology, 70*(3), 461-475.

Elliot, A. J. & McGregor, H. A. (1999). Test anxiety and the hierarchical model of approach and avoidance achievement motivation. *Journal of Personality and Social Psychology, 76*(4), 628-644.

Elliot, A. J. & McGregor, H. A. (2001). A 2 × 2 achievement goal framework. *Journal of Personality and Social Psychology, 80*(3), 501-519. doi: 10.1037/0022-3514.80.3.501

Elliot, A. J. & Moller, A. C. (2003). Performance-approach goals: good or bad forms of regulation? *International Journal of Educational Research, 39*(4-5), 339-356. doi: 10.1016/j.ijer.2004.06.003

Elliot, A. J. & Murayama, K. (2008). On the measurement of achievement goals: Critique, illustration, and application. *Journal of Educational Psychology, 100*(3), 613-628. doi: 10.1037/0022-0663.100.3.613

Elliot, A. J. Sheldon, K. M., & Church, M. A. (1997). Avoidance Personal Goals and Subjective Well-Being. *Personality and Social Psychology Bulletin, 23*(9), 915-927. doi: 10.1177/0146167297239001

Elliot, A. J. & Thrash, T. (2001). Achievement Goals and the Hierarchical Model of Achievement Motivation. *Educational Psychology Review, 13*(2), 139-156. doi: 10.1023/a:1009057102306

Field, A. (2009). *Discovering statistics using SPSS: (and sex and drugs and rock 'n' roll)* (3 ed.). Los Angeles, CA: Sage.

Gjesme, T. & Nygård, R. (1970). Achievement-related motives: theretical considerations and constructions of a measuring instrument. Oslo, Norway: University of Oslo.

Halvari, H. (1991). Effects of goal distance in time on relations between achievement motives and energy consumption by aerobic processes during 1500 m running. *Perceptual and Motor Skills, 72*(3c), 1143-1165. doi: 10.2466/pms.1991.72.3c.1143

Halvari, H. (1997). Moderator Effects of Age on the Relation between Achievement Motives and Performance. *Journal of Research in Personality, 31*(3), 303-318. doi: 10.1006/jrpe.1997.2185

Halvari, H. & Kjormo, O. (1999). A structural model of achievement motives, performance approach and avoidance goals, and performance among Norwegian olympic athletes. *Perceptual and Motor Skills, 89*(3 Pt 1), 997-1022. doi: 10.2466/pms.1999.89.3.997

Halvari, H. Skjesol, K., & Bagøien, T. E. (2011). Motivational climates, achievement goals, and physical education outcomes: A longitudinal test of achievement goal theory. *Scandinavian Journal of Educational Research, 55*(1), 79-104.

Halvari, H. & Thomassen, T. O. (1997). Achievement motivation, sports-related future orientation, and sporting career. *Genetic, Social and General Psychology Monographs, 123*(3), 343-365.

Jones, G. (1995). More than just a game: research developments and issues in competitive anxiety in sport. *British Journal of Psychology, 86* 449-478. doi: 10.1111/j.2044-8295.1995.tb02565.x

Karterolis, C. (1997). *The factorial validity of SCAT in Greek students: Testing the assumption of equivalent structure and mean differences across gender.* Paper presented at the Innovations in sport psychology: Linking theory and practice, Israel.

Li, C.-H. (2010). Predicting subjective vitality and performance in sports: The role of passion and achievement goals. *Perceptual and Motor Skills, 110*(3, Pt 2), 1029-1047.

Man, F. Nygård, R. & Gjesme, T. (1994). The Achievement Motives Scale (AMS): Theoretical basis and results from a first try-out of a Czech form. *Scandinavian Journal of Educational Research*, 38(3-4), 209-218. doi: 10.1080/0031383940380304

Martens, R. (1977). *Sport Competition Anxiety Test*. Champaign, IL Human Kinetics.

Martens, R., Vealey, R. S. & Burton, D. (1990). *Competitive anxiety in sport*. Champaign, Il: Human Kinetics.

McClelland, D. C., Atkinson, J. W., Clark, R. A. & Lowell, E. L. (1953). *The achievement motive*. New York: Appleton-Century-Crofts.

Midgley, C., Kaplan, A. & Middleton, M. (2001). Performance-Approach Goals: Good For What, For Whom, Under What Circumstances, and At What Cost? *Journal of Educational Psychology, 93*(1), 77-86. doi: 10.1037//0022-0663.93.1.77

Moller, A. C. & Elliot, A. J. (2006). The 2 × 2 Achievement Goal Framework: An Overview of Empirical Research. In A. V. Mittel (Ed.), *Focus on educational psychology.* (pp. 307-326). Hauppauge, NY: Nova Science

Muthén, B. & Kaplan, D. (1985). A comparison of some methodologies for the factor analysis of non-normal Likert variables. *British Journal of Mathematical and Statistical Psychology, 38*(2), 171-189. doi: 10.1111/j.2044-8317.1985.tb00832.x

Ommundsen, Y. (2004). Self-Handicapping Related to Task and Performance-Approach and Avoidance Goals in Physical Education. *Journal of Applied Sport Psychology, 16*(2), 183-197.

Roberts, G. C., Treasure, D. C. & Conroy, D. E. (2007). Understanding the dynamics of motivation in sport and physical activity: An achievement goal interpretation. In R. Eklund & G. Tenenbaum (Eds.), *Handbook of sport psychology* (pp. 3-30). New York, NY: Macmillan.

Skjesol, K. & Halvari, H. (2005). Motivational climate, achievement goals, perceived sport competence and involvement in physical activity: Structural and mediator models. *Perceptual and Motor Skills, 100*(2), 497-523. doi: 10.2466/pms.100.2.497-523

Smith, R. E., Smoll, F. L. & Schutz, R. W. (1990). Measurement and correlates of sport-specific cognitive and somatic trait anxiety: The sport anxiety scale. *Anxiety Research, 2*(4), 263-280. doi: 10.1080/08917779008248733

Smith, R. E., Smoll, F. L. & Wiechman, S. A. (1998). Measurement of trait anxiety in sport. In J. L. Duda (Ed.), *Advances in sport and exercise psychology measurement* (pp. 105-127). Morgantown, WV: Fitness Information Technology.

Thomassen, T. O. & Halvari, H. (2007). A hierarchical model of approach achievement motivation and effort regulation during a 90-min. soccer match. *Perceptual and Motor Skills, 105*, 609-635. doi: 10.2466/pms.105.2.609-635

Van Yperen, N. W., Elliot, A. J. & Anseel, F. (2009). The influence of mastery-avoidance goals on performance improvement. *European Journal of Social Psychology, 39*(6), 932-943.

Vansteenkiste, M., Smeets, S., Soenens, B., Lens, W., Matos, L. & Deci, E. (2010). Autonomous and controlled regulation of performance-approach goals: Their relations to perfectionism and educational outcomes. *Motivation and Emotion, 34*(4), 333-353. doi: 10.1007/s11031-010-9188-3

Weinberg, R. S. & Gould, D. (2011). *Foundations of sport and exercise psychology* (5 ed.). Champaign, Ill.: Human Kinetics.

White, R. W. (1963). Motivation reconsidered: The concept of competence. *Shoben, Edward Joseph*, 33-59.

SUMMARY

In the literature achievement goals have been associated with both positive and negative outcomes, where consequences of adopting mastery goal is positive, performance-avoidance goal is negative, and performance-approach goal is a mix of negative and positive. This study investigated the predictive ability of achievement goals and competition trait anxiety on performance levels (local, regional, national), using multinomial logistic regression, among cross-country and biathlon athletes (M age = 17.65, SD = 1.8). The results showed that only performance-avoidance goal and competition trait anxiety were significant predictors of performance levels, while performance-approach goal and mastery goal were non-significant. Performance-avoidance goal predicted whether athletes competed regional- or national level, whereas competition anxiety predicted if athletes competed on a local or nationally level. The study used a modified version of the trichotomous achievement goal framework, which does not have the approach/avoidance distinction for the mastery goal. Future studies should investigate how successful the 2 x 2 achievement goal model predicts sport performance.

STRESZCZENIE

W literaturze przedmiotu osiąganie celów wiąże się z pozytywnymi i negatywnymi rezultatami. Konsekwencje przyjęcia orientacji na osiągnięcie mistrzostwa są pozytywne, dla orientacji unikowej są one negatywne, a dla orientacji na poziom wykonania są one zarówno pozytywne jak i negatywne. W niniejszym badaniu, za pomocą wielowymiarowej regresji logistycznej, zmierzono zdolność predykcyjną osiągania celów i cechę lęku przed współzawodnictwem w odniesieniu do poziomów osiągnięć (na szczeblu lokalnym, regionalnym, krajowym) wśród uczestników zawodów przełajowych i biatlonistów (M wiek = 17.65, SD = 1.8). Wyniki wskazały, że tylko orientacja unikowa i cecha lęku przed współzawodnictwem były znaczącymi wskaźnikami poziomów osiągnięć, podczas gdy orientacja na poziom wykonania i orientacja na osiąganie mistrzostwa nie miały znaczenia. Orientacja unikowa przewidywała, czy sportowcy brali udział w zawodach na poziomie regionalnym lub krajowym, natomiast lęk przed współzawodnictwem przewidywał, czy sportowcy startowali w zawodach na poziomie lokalnym, czy krajowym. W badaniu zastosowano zmodyfikowaną wersję trzystopniowej teorii osiągania celów, która nie czyni rozróżnienia na podejście/unikanie dla osiągania mistrzostwa. Przyszłe badania powinny zmierzyć skuteczność czterostopniowego modelu osiągania celów dla osiągnięć sportowych.

SAMMENDRAG

I litteraturen har ulike målperspektiv blitt assosiert med både positive og negative resultat, der konsekvenser ved å velge mestringsmål har gitt positive, prestasjons-unngåelsesmål har gitt negative, og prestasjons-tilnærmingsmål har ført til en blanding av negative og positive resultat. Dette studiet undersøkte sammenhenger mellom ulike målperspektiv, konkurranseangst og prestasjonsnivå (lokalt, regionalt, nasjonalt) ved å bruke multippel regresjonsanalyse. Deltakerne i undersøkelsen var langrennsløpere og skiskyttere (M alder = 17,65, SD = 1.8). Resultatene viste at prestasjons-unngåelsesmål og konkurranseangst predikerte signifikant prestasjonsnivå, mens prestasjons-tilnærmingsmål og mestringsmål ikke var signifikante predikatorer for prestasjonsnivå. Prestasjons-unngåelsesmål predikerte om utøverne hevdet seg på regionalt eller nasjonalt nivå, mens konkurranseangst predikerte om utøverne hevdet seg på lokalt eller nasjonalt nivå. Studiet anvendte en modifisert versjon av en tredeling på målperspektiv, hvor en ikke splitter mestringsmål i tilnærming/unngåelse. Fremtidige studier bør undersøke hvordan 2x2 modellen for målperspektiv predikerer idrettsprestasjoner.

DR. PIOTR PRÓCHNIAK, PHD

Pomeranian University
Department of Psychology
Westerplatte 64
Slupsk 76-200, Poland
E-mail: piotrprochniak@wp.pl

PERSONAL VALUES AS MOTIVES OF CLIMBERS

INTRODUCTION

Risky recreational sports are growing in popularity. Examples of such sports are: parachuting, snowboarding, motorcycling, SCUBA diving, climbing etc. Risky recreational sports include the following characteristics: (1) involvement with the natural environment, (2) elements of risk and danger, (3) uncertain outcome and (4) influenced by the participant or circumstance. In fact - day after day, month after month, year after year hundreds of people are injured and killed while engaging in high-risk sports (Ewert, 1993).

Climbing is an adventurous activity that carries a risk of serious injury or even death. For example, the world's second highest mountain, K2, is also one of the most dangerous mountains in the world. K2 has a summit/fatality rate of nearly 26 per cent, meaning that for every 100 climbers returning after having successfully reached the summit, 26 have died trying (Peron, 2009).

Motivation is the need that drives an individual to act in a certain way to achieve the desired satisfaction (Moutinho, 2000). Many different reasons and motivational factors compel people to choose risky recreational sports. Climbers often have multiple motives for participation in mountains sports too (Ewert, 1994; Levenson, 1990). For example, McIntyre (1992) identified six motives among climbers: challenge, control creativity, escape, physical setting and recognition. Similarly, climbers at Mt. Rainer (Washington) were moti-vated to climb due to: challenge, catharsis, creative, locus of control, opportunities, physical setting and recognition (Ewert, 1993); while climbers at Mt. McKinley (Alaska) noted five factors: aspects of climbing, catharsis/escape, exhilaration/excitement, image and social aspects (Ewert, 1994).

Researchers are also looking for subjective personality traits of people who decide to engage in risk action because personality traits direct and motivate behavior (Pervin, 1994). For example, Marvin Zuckerman's (1994) research on the sensation-seeking trait, explains to at large extent the motives behind participation in high-risk activity. The sensation Seeking trait was "defined by the seeking of varied, novel, complex, and intense sensations and experiences, and the willingness to take physical, social, legal, and financial risks for the sake of such experience" (Zuckerman, 1994, p. 27). Sensation seeking is a sensory need which is based on the optimal level of stimulation. If the level of stimulation is too low or too high sensation seeking leads to impropriety. Every person has his/her own individual level of the sensation seeking need. The intensification of this need depends on a person's age, sex and situational factors. Furthermore, it should be highlighted that this need has a strong biological basis. Zuckerman (1994) claims that it is also influenced by the environment, but this influence is not a decisive one.

The sensation seeking trait can be measured via standard self-report questionnaires. This trait can be partitioned into four dimensions: thrill and adventure seeking (TAS), experience seeking (ES), disinhibition (Dis), boredom susceptibility (BS), and total sensation seeking (total SSS) (Zuckerman, 1994).

The numerous studies on the sensation seeking personality of people who participate in risky recreation activities (e.g. divers, climbers, surfers) showed that these people had higher scores in the sensation seeking scales in comparison to those, who did not take part in such risky activities (Breivik, 1996; Cronin, 1991; Goma-i-Freixanet, 1991; Schroth, 1995). For example, Cronin (1991) administered the Sensation Seeking Scale V to 20 members of a university mountain-climbing club and 21 control volunteers. Mountain climbers scored higher on the Total Score, Experience-Seeking, and Thrill and Adventure Seeking sub-scales. Rossi and Cereatti (1993) tested the hypothesis that high-risk sports are chosen by high sensation seekers, and compared five groups of athletes (control, physical education students, free-climbers, speleologists, and ski jumpers). The mountain athletes scored higher than controls in the Total Score and in every sub-scale of the Sensation Seeking Scale V except Boredom Susceptibility. The number of accidents these athletes suffered correlated with the Total Score and Thrill and Adventure Seeking, verifying the relationship between risk taking and sensation seeking. A third study (Breivik, 1996) examined sensation seeking and risk taking in successful Norwegian Everest expedition members. Elite climbers, sports students, and military recruits were reference groups. The Everest expedition members attained very high results in the SSSV Total score and on every subscale except disinhibition, and these scores were significantly higher than those of the students and military recruits. The elite climbers also demonstrated significantly higher scores than controls on all factors except disinhibition. Other factors investigated by the author indicated that, as expected, Everest climbers are risk takers as well as sensation seekers.

Personal sensation seeking traits are not the only motives of climbing (Egan & Stelmack, 2003). However, studies on climbers are not focused on their personal values system.

Values motivate behavior. For example, Rokeach (1973) found that people act according to their values because there is a need for consistency between one's beliefs and one's behavior. Important values induce stronger motivation, increasing the probability of goal directed behavior (Gollwitzer, 1996). However, values do not explain specific behavior but rather behavioral patterns (Bond, Leung & Schwartz, 1992).

I believe, it is possible to understand the motives of people who participate in high-risk recreational activities only if we study the biologically determined personality traits as well as other conditions (of cognitive character), among which we can list, personal aspirations and personal structure of values. The personal analysis of high-risk activities should include what is of importance to the respondents, what are the motives which animate their lives, what they would like to give up. In other words, a study of the personal values of climbers can enrich the knowledge about people who risk their own health and even their lives.

PERSONAL VALUES AS MOTIVES (S. SCHWARTZ'S POINT OF VIEW)

Values can be treated as existential; they possess specific meaning in specific situations and contexts as well as cross situational character (Chernoff & Davison, 1999; Schwartz, Sagiv & Boehenke, 2000). They make up the essential criterion which allows to estimate someone's behavior as well as to characterize the particular order. Some values are very important for the subject, while others are less important.

Values make up a cognitive representation of challenges, which an individual would undertake in order to survive biologically, to function as best as possible in a group as well as to live a satisfying life. Shalom Schwartz treats values as personal goals, meaning that values possess the character of sensible goals which all people try to reach in their lives. They represent stable but sensible preferences. Values motivate people to act as well as to undertake ventures (Madrigal & Kahle, 1994; Schwartz, 1992; Schwartz, Sagiv & Boehenke, 2000). The researchers are searching for the universal, culture-free contents, in spite of their essential differences. According to Shalom Schwartz, values construct the cognitive representations of challenges (goals), which people face in all cultures: biological challenges which make people survive; social challenges, which make people interact as well as challenges placed on an individual by the community, in which the given individual exists. These values are the basic principles that guide individual behavior throughout life (Schwartz, 1992). Thus, the researcher treats values as personal goals. This means that if we know the values of a person, we can more or less foresee what goals, including risky goals, he or she will be commit to in practice. Schwartz's Value Survey allows distinguishing the following types of values:

Achievement: Successful, capable, ambitious, influential, intelligent, self-respect.

Benevolence: Helpful, honest, forgiving, loyal, responsible, true friendship, a spiritual life, mature love, meaning in life.

Conformity: Politeness, honoring parents and elders, obedient, self-discipline.

Hedonism: Pleasure, enjoying life.

Power: Social power, authority, wealth, preserving my public image, social recognition.

Security: Clean, national security, social order, family security, reciprocation of favors, healthy sense of belonging.

Self-Direction: Creativity, curious, freedom, choosing own goals, independent, private life.

Stimulation: Daring, a varied life, an exciting life.

Tradition: Devout, accepting my portion in life, humble, moderate, respect for tradition.

Universalism: Protecting the environment, a world of beauty, unity with nature, broad-minded, social justice, wisdom, equality, a world at peace, inner harmony (Schwartz & Bilsky, 1987; Schwartz, 1992).

Different combinations and hierarchies of the values represented in Schwartz's theory motivate behavior for different reasons, and guide behavior in a different manner. The particular categories of values create the so-called "meta-categories", which may be introduced in two polarized dimensions:

1) Self-oriented (self-enhancement/openness to change);
2) Other-oriented/stability (self-transcendence/conservation).

These can be grouped into four meta-categories, which include the following groups of values:

a) Self-Transcendence: Universalism and Benevolence;
b) Self-Enhancement: Hedonism, Achievement, Power;
c) Openness to Change: Stimulation, Self-Direction;
d) Conservation: Security, Conformity, Tradition.

Until now there has been very little research on the personal values of risk takers (including climbers). For example, Shoham et al. (1998) found that thrill-seeking respondents scored higher than thrill-avoiders on the importance of three values: "warm relationships with others"; "fun and enjoyment"; and "self respect".

The purpose of this study was to compare the climbers' and control group's personal values manifested in The Schwartz Model. As discussed earlier, findings in this area prove that climbers display specific traits (Cronin, 1991; Jack & Ronan, 1998). The hypothesis, based on The Schwartz Value Model was that climbers would score higher in such meta-categories as Stimulation Value and Openness to Experience than the low risk activity group.

25

METHODS

Participants. The total sample was made up of two groups. The first group consisted of 66 male climbers who voluntarily participated in this study (M = 26.5; SD = 10.1). The respondents had an average of 9 years of climbing experience. This group was recruited via high risk activity associations or climber clubs in the south of Poland. All members of the group had experience in high mountains: the Tatra Mountains, the Alps and some of them – in the Himalayas. The second group was a control group of 57 men (M = 28.4; SD = 4.4), none of whom had ever participated in any high-risk activity. The controls had an average of 7 years of activity experience.

Procedure. The groups taking part in this examination were asked to fill in the Questionnaire section of the Schwartz Survey Instrument. Each group was informed about the aim of the research. Participation was voluntary. Apart from filling the form, the respondents had to answer questions concerning their age, sex and time of practicing their discipline. The members of the control group were additionally asked if they had any experience connected with practicing a risky activity.

Questionnaire. The present study was conducted with the application of the Schwartz Survey Instrument. This questionnaire allows measuring the values as goals, in accordance with Scwartz's theory. The questionnaire consists of a list of 57 values, which are connected with individual or group goals. These values were grouped into 10 categories. The participants were asked to rate them as "life-governing values" on a scale of -1 to 7. The -1 level means that the presented value is against participant's principles, 0 – the given value is not important for participant, 3 – the given value is important for the participant, 6 – the given value is very important; 7 – the given value is the most important one in the participant's life.

The coefficient of preference of a given category or meta-category is the average value, ascribed to the particular category or meta-category chosen by the participant.

RESULTS

First, the differences in 10 categories of values between the group of climbers and the control group were studied. The results are presented in table 1.

Table 1. Personal values - comparison between the climbers and control groups, student test (t)

Variables	Climbers		Control group		t Student
	M	SD	M	SD	
PERSONAL VALUES					
Power	3.65	1.24	3.55	1.34	.91
Achievement	4.50	.80	4.35	1.05	.37
Hedonism	3.85	1.10	3.74	.85	.94
Stimulation	4.66	1.11	3.40	1.16	**5.72****
Self-Direction	5.05	.67	4.63	.81	**2.43***
Universalism	4.15	1,07	4.30	.87	-.58
Benevolence	4.55	.94	4.44	.83	-.56
Tradition	3.35	1.10	3.76	1.01	-.78
Conformity	4.45	1.05	4.65	1.08	1.24
Security	4.43	.91	4.66	.75	1.48

p<.05*; p<.01**

Climbers were characterized by significantly higher results in comparison to the control group in such scales as: Stimulation (p < .001), Self-Direction (p < .05). In other cales of values the climbers' results did not differ from those of the control group.

As it was mentioned by Schwartz (1992) different combinations and hierarchies of values motivate behavior for different reasons, and guide behavior in a different manner. The particular categories of values create the so-called "meta-categories". That is why the differences in the meta-categories of values between the climbers and control groups were included in our study. The results are presented in table 2.

Table 2. Meta-categories of values – comparison between the climber and control groups, student test (t)

Variables	Climbers		Control group		t Student
	M	SD	M	SD	
METACATEGORIES OF VALUES					
Self-Enhancement	4.00	.84	3.88	1.04	1.23
Openness to Change	4.85	.73	4.01	.82	5.34***
Self-Transcendence	4.35	.93	4.37	.85	-.61
Conservation	4.07	.92	4.35	.83	-1.43

p<.001***

Climbers were characterized by significantly higher results in comparison to the control group, in the meta-category Openness to Change (p < .001).

DISCUSSION

The obtained results show that the personal values of climbers differ from the personal values of the control group. According to Schwartz (1992), values are the variable motivation of people which leads to concrete choices in the concrete situational context. The intensity of particular values informs us about an individual's goals in concrete activities as well as in high-risk activities. It was found, that extreme individual's rated the value Stimulation higher in comparison to the control group. Our results confirmed the findings of previous studies on sensation seeking (Hymbaugh & Garett, 1974; Jack & Ronan, 1998; Zuckerman, 1994). Climbing satisfies the need for stimulation in the climber group. Climbers are people who appreciate challenges, seek experiences and adventures, like living varied lives. They can be charac-terized by positive attitudes towards emotion, especially towards positive or joyful affect (Zuckerman, 1994).

Sensation stimulation related negatively to specific fearfulness, especially in situations where there is danger of physical harm (Zuckerman, 1994). That is probably why climbers seek challenges, risk or even extreme situations in the mountains.

Higher intensity of Stimulation in the climber group may also have negative consequences. Studies on sensation seekers illustrate that they not view the environment as threatening. They usually underestimate the level of risk (Trimpop, 1994; Zuckerman, 1994). This means that, in risky situations, climbers can minimize the risk associated with climbing or even fail to recognize such risks.

It needs to be emphasized that Self-Direction is the value that distinguishes climbers from the control group. Climbers are people with a high need for autonomy, independence in thinking and acting, as well as rivalry. It seems that the specifics of aerial recreation are at odds with the personal goals of the participants - climbers feel free in mountains.

27

Climbers are people with a strong set of values, who listen to others but make the ultimate decision themselves. Moreover, climbers will never act against their most important values, regardless of other's actions or opinions. A higher Self-Direction score in the climber group may also mean that they act in accordance with their own needs rather than social conventions or the needs and attitudes of others. They know exactly what their goals are. Climbers are competent and strong people and perhaps one of their most important features is that they do not give up until they have reached their desired goals.

An interesting issue for future research would be to analyze the personal values of people who participate in other high-risk recreational activities e.g. alpinists, rock climbers, surfers, glider pilots or scuba-divers.

REFERENCES

Bond, M. H., Leung, K. & Schwartz, S. (1992). Explaining choices in procedural and distributive justice across cultures. *International Journal of Psychology, 27*, 211-225.

Breivik, G. (1996). Personality, sensation seeking and risk taking among Everest climbers. *International Journal of Sport Psychology, 27* (3), 208-230.

Chernoff, R. A. & Davison, G. C. (1999). Values and their relationship to HIV/AIDS risk behavior among late-adolescent and young adult college students. *Cognitive Therapy and Research, 23 (5)*, 453-468.

Cronin, C. (1991). Sensation seeking among mountain climbers. *Personality and Individual Differences, 12 (6)*, 653-654.

Egan, S. & Stelmack, M. R. (2003). A personality profile of Mount Everest climbers. *Personality and Individual Differences, 34 (8)*, 1491-1494.

Ewert, A. (1993). Differences in the level of motive importance based on trip outcome, experience level and group type. *Journal of Leisure Research, 25*, 335-349.

Ewert, A. (1994). Playing the edge: Motivation and risk taking in a high-altitude wilderness like environment. *Environmental. Behavior,* 26, 3 – 7.

Gollwitzer, P. M. (1996). The volitional benefits of planning. P.M. Gollwitzer & J. Bargh (eds.). *The psychology of action: Linking cognition and motivation to behavior.* New York: Guilford Press, 287-312.

Goma-i-Freixanet, M. (1991). Personality profiles of subjects engaged in high physical risk sports. *Personality and Individual Differences, 12 (10)*, 1087-1093.

Hymbaugh, K., & Garrett, J. (1974). Sensation seeking among skydivers. *Perceptual and Motor Skills, 38,* 118.

Jack, S. J. & Ronan, K. R. (1998). Sensation seeking among high- and low-risk sports participants. *Personality and Individual Differences, 25,* 1063-1083.

Levenson, M. R. (1990). Risk taking and personality. *Journal of Personality and Social Psychology 58 (6),* 1073-1080.

Madrigal, R. & Kahle, L. R. (1994). Predicting vacation activity preferences on the basis of value-system seg-mentation. *Journal of Travel Research 32 (3),* 22-28.

McIntyre, N. (1992). Involvement in risk recreation: A comparison of objective and subjective measures of engagement. *J. Leisure Res., 24,* 64-71.

Moutinho, L. (2000). *Strategic Management in Tourism.* New York: CABI Publishing.

Peron, R.G. (2009). Everest & Himalaya climbing end report. http://www.explorersweb.com/everest_k2 /news.php?id=18602

Rokeach, M. (1973). *The Nature of Human Values.* New York: Free Press.

Rossi, B. & Cereatti, L. (1993). The sensation seeking in mountain athletes as assessed by Zuckerman's Sen-sation Seeking Scale. *International Journal of Sport Psychology, 24,* 417-431.

Schroth, M. L. (1995). A comparison of sensation seeking among different group of athletes and non-athletes. *Personality and Individual Differences, 18 (2)*, 219-222.

Schwartz, S. H. (1992). Universals in the content and structure of values: Theoretical advances and empirical tests in 20 countries. In M.P. Zanna (Eds.),.*Advances in experimental social psychology, 25,* (pp.1-65) New York: Academic Press.

Schwartz, S. H. & Bilsky, W. (1987). Toward a universal psychological structure of human values. *Journal of Personality and Social Psychology, 53*, 550-562.

Schwartz, S. H., Sagiv, L. & Boehenke, K. (2000). Worries and values. *Journal of personality, 68, 2,* 309-346.

Shoham, A., Florenthal, B., Kropp, F. & Rose, G. M. (1998). The relationship between values and thrill- and adven-ture-seeking in Israel. *European advances in consumer research, 3,*333-338.

Trimpop, R. M. (1994). *The psychology of risk taking behavior.* Amsterdam: Elsevier Science.

Zuckerman, M. (1994). *Behavioral expressions and biosocial bases of sensation seeking.* New York, Cambridge: University Press.

SUMMARY

The aim of the present study was to identify the personal values of climbers and persons who do low risk activity in the frames of the Schwartz's Values Model. The sample group consisted of 66 climbers (*M* age = 26.5, *SD* = 10.1) and 57 low risk activity takers (*M* age = 28.4, *SD* = 4.4). The Survey Instrument by Schwartz was used as a method of the study. It was found out that climbers scored significantly higher on Stimulation and Self-Direction in comparison to the control group, as well as climbers also scored significantly higher on meta-category Openness to Change.

STRESZCZENIE

Celem prezentowanego badania było poznanie wartości osobowościowych alpinistów oraz ludzi niepodejmujących aktywności ryzykownych, zbadanych w ramach Modelu Wartości Schwartz'a. W badaniu wzięło udział 66 alpinistów (*M* age = 26.5, *SD* = 10.1) oraz 57 osób nie podejmujących ryzyka (*M* age = 28.4, *SD* = 4.4). Jako narzędzie badawcze wykorzystany został Kwestionariusz Wartości Schwartza. Rezultaty badań pokazują, że alpiniści mają istotnie wyższe wyniki w skali Stymulacja i Kierowanie Sobą w porównaniu z grupą kontrolną. Alpiniści uzyskali również istotnie wyższe wyniki w meta-kategorii Otwartość na Zmiany.

SAMMENDRAG

Undersøkelsen har hatt som målsetning å identifisere personlige verdier til klatrere og personer som driver med lav-risiko aktiviteter, i forhold til S. Schwartz *Values Survey Modell.* Undersøkelses gruppe var 66 klatrere (*M* alder = 26.5, *SD* = 10.1) og 57 utøvere med lav-risiko aktiviteter (*M* alder = 28.4, *SD* = 4.4). Måleinstrumentet var spørreskjema av S. Schwartz. Resultatene viser at klatrerne skåret signifikant høyere på *stimulation* og *Self-Direction* i forhold til kontroll gruppen. Klatrerne skåret også signifikant høyere på meta-kategorien *openess to change.*

DR. DAGMAR DAHL, PHD

Finnmark University College
Department for Sport and Science
Follumsvei 31
9509 Alta, Norway
E-mail: Dagmar.Dahl@hifm.no

WHEN THE MEDAL IS IN HEAVEN.
RELIGIOUS BELIEF –
MOTIVATIONAL BASIS FOR SPORTS PERFORMANCE?

INTRODUCTION

The German Sports philosopher and sociologist Sven Güldenpfennig used the term "Glaubensdoping" (Belief-Doping) when talking about athletes who put their performance in God's trust and support. Since he has used this term in 2000 it has become common for athletes to talk about more intimate subjects such as their personal beliefs. Some have gone as far as showing their religious conviction with a missionary zeal, which caused a ban from the official body. The IOC and the FIFA were concerned about their own credibility as an open arena, independent of the participants' philosophy of life. In sports' pedagogical contexts, the confrontation as well as the cooperation within the area of religion has become an issue.

In this article we will look at this topic from two perspectives. First, we ask the question, is there a connection between religion and sports that allows this close link between motivation and sports performance? Secondly, how can the theoretical-philosophical basis of this connection be interrelated to personal experiences? We will embed those questions in a sports pedagogical approach and give some suggestions, which may lead to further investi-gation. The question whether religious belief can represent a motivational basis for sports performance shall therefore be discussed by presenting aspects from a Sports Pedagogical and Sports Philosophical point of view.

METHOD

To examine these questions we have used a qualitative approach in form of text analysis of not only core religious texts and interpretations of them but also some relevant literature from the field of sport pedagogy and psychology from which comparisons made and conclusions drawn. Furthermore, we analyzed biographical material presented in different studies and books. Additional text based data material has been generated by qualitative interviews and dialogues with experts from both areas (sport and religion) and representatives from different religions. The choice of interview partners and sources where supported by expert rating. Parts of this data had been collected in connection with a larger research project in the field of Sport and Religion (cf. Dahl, 2009).

After a short introduction to the terms "sports" and "religion", the resemblances and the connection between sport/ sports pedagogy and religion are addressed. The term "motive" is important in the context of this work and leads to religion's attitude towards sport. This prepares the ground for discussion about our main question: "can religious belief be a motivationnal basis for sports performance?"

SPORT AND RELIGION AS MULTIFACET PHENOMENA

Both terms, "sport" and "religion" are quite complex and neither clearly nor uniformly defined by scholars. Due to developments in a globalized society, both phenomena need constant discussion. Sports sociologist Heinemann distinguishes between different sport models and mentions as constructive elements bodily activity, performance principle, typical rules for different sports, unproductiveness (cf. Heinemann, 1998, 35). The American sports philosopher Suits considers the following elements as "determinable" elements of sports: a "goal", means for achieving the goal, rules, lusory attitude, and physical skills as characteristic of sports. The introductory comprehensions in this inquiry are sports including physical activity in a "sports-for-all" setting. In addition we look at the special form, top-level-sports, which are known from media and international sporting events and practised in clubs and training groups in European countries. Top-level- Sports is a system in the complex of sports and distinguishes itself by its very focus on top-level performance aiming at new records, mediatization and globalization (cf. Dahl, 2008). We will take a more detailed look at the complex topic "sport" from the sports pedagogical point of view which is presented by Balz/Kuhlmann. Their concept offers a pragmatic approach to compare the interconnections between sports and religion in terms of motivational support.

Religion is as complex a phenomenon as sport. It is an ambiguous term that is not clearly defined. Generally, religion is seen as a shared cultural belief system with rituals, mystical language and symbols, devotion to gods/deities or trans-empirical power, rules for ethical conduct and guidelines for interpretation of life and existence. In this research, those religions generally accepted as "world religions" were chosen. Regarding the specific examples cited in this text, the selected religions are Christianity, Islam and Buddhism. Christianity represents the main religion in both Germany and Norway, the two countries where this inquiry mainly has taken place and which are part of the cultural background for today's top level sports. Islam is today's most discussed religion and Buddhism, a represent-tative for eastern philosophy and alternative thinking, has gained more popularity in Western countries during recent decades. For the purpose of this study we are including a broader comprehension of religion with includes also a personal performed spirituality which is not necessarily linked to the institutional religion.

SPORT PEDAGOGY AND RELIGION: LINK BETWEEN MOTIVATION, PERFORMANCE, SPORT AND RELIGION

Sport pedagogy as an academic discipline deals with "questions, problems, contexts of sport and teaching (or movement culture and education)" (Balz & Kuhlmann, 2006, p.20). Balz and Kuhlmann underline the focus on application in practical situations. They differ in addressing one of two options: first, to better one's sports performance that means the main interest is the "sport," or secondly, to develop human beings as fully human, the focus is on human beings themselves. The last point especially emphasizes the importance of the inclusion of one's philosophy of life in sport pedagogical considerations. When asking religions (which, in this text, refers to representatives and experts in this field) about their attitude towards sports, it is useful to keep these two aspects in mind. We will see that some of the answers address both of them.

SPORT AND RELIGION - A SPECIAL RELATIONSHIP

In discussing sport and religion it is interesting to discover how far sport can be considered as a religion, i.e., the debate about resemblances and differences between sports and religion. The resemblances are related to formal and functional similarities and include aspects such as the following. Both sport and religion are similar as core elements of most cultural systems. They regard the human being in its entirety and create "time-outs" from the stress of everyday life. Both include rituals and ritual actions in a similar way. In both the members are obliged to follow a set of rules and both "offer" "saints" which the individual/common member can worship. They are social institutions that convey norms and meaning. Both are engaged in general social life even if that is not directly concerned with either sport or religion. Both have been considered and "used" as state religion/folk religion or state sport/folk sport and have been abused by political exploitation.

Nevertheless there are clear differences concerning contents and scope of sports and religion that are important and need to be emphasized. All the representatives from the world religions interviewed for this study stress the differentiation as necessary. Some of the dissimilarities include:

(i)   Religions cover a broader perspective than sports and are related to the whole of human life. Religions offer support and possibilities of interpretation at the "turning points," the times of crises in life.

(ii) Sport is a "thing" "in" the world, while religions also focus on the transcendental. Religions want to also take care of those who do not believe and – at least the world religions – are expecting to be valid for all human beings. Any sport event is usually a short-term experience, whereas a religious experience tends to be more long-lasting, often connected with constant changes in life. Sport was meant to be for leisure-time entertainment for the spectators, which is not the aim of religious events.

When looking in the context of this inquiry on the motivational basis, it seems to be useful to have the structural similarities in mind. Those can represent a common ground for motivation in sports participation, e.g. the engagement in social life.

MOTIVE – RELIGION AS AN AIM

When looking at different approaches to mental training and performance psychology we can find that the concrete exercise task used is to be placed in a comprehensive context. Eberspächer (2001) described the process of focusing in exercise with concentric circles starting with the individuals "I" and the task proceeding with the nearby surrounding, the performance expectation and the consequences whereas the last circle gathering the whole, is the general question of meaning. This question can, for some athletes, be answered by their religious belief. That is to say, the motive for a good performance can be in the final end to serve or honour their religious conviction. Several athletes can be observed, especially after a good performance, sending prayers of gratitude up to heaven or making the sign of cross or other religious symbol in order to show their conviction.

Furthermore in those examples, the movement activity itself can be considered as part of a religious action. That means that an underlying motive for the sport event is not a sport immanent but is reasoned in the religious context. Somebody is doing sports as a part of one's religious commitment.

A famous example is the ancient Olympic Games. Even though the competitions were important in terms of an ideal of citius – altius - fortius and the winner was acknowledged in society for his athletic performance, the Games were also part of honouring Zeus, the main god in the ancient Greek religion (Decker, 1995). Some religions have movement activities as part of their religious practice like dancing or, as some Muslims like to emphasize, prayers which contain a set of different movement activities (cf. Dahl, 2009).

If we want to address the possibility of increasing motivation for sports practice by one's religious belief, first, we have to consider attitude of religion towards sports. In this paper we present Christianity as the main example as it is still the prominent religion in the countries where the research took place and also a kind of cultural background for top-level sport as we do know it from events like the Olympic Games. In addition, Islam and Buddhism as to set of beliefs which has become more impact also in western societies in the recent years are described.

RELIGION'S ATTITUDE TOWARDS SPORT

Christianity. The human body is seen as a creation by God and therefore has to be taken care of. Today body and soul are viewed as equal parts of the whole human being. Earlier interpretations of the New Testament, especially the Epistles of Paul, were based on a Platonic view that degraded the body by calling it "the prison of the soul" and the place which leads to sin. Those attitudes no longer guide (lead) the Christian perspective on body, movement and sport. In recent decades, theological understanding takes into account the Jewish context from the Old Testament with a holistic perspective on body and soul. The bodily resurrection of Jesus underlines the high regard of the human body in the Christian religion. Movement in context with the body is regarded as useful and natural, "we are created to be in movement" (Austad, 2004). Paul knew the sports of his age and used allegories and examples from the ancient world of sports for his explanations. Today Christian churches have a positive attitude towards sports. Sporting activity is recommended if used in a balanced way in order to live a meaningful life, enjoying yourself and the company with others. In addition, top-level sport is regarded positively as long as human dignity is respected and one's 'addiction' to sport does not infringe on ethical and fair behaviour because of a "winning-at-all-costs" attitude. Modern Christianity acknowledges the meaning of sport in terms of bodily welfare. Talent in sport can be seen as a gift from God. In terms of pedagogical reflections, the Roman Catholic Church especially draws a line between "discipline as a Christian and the discipline as an athlete".

In a common declaration, evangelical and catholic churches in Germany pointed out the following positive aspects of modern sports.

- Joy and human fulfillment *(Freude und menschliche Erfüllung)*
- Exploration of one's own limits of performance *(Auslotung der Grenzen der eigenen Leistungsfähigkeit)*
- Social career *(Sozialen Aufstieg)*
- Rolemodel for young athletes *(Vorbildfunktion für junge Sportlerinnen und Sportler)*
- Value of entertainment for spectators *(Unterhaltungswert für die Zuschauer)*
- Overcoming of national borders *(Überwindung nationaler Grenzen)*

But these churches caution against

- Victory and success at any costs *(Sieg und Erfolg um jeden Preis)*
- Athletes as „tools" or means in the hands of others *(Sportlerinnen und Sportler als „Instrument" in der Hand anderer)*
- Manipulative interventions and performance enhancing drugs *(Manipulative Eingriffe und Doping)*
- Difficulties to integrate sports in the whole life span *(Schwierigkeiten der Einordnung des Sports in das Lebensganze)*

- Lack of social safeguard (especially for those who never reach the top) *(Mangelnde so-ziale Absicherung (vor allem für diejenigen, die nie ganz an die Spitze kommen))*
- Risk of social descent after one's sports career has ended *(Gefahr des sozialen Abstiegs nach dem Ende der „Karriere')*
- Commercialization, politization, nationalization *(Kommerzialisierung, Politisierung und Nationalisierung)* (EKD, 1990, p.5)

Islam. Muslims too are convinced that human beings are created by God and that tak-ing care of the body is important. The body is called the "mount of the soul" and both the Quran and Hadith give lots of guidance on how to deal with one's body.

In those texts movement and sports are regarded as positive. One should use one's body and take care of it in a balanced way without exaggeration. Muhammad himself prac-tised the sports of his culture and recommended instructing children in swimming, horse-riding and arch-ery. Also top-level sports are accepted in this sense as long as they do not prevent one from be-ing a good Muslim, i.e., following Islamic ethical guidelines. For sports practice, several sources paid special attention to the relation and intermingling of the sexes and the question of appropriate clothing. Different ways of interpreting the rules regarding this question depend on the cultural diversity. In correspondence to Sura 2 in the Quran, many representatives consulted in this study emphasized that there should not be compulsion in the religion, but an individual Muslim should choose the right ethical conduct in accordance to his/her devotion to God, to Islam. More extreme or strict positions, which, for example, consider sports as preparation for the physical "jihad", are rooted in cultural-political circumstances.

As a demonstration of a close connection between Islam and top-level sports, but even more, the unity of the "Islamic world as defined in the founding documents of this religion, was shown when the "Islamic Solidarity Games" were established and took place for the first time in this form in 2005.

Buddhism. Taking care of your body is important, as "your relationship to your body defines your relationship to the world" (Fuchs in interview, May 2006). The body is seen in a holistic way and differs from the Western dualistic perspective. Considering sports, Buddhism as a religion with bodily activity in some of the meditations takes a positive attitude as long as it does not lead a person to get "addicted" or dependant. Buddha himself practised the sports of his age when he was young. In the martial arts the link between sports and Buddhism may be clearer than in other religious concepts. In the original ancient form of the martial arts practice, the Buddhist ethics and spirituality are obvious. Nowadays, the "Olympic" forms of martial arts sports have mainly lost their religious roots, but they still highlight important as-pects, especially from the Zen-Buddhist tradition, regarding both body and mind in sports. Buddhist meditation and psychology are linked to Csikszentmihalyi's concept of "flow", which he mentioned in his work (Csikszentmihalyi & Jackson, 1999), and may explain the increased interest of top-level athletes in Buddhism as was mentioned by one of the represent-atives interviewed. The positive aspects for practising sport include, for instance, health, well-being, improvement and optimizing one's performance, developing human potential, cooperation and fair-play, and the flow-experience.

MOTIVATIONAL BASIS - RELIGIOUS BELIEF AND THE CORRESPONDING SET OF VALUES AS BASIS FOR PERFORMANCE

Motivation is a very complex term to define. In everyday language we are talking about one's motivation or lack of it, when describing a person's pursuit for attaining his/her aim. In this inquiry we briefly outline some of the principal points, without going into a detailed debate about the sport psychological term of motivation.

"Motivation is the direction and intensity of effort" (Weinberg & Gould, 2003, p.82). This definition indicates that motivation involves a person being attracted to certain situations (direction) and puts forth a certain amount of effort in those situations (intensity). Regarding the situation in sports does this mean that an individual chooses to participate in an activity with at least a basic engagement. The "reason" behind that, i.e. the motive often is composed of several aspects, but as mentioned before, one motive can be the athlete's religious belief. When looking at motivation, psychologists generally hold one of three different views, that is, the trait-centred view, the situation-centred view, or the interactional view. Weinberg & Gould (2003, p.53) mention that the "trait-centred view (also called the participant-centred view) contends that motivated behaviour is primarily a function of individual characteristics. That is, the personality, needs, and goals of a student, athlete, or exerciser are the primary determinants of motivated behaviour."

On the other hand, the situation-centred orientation implies that the situation, the setting determines the level of motivation. In application, it is mostly a kind of combination, that is, the interactional view, which contends that "motivation results neither solely from participant factors, such as personality, needs, interests, and goals, nor solely from situational factors. (…) The best way to understand motivation is to consider both the person and the situation and how the two interact" (ibid, pp.54f.)

The term "motivational basis" is used here in order to cover a broader approach, including both terms, motive and motivation, with all mentioned aspects.

Thus, why religion in particular is well suited as a motivational basis is addressed first by comparing and connecting aspects from sports pedagogy and the attitude of religions towards sport, and, secondly, by looking at the athlete's personal experience (in the next paragraph). The relevant perspective that warrants close scrutiny is the "direction" aspect, in other words, why is it possibly attractive for a religious person to seek a sport situation. At the same time, it may also be of interest to look at the "effort" aspect, that is, the reasons behind athletes' and others of religious persuasion participation in competitive sporting events. For this purpose, it seems useful to compare sports and religion in terms of the different perspectives on motivation, that is, the personal, situation-centred, and interaction views.

Let us now have a closer look at the sports phenomenon – both as top-level sports and sports for all – from the pedagogical point of view. According to sports pedagogues Kuhlmann and Balz (2006), sports participants are typically confronted with requests of movement, interaction, and realization. That means the core element in sports is movement, which is more or less performed in social interaction and can serve for interactive contact and communication. Finally those aspects have to be realized and figured out in terms of training, exercise, game, competition or play. Kuhlmann and Balz (2006) outline special experiences which can be applied in sports: bodily experiences including both performance vs. relaxation, power and sensitivity gained through movement activities; personal experiences regarding our own personality and our being an individual, when, for example, joining challenging actions; social experiences when playing together, meeting others practicing sports and undergoing cooperation and competition in fellowship; and finally, material experiences, which means the direct contact with the natural and material surroundings, such as feeling the water, grabbing a ball, running on forest soil.

Of interest in this study is that the former leader of the Evangelical Churches in Germany (EKD), Bishop Wolfgang Huber, describes and appreciates the natural, the personal and the social dimension of sport and physical activities (Huber, 2000). But one can equally compare the identified range of experiences to religious practice: bodily experiences in forms of prayer-movements, ritual dances and washings, Lenten-fast or other ritual movements combine the personal experiences which are accomplished by spiritual incidents. The social dimension is a basic one in all world religions: being a fellowship of co-religionists is one of the defining markers of a religion and most religions have a certain focus on social activities and forms of charity. Also the meeting with the "material world" is important in most known philosophies, even though religions have occupied interests in the immaterial world. The world religions contain interpretations of the nature around us, show a certain responsibility toward it, and give guidelines in how to live in harmony in the surrounding world. As an example, one can find the intertwining of sport and religion in experiencing the combination material world – immaterial world and the person's conception of the setting when going a long cross country ski tour in a splendid landscape and weather conditions.

Sport pedagogical and psychological research regarding the "meaning" a person associates with practicing sports outlines, amongst others, the following aspects: experience of performance and self value, health and well-being as well as social contact with other people. In addition people are looking for a kind of excitement, impressions and nature-experience and the possibility for expression and aestheticism and an experience of happiness. Of course not all of the areas of meaning are given in all situations and are valuable for all athletes. How do these aspects fit in with a devout athlete?

All the examined religions underline the importance of taking care of bodily and social health and acknowledge the possibilities exercise and movement can offer. As we have seen before, Christian churches appreciate those aspects as positive points in their statement.

When comparing religious practice with sports, there are in particular the parallels on the experiential level, that is, experience of self value, health and well-being as well as the respect for nature and social life, which obviously make it easy to associate one's religious with one's sporting activity. Both religion and sports have a common ground of values, supplementary for a believer is the sense of belonging to a truth system which provide a kind of extra responsibility in terms of living a good/right life.

But where sports can provide many of the same values and experiences as religion, one point it lacks: the spiritual aspect. This lack of inclusion of the spiritual in sports leads us to the other perspective: the athlete's point of view.

THE PERSONAL EXPERIENCE – ATHLETES IN ACTION

Most people watching sport have seen them: athletes making the sign of cross or lifting up their heads and folding their hands to prayer, Muslims kneeling down on the ground or – before the rules were changed – soccer players showing their message on their t-shirts under the tricot. No doubt, for some of those their religious belief has a basic meaning for their whole lifestyle. As we have seen that motivation is defined as the direction and the intensity of effort. Especially when we consider the personal trait oriented view, one's faith can have great influence on the individual athlete. Because of a set of shared values, for example, health, well-being, social, experience of self-worth and value of one's performance, both the leaning to sports activities as such and the grade of engagement can be interpreted by an athlete as a special addiction to one's religion. But athletes also find support in their faith to overcome difficulties and dark sides which sports can present. One can get motivation back when having directed the engagement to a greater aim, than just winning the gold medal in the stadium.

In biographies and interviews with Christian athletes, many of them emphasize the importance of their faith and what it means. It helps them to understand the deeper meaning of life and their role as a top level athlete. The Christian Association "Sportler ruft Sportler" (SRS) (the German partner of "Athletes in Action") which looks after Christian athletes and offers pastoral welfare, mentions different anxieties athletes struggle with. Amongst others, they refer to the anxiety associated with injuries and failure or being dropped from the team and not being part of the "sport system" because of injuries or failure. Athletes may be afraid of unpopularity and the special status in society at the end of their sporting career, of suffering the humiliation of not being able to fulfil their full potential while under the limelight of the media during important competitions (SRS, 2010). In contrast, SRS emphasizes the following as motivational factors for joining top level sports, amongst others: being somebody special, receiving accolades/ appreciation, proving one's ability and impressing parents, trainers, friends, and club, being a part of a team, having an athlete's body, escaping from other "weaker" parts of life and showing strength. And they also mention the reason for participating in top level sports is the desire to develop one's full potential and experience "flow". Those two last points shall be underlined, as they are important from the Buddhist point of view on sports. Michael Fuchs, who was representative for Buddhism at the Athens Olympic Games in 2004, reports that an increasing number of western top-athletes are interested in Buddhism. He explained this phenomenon as the search for the spiritual experience, aiming the "flow" without an exhausting sports performance. Difficult and challenging situations are generally part of life. Religions claim to provide interpretations that cover the whole life span, including the "crises" in existence. Thus, Conrad and Lau (2010) reveal in their study that religious athletes use their faith as a kind of psychological support when coping with difficulties and demands in training and competition. These authors conclude that religiosity has an impact on athletes' experiences in top-level sport and underline the evidence of organisations like "Sportler ruft Sportler", which cares about the spiritual aspect of the sportsperson. Breitmeier (2010), as representative of this organization, explains their Christian perspective, which implies that a human being is an entity of body, psyche and spirit. This indicates three levels of perception: body: the surrounding, psyche: my Self, spirit: something larger than me/God. In his article, Breitmeier criticizes that in common sport training context the focus is on the body and psyche, while the spiritual aspect and the deeper search for meaning are neglected. The main concern is success and winning. In the long term, this focus may incur problems with the athlete's self-esteem, questions of personal identity, and meaning of life (Breitmeier, 2010). He underlines the desire of athletes of strong personality who are able to transfer meaningful values from sport to the rest of their life and vice versa. The reports from athletes about the significance of their faith for their sporting career support those points. Kadel & Volke (2006) collected and presented interviews in their books with several Christian athletes, most of them from the field of soccer. Despite their different background in their life stories, one can find some parallels within their own evaluation of the importance of their religious truth for their life as top-level athletes. Aspects cited for appreciating their belief are, for example, the quest of meaning and the search for reliable happiness. Other points are coping with difficulties and failures, but also with being famous and wealthy, a condition which is not necessarily associated with a happy, meaningful life. Others are grateful for their talent and underline the consciousness of feeling under the shelter and support by their faith.

RESUME AND CONCLUSION

„Glaubensdoping" does exist if one wants to use this 'ironical term' for the special motivation religious athletes may experience. It is grounded in philosophy and the attitude of religion towards sport. In this article Christianity, Islam and Buddhism were researched, with the main emphasis on Christianity and Christian athletes. A line can be drawn between one's religious commitment, sports and sports pedagogical aims and the motivational basis for exercise and sports performance.

There are similarities/resemblances between sport and religion. Furthermore there are parallels in sports pedagogical approach towards exercise performance and the attitude and appreciation religion show concerning sports, which brings us to the conclusion that being religious supports rather than prevents athletes and trainees/exercisers from sports participation. On the personal level and seen from the trait centred view of motivation, an athlete may be attracted to exercise (direction aspect of motivation) because of these similarities, and he/she may want to display a certain effort in order to strengthen his or her religious faith. A believer recognizes that sports have values and elements which fit quite well with one's religions attitude. As an explanatory example: Religions regard taking care of the body as important, that can be translated for an athlete as „showing a good bodily per-formance – a means to demonstrate being a good Christian". Also the interactive and situation-centred view on motivation lets us conclude the link to religion. When looking at the resemblances there are lots of similarities on the situational plan, the setting and scenery. People belonging to a religion may experience a certain religious-like setting under a sporting event or their exercise. While the first conclusions here can be seen as directly encouraging for motivation in and to sports, there is also the indirect way to strengthen the motivation, as we will explain not. In addition to the similar fields of experiences, there is one added in religion: the spiritual experience which considers the human being as a unity of body, soul *and* spirit. This spiritual level obviously contribute to develop resilience in endeavouring situations by offering meaning in otherwise meaning-less experienced situations. That means an indirect support for motivation to sports in terms of enable the athlete to cope with difficulties which otherwise might have diminished the engagement to sports activities.

This study had been carried out on a general level. Sport and Religion are not closed systems. There might be differences in the personal experiences of motivation where aspects like identity, gender, culture and relationship can play important parts. Further research is also needed for example to reveal more clearly strategies and processes how religious athletes deal with challenges different from atheists. At the same time it is important to discuss and be aware of the process of instrumentalization: religion cannot be "used" as doping, cannot be instrumentalized for performance enhancing. The term „Glaubensdoping" should therefore be refused. However, the motivational basis for „the medal in heaven" is given.

REFERENCES

Austad, T. (2004). I bevegelse – til fornyelse. Kristent syn på idrett. *DIN – tidsskrift for Religion og Kultur (6), 1*, 75-82.

Baker, W. J. (2007). *Playing with God – Religion and Modern Sport*. London.

Balz, E. & Kuhlmann, D. (2006). *Sportpädagogik*. Aachen: Meyer & Meyer.

Benn, T., Pfister, G. & Jawad, H. (eds.) (2010). *Muslim Women and Sport*. New York.

Benz, C. (2011). *Moral Values and Beliefs of Christian Athletes in Competitive Sports*. Unpublished Manuskript, Stuttgart.

Breitmeier, B. (2010). Der Sport /Ganzheitliche Sportlerförderung. SRS Sportler ruft Sportler e.V: *Christ und Sport*. Version 2.3. Altenkirchen, 11-15.

Brockhaus, R. SCM (Hg.) (2010). *Mit vollem Einsatz*. Das Neue Testament mit Lebensberichten internationaler Spitzensportler. Witten.

Conrad, J. & Lau, A. (2010). Einfluss religiöser Einstellungen von Athletinnen und Athleten auf ihr leistungs-sportliches Leben. Vortrag. Körper, Kult und Konfession. Religiöse Dimensionen des Sports und Körperkults. Jahrestagung 2010 der dvs-Sektion *Sportsoziologie* in Kooperation mit den DGS-Sektionen Soziologie des Körpers und des Sports und Religionssoziologie. Frankfurt/Main.

Cooper, A. (1998). *Playing in the Zone. Exploring the Spiritual Dimensions of Sports*. London/Boston.

Csikszentmihalyi, M. & Jackson, S. (1999). *Flow in Sports*. Leeds: Champaign.

Dahl, D. (2008). Sport und Religion/en. M. Klöcker & U. Tworuschka (eds.). *Praktische Religionswissenschaft.* Köln, 177-188.

Dahl, D. (2009). *Zum Verständnis von Körper, Bewegung und Sport in Christentum, Islam und Buddhismus – Impulse zum interreligiösen Ethikdiskurs zum Spitzensport.* Berlin.

Decker, W. (1995). *Sport in der griechischen Antike.* München.

Deutsche Vereinigung für Sportwissenschaft 10-23 Sportsoziologie 2010 auf: http://www.sportwissenschaft.de/ index.php?id=1131, actualized 16.9.2011.

Eberspächer, H. (2001). *Mentales Training.* München: Stiebner Verlag.

Evangelische Kirche in Deutschland (ed.). *Sport und christliches Ethos – Gemeinsame Erklärung der Kirchen zum Sport.*

Evangelische Kirche in Deutschland (ed.) (1991). *Gott ist ein Freund des Lebens,* Hannover (www.ekd.de/EKD-Texte/2064_gottistfreund_1989_freund4.html)

Evangelische Kirche in Deutschland: Arbeitskreis "Kirche und Sport": http://www.ekd.de/kirche-und-sport/ arbeitskreis.html actualized 16.9.2011

Evangelische Kirche in Deutschland (ed.). *Zum Wohl der Menschen und der Gesellschaft. Perspektiven der Zusammenarbeit von Kirche und Sport in Deutschland.* http://www.ekd.de/kirche-und-sport/daten/ Zum_Wohl_der_Menschen_und_der_Gesellschaft.pdf; 7.2.2012

Felmberg, B. (2010). Sportbeauftragter der Evangelischen Kirche in Deutschland. Gesprächsnotiz. Berlin.

Fuchs, M. (2006). Repräsentant für den Buddhismus während der Olympischen Spiele 2004. Gesprächsnotiz. Hamburg .

Grupe, O. & Mieth, D. (eds.) (1998). *Lexikon der Ethik im Sport.* Schorndorf: Hofmann..

Gruppe, O. & Huber, W. (eds.) (2000). *Zwischen Kirchturm und Arena – Evangelische Kirche und Sport.* Stuttgart.

Güldenpfennig, S. (2000). *Sport: Kritik und Eigensinn. Der Sport der Gesellschaft.* Sankt Augustin.

Heinemann, K. (1998). *Einführung in die Soziologie des Sports.* Schorndorf. Hofmann.

Hoffman, S. (ed.) (1992). *Sport and Religion.* Champaign.

Huber, W. (2000). Sport als Kult – Sport als Kultur. O.Gruppe & W.Huber (eds.). *Zwischen Kirchturm und Arena – Evangelische Kirche und Sport.* Stuttgart, 15-28.

Jacobi, P. & Rösch, H.-E. (eds.) (1986). *Sport und Religion. Christliche Perspektiven im Sport.* Mainz.

Klöcker, M. & Tworuschka, U. (eds.) (2005). *Ethik der Weltreligionen.* Darmstadt: Wissenschaftliche Buch-gesellschaft.

Moegling, K. (1987). *Zen im Sport.* Haldenwang.

O'Gorman, K. (2010). *Saving Sport: Sport, Spirituality and Society.* Dublin.

Parry, J. & Watson, N. (eds.) (2007). *Sport and Spirituality.* New York.

Prebish, C. (1993). *Religion and Sport. The Meeting of Sacred and Profane.* London.

Schwank, W. & Koch, A. (eds.) (1999-2003). *Begegnungen.* Schriftenreihe zur Geschichte der Beziehung Christentum und Sport (4 Bde.). Aachen.

Sportler ruft Sportler e.V. http://www.srsonline.de/index.php?id=692, actualized 10.3.2012

SRS Sportler ruft Sportler e.V (2010). *Christ und Sport.* Version 2.3 Altenkirchen.

Ulrichs, H.-G., Engelhardt, T. & Treutlein, G. (eds.) (2003). *Körper, Sport und Religion.* Idstein.

Volke, S. & Kadel, D. (2006). *Wenn Fußballer glauben.* Asslar.

Weinhold, K.-P. (2000): Kirche und Sport in der Evangelischen Kirche in Deutschland. O. Gruppe & W. Huber (eds.). *Zwischen Kirchturm und Arena – Evangelische Kirche und Sport.* Stuttgart, 72-94

SUMMARY

In the last decade religion has become more present also in the field of sports. A line can be drawn between one's religious commitment, sports, the pedagogical aims of teaching sport, and the motivational basis for exercise and sports performance. There are resemblances between sport and religion. Furthermore, there are parallels between sports pedagogical approach towards exercise performance, and the attitude and appreciation religion shows with regard to sports. Reports from religious athletes reveal the importance of their faith for their sport career. The results of the study bring us to the conclusion that being religious supports rather than prevents athletes from exercises or from sports participation. Obviously religious faith can be an important factor for motivation of performance.

STRESZCZENIE

W ostatnich latach coraz bardziej dostrzegalna staje się obecność religii w dziedzinie gier sportowych. Możemy połączyć jedną linią wiarę w Boga, sport, pedagogiczne cele w nauczaniu sportu oraz podstawę motywacyjną do treningu i występowania w zawodach sportowych. Według autora występują podobieństwa pomiędzy sportem a religią. Co więcej, istnieją paralele pomiędzy sportowym podejściem pedagogicznym w organizacji treningów a stosunkiem i aprobatą, jaką religia darzy sport. Sprawozdania wierzących sportowców odsłaniają ważność wiary dla ich sportowej kariery. Wyniki badania prowadzą autora do wniosku, że wiara w Boga raczej wspiera niż przeszkadza sportowcom w ćwiczeniach i udziale w sportowych występach. Widocznie wiara może być istotnym czynnikiem motywacji osiągnięć.

SAMMENDRAG

I det siste ti årene har religion som tema blitt mer og mer synlig også på idrettsarenaen. Det kan dras forbindelser mellom religiøs engasjement, idrett, idrettspedagogiske mål og motivasjonsbakgrunn for å trene og prestere i idrett. Likheter mellom idrett og religion kan sees. Dessuten finnes det samspill mellom idrettspedagogiske tilnærminger til idretts-prestasjon og holdningen som religion har til idrett. Fortellinger fra religiøse idrettsutøvere viser at troen har betydning for idrettskarrieren deres. Forskningsresultatene antyder konklusjonen at det å være religiøs som toppidrettsutøver er mer hjelp enn et hinder for trening og idrettsutøvelse. Dette avhenger selvsagt av den enkeltes religionsforståelse. Mye tyder på at tro kan være en viktig faktor for motivasjon og prestasjon.

41

DR. HERBERT ZOGLOWEK PHD

Finnmark University College
Department of Sport and Science
Follumsvei 31
9509 Alta. Norway
E-mail: herbert@hifm.no

Pomeranian University
Department of Psychology
Westerplatte 64
Slupsk 76-200, Poland
zoglowek@o2.pl

FRILUFTSLIV AS A
NATURE-RELATED CONCEPTUALIZATION OF LIFESTYLE

INTRODUCTION

Why do young people today feel enamoured with nature? Why do they look for re-laxation and contemplation in nature? Why does nature give them something special that they feel the need of in their daily lives? Why the connection to nature is so strong in one of the richest nations that boasts the highest degree of welfare support, a very high standard of tech-nology, and the highest life quality[1] (UNDP, 2011) in the world? Typically, Norwegians have a strong connection to nature, which finds its expression in a lifestyle they call *friluftsliv*. How is this phenomenon understood and explained?

Based on general research, my own research with young people, and informal talks and discussions with students, I reflect on and discuss first the central issues that may provide an answer to these questions. Second will be to see on these results in the light of the biophilia hypothesis and to discuss some pedagogical implications.

THE PHENOMENON *FRILUFTSLIV*

Friluftsliv is a special Norwegian phenomenon. It is not easy for other people to un-derstand what *friluftsliv* means. Translation to other languages is difficult because it is more than just outdoor life, as the verbatim translation suggests. For most Norwegians, *friluftsliv* has many other special emotional, social and cultural connotations. Often Norwegians them-selves cannot express very clearly why they engage in these nature-related activities.

The magnificent national poet, Henrik Ibsen[2], created this special term *friluftsliv* in 1861, which gives Norwegians the possibility to express their feeling, meaning, experience and reason in relation to the nature in just one word: *friluftsliv*. During the last century *friluftsliv* has developed as a certain lifestyle of the Norwegian people, which has enormous importance not only for national identity and individual finding one's self, but also for health-care and welfare policy, as well as an increasing significance in the Norwegian education system.

Friluftsliv is mostly related to experiences in nature. This aspect is also explicit accen-tuated and underlined in all relevant definitions, both in official papers of the government and in pedagogical and psychological based approaches and perspectives. In the white papers of the Norwegian government – and not only one addresses *friluftsliv* - it is written that *friluftsliv* is "being in and physical activities outdoors during leisure time with the intention of changing

---

[1] Since 2001 Norway is - with two exceptions (2007 and 2008) - continuously ranked as first on the Human Development Index (HDI), determined by the UNDP. Norway's index in 2011: 0.943
[2] Henrik Johan Ibsen (1826-1906), Norwegian dramatist and lyric poet.

the environment and experiencing nature"[1] (MD 1987, p.12). This over-all aim is emphasized again later in a more concrete description: "Experience of nature is the core of *friluftsliv* and includes experiences of flowers and trees, birds and animals, water, taste-, sound- and scent-experiences, and the changing of seasons in nature"[2] (MD 2001, p.31).

In this article, this phenomenon is discussed from a nature-philosophic and pedagogic perspective, with the aim to answer why nature has such importance in the lives of these people on the northern border of Europe.

In the first part of this chapter, interest in this question is explained, with the starting point of research in *friluftliv* as leisure and lifestyle activity. The second part is a philosophic approach to nature that subsequently provides the background for a deeper interpretation and explanation of the research. And finally, in the conclusion of the chapter, a reflection on the pedagogical importance of *friluftliv* is provided.

WHY PEOPLE LIKE TO BE OUTDOORS - MOTIVATION TO *FRILUFTSLIV*

Friluftsliv is a very popular research area. Motive factors and different activities are the most common foci of periodic research in this field. In the last two-three decades, the meaning, understanding, and leisure motives of *friluftsliv* in Norway and other Scandinavian countries have been researched with different perspectives and approaches (see e.g. Kaltenborn, 1989; Vaagbø, 1990; Kaltenborn & Vorkinn, 1993; Pedersen, 1999: Teigland, 2000; SSB, 2001; Nerland, 2002; Nerland & Vikander, 2002; Odden & Aas, 2002; Odden, 2008).

Initially I want to refer to a large survey of the Norwegian statistic office (SSB) in 2001 in which 1378 people were asked about their attitudes toward and activities in *friluftsliv*. The design was by the so-called REP-scale[3] (Driver et al., 1991). Table 1 is a short excerpt of the results, which shows the ten most important reasons for *friluftsliv*[4]. These ten statements are identified as the important or most important motives of 60% or more of the population.

Table 1: Mean of the 10 most important motives to be engaged in friluftsliv
(SSB, 2001, after Odden, 2008; translation of the author)

Motivic statements	Mean	Important/very important in %
(1) I can accumulate new strength and mental boost	4.1	79
(2) I get away from stress and everyday life	4.0	78
(3) I get movement and training	4.0	77
(4) I can take care o my health	4.0	76
(5) I can experience the quietness and peace of nature	4.0	74
(6) I can use my body in many different ways	3.9	72
(7) I get a change from everyday routines	3.9	70
(8) I can experience the landscape and spirit in nature	3.8	68
(9) I can be together with my family	3.9	66
(10) I can be together with friends	3.7	61

---

[1] Original: "… opphold og fysisk aktivitet i friluft i fritiden med sikte på miljøforandring og naturopplevelse" (translation of the author).
[2] Original: "Naturopplevingar er sjølve kjernen I friluftslivet og inneheld opplevingar knytt til både blomster og tre, fugl-og dyreliv, vatn, smak, lyd og luktopplevingar, og til vekslingar i naturen gjennom året" (translation of the author).
[3] The Recreation Experience Preference Scales were introduced of Driver et al. (1991). They are used in a lot of big surveys about *friluftsliv*. A good overview and summarizing of critical points of this method is given in Odden & Aas (2002).
[4] The whole table of results is shown in Odden, 2008, p.69.

Most research about *friluftsliv* results in a kind of categorizing of *friluftsliv* activities or motive factors, which was done before or after the survey. The first national survey of SSB (1975) differentiated three main categories: fitness and physical health, break and recreation, and experience of nature. Other classification patterns can be, depending on the focus of the research, more or less different, for example, they referred to first, the activities of "wanderers, gatherers, and specialists" (Pedersen, 1999; translation of the author); secondly, cultural-historical categories, that is, traditional *friluftsliv*, classical *friluftsliv* and activity-oriented *friluftsliv* (Waaler 2013); or, thirdly, more specified and differentiated categories, namely, contemplation, experience of nature, social togetherness, physical activity, happiness, fishing-related motives, and mastery/excitement (e.g., Aas & Kaltenborn, 1995; translation of the author).

The *friluftsliv*-motive-research related to the REP-scale can be critiqued for its use of closed questions, an individualistic approach, and not attending to culture differences and level of consciousness. In contrast, the survey of *friluftsliv* students in Alta consisted of open questions, which were categorized afterwards. The categories are addressed in the next section of this chapter.

MOTIVATION STRUCTURE OF *FRILUFTSLIV* STUDENTS

The last ten years (from the academic year 2003/04 to 2011/12), I have collected information from the students who started *friluftsliv* studies at Finnmark University College in Alta. This group can be described as young people aged 18-30 years, who are especially interested in *friluftsliv*. In the beginning and during the study year they are asked certain questions connected to the subject they are learning and related to their motivation, meaning, knowledge, and experience. One main question in the first lecture is: why do they like to be outdoors "on tour". To this open question, students could respond in self-formulated keywords or short sentences, which describe their main motives. Subsequently their answers were evaluated and categorized. The first categorization, created on the basis of the given answers, provided a differentiation in "contemplative or mental grounding", "social grounding" and "physical grounding". Later this category scheme was enhanced according to the categories in Table 1. In further discussion with students, the following five categories were used:
(1) Experience of nature
(2) Contemplation
(3) Physical activities
(4) Social relations
(5) Mastery/excitement.

The collected results for the period 2003 - 2012 are shown in Figure 1.

These results open up some new reflections, questions and hypotheses, for example, it is interesting that in this age-group "contemplation" is named twice as often as physical activity or mastery/excitement. It is also noteworthy that despite the fact that *friluftsliv* is prac-ticed predominantly in groups, "social togetherness" is named the least frequently. But the focus should here be placed on the first point: "experience of nature". Later in the discussion of this category, other points are also addressed.

45

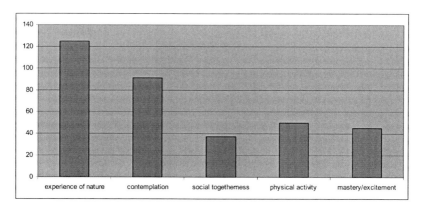

Figure 1: Why students go "on tour" in *friluftsliv* (N=180 (= basic population))

That the motive "experience of the nature" is most frequently named is not really a surprise. Indeed, outdoor experience, connected to nature, is already identified as a special aim, which *friluftsliv* undertakes to address. But what the "experience of nature" includes is a summary of partly different associations, understandings and feelings. These connections and connotations should become evident in the students' responses to the second question.

EXPERIENCE OF NATURE – LEARNING AND DEVELOPMENT

Experience of nature should be considered here in a nature-philosophical way with a pedagogical perspective. The pedagogical inspired starting point for this article is pedagogical reflection on experience and the role of experience in learning and development. The importance of experience, especially primary, unmediated experience with teaching and learning contents is widely accepted and acknowledged as an effective way of learning. Already Roth (1969) had emphasized the "original encounter" as an important pedagogical concept. Thus the experience of nature must have relevance and purport not only in subjects related to nature like biology. The pedagogical and didactic concepts are going well beyond the biological perspective, when they attribute three main assumptions to the relevance of the experience of nature:

(1) Encouragement of social and mental competence (personal development).
(2) High motivation because of first hand experience (outdoor education).
(3) Appreciation of nature, and feeling of responsibility (environment awareness) (s.a. Gebhard, 2001; Mayer, 2005).

From early childhood children have experience with nature. These experiences are most widely connected to unmediated and holistic perception. Even if the child's first impressions and experiences of nature are mostly unconsciously saved, the human being retains an affinity and bond with one's natural roots, which leave behind long-term spoors. Fortunate living conditions, which allow varied and intensive experience in nature, accomplish an intensive relationship to nature. The subsequent concept of nature will be the expression of the personal endowment of life and development of identity, with other words: a meaningful aspect of the biographic identity. The conceptualization of the nature can be thought of and described as a cognitive-affective-motivational scheme, which is an important part of an "inner working model" (Berman & Sperling, 1994) or a "subjective theory" of life (Groeben et al., 1988; s.a. Gergen, 1994).

THE "NATURE OF EXPERIENCE"

The "nature" of experience, that means the substantial content of experience, is not really obvious. The importance of experience is in contrast to the vagueness of the term. The Oxford English Dictionary gives different definitions of "experience" such as "the fact of being consciously the subject of a state or condition, or of being consciously affected by an event" or "the state of having been occupied in any department of study or practice, in affairs generally, or in the intercourse of life; the extent to which, or the length of time during which, one has been so occupied; the aptitudes, skill, judgment, etc. thereby acquired" (OED, 1989). A well-recognised explication of the term remains to be realized, which is to say that it may never be possible. What Gadamer said more than 50 years ago hold true, that is, experience seems "to belong to the most unclear terms we know" (Gadamer, 1960, quoted in Prange, 1978, p.329; translation of the author). In scientific as well as everyday language the term *experience* is used with different connotations (s.a. Zoglowek & Rolland, 2007a; 2007b; 2009; 2010). From a learning perspective, experiential knowledge is distinguished from theo-retical knowledge. This point will be emphasized when the results of experience are identified as more that cognitive. Experience can have the meaning of "being at home in a subject". If someone knows what he can expect and how to behave or to react, then he can be said to have experience in this case. But experience is more than perception because, although based on perception, experience includes implications, conclusions, consequences, and other inter-pretations. In the case of the experience of nature, we denote experience as the result of an un-mediated relation between a person and the environment (nature), which is usually based on activity (see Figure 2). Sometimes, however, already the process is identified as experience.

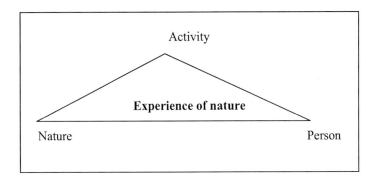

Figure 2: Experience of nature

THE EXPERIENCE OF NATURE – A SOCIO-CULTURAL APPROACH

The person's relation to nature is determined in a significant way by the tension be-tween nature and culture. The relation of the human being to nature is more than a biological determination – part of the nature and satisfaction of needs by nature – the relation to nature is also determined culturally and psycho-socially. People in different times and cultures have their unique relationships with nature and different approaches to it. And these relationships can be shaped individually. Thus, for human beings, nature does not exist as "nature by itself", but it is the result of cultural mediated relation between the person and nature. The relation can have qualitatively different dimensions of the cognitive, mental and acting involvement in and with nature (s.a. Mayer, 2005).

Mayer (1992) distinguished eight different related dimensions of the person's relations with nature:

- Agricultural or beneficial dimension:
    Nature is source of life. This utility function is still present in a lot of leisure activities in the nature.
- Scientific dimension:
    Nature is object of rational knowledge of the world. Natural sciences observe, classify, research and experiment in and with the nature.
- Social dimension:
    Especially animals, but also the flora, are friends of people, sometimes in a way really as social partners.
- Recreative dimension:
    Sojourn in the nature can be rest and recovery, and gives emotional or psychosomatic satisfaction.
- Protecting dimension:
    Nature protection and ecological awareness is contingent on that the nature and the biodiversity is something worthy of protection.
- Ethical-religious dimension:
    Biocentric attitudes like totemism lead to the understanding of integrity of creation, which can find expression in activities of protection of species.
- Aesthetic dimension:
    Sense perceptions in connection with the feeling of beauty or feeling of well-being are sensed as enrichment of life.
- Symbolic-allegoric dimension:
    Animals, plants and nature phenomena can be used as mirrors or media for psychological or sociological phenomena and features or characteristics of people and society.

To call these relations "dimension" means that they are not clearly described, definitive realms, but rather more aspects that arise because of a special perspective to the object "nature". Thus, there can be also a lot of overlap among these dimensions.

EXPERIENCE OF NATURE - A SOCIO-BIOLOGICAL APPROACH

Kellert and Wilson (1993) gave a similar catalogue of dimensions of the person's relation to nature, based on a more biological approach. The description is quite similar to Meyer's (1992) dimensions, although not exactly the same. Kellert and Wilson used other terms, and with "negativistic" perspective it is added one dimension more. This classification of perspectives traces back to the American biologist Edvard O. Wilson, who presented the controversial *Biophilia Hypothesis* in 1984. Following this train of biophilic thought, Kellert and Wilson (1993) proposed that there is only a limited number of human values of nature, of typological dimensions, which describe the relation of the human being and nature. They present a classification of nine dimensions of human nature relatedness (see Table 2).

Table 2: Typology of Biophilia Values (Kellert & Wilson, 1993, p. 59)

Term	Definition	Function
Utilitarian	Practical and material exploitation of nature	Physical sustenance/ security
Naturalistic	Satisfaction from direct experience / contact with nature	Curiosity, outdoor skills, mental/physical development
Ecologistic-scientific	Systematic study of structure, function, and relationship in nature	Knowledge, understanding, observation skills
Aesthetic	Physical appeal and beauty of nature	Inspiration, harmony, peace, security
Symbolic	Use of nature for metaphorical expression, language, expressive thought	Communication, mental development
Humanistic	Strong affection, emotional attachment, "love" for nature	Group bonding, sharing, cooperation, companionship
Moralistic	Strong affinity, spiritual reverence, ethical concern for nature	Order and meaning in life, kinship and affiliational ties
Dominionistic	Mastery, physical control, dominance of nature	Mechanical skills, physical prowess, ability to subdue
Negativistic	Fear, aversion, alienation from nature	Security, protection, safety

THE BIOPHILIA HYPOTHESIS

The biophilia hypothesis suggests that human beings have an emotional fixation on nature and especially on living organisms. Moreover, this fixation is universal and belongs to the evolutionary heritage: "The Biophilia Hypothesis boldly asserts the existence of a biologically based, inherent human need to affiliate with life and lifelike processes. This proposition suggests that human identity and personal fulfilment somehow depends on our relationship to nature. The human need for nature is linked not just to the material exploitation of the environment but also to the influence of the natural world on our emotional, cognitive, aesthetic, and even spiritual development. Even the tendency to avoid, reject, and, at times, destroy elements of the natural world can be viewed as an extension of an innate need to relate deeply and intimately with the vast spectrum of life about us" (Kellert & Wilson, 1993, p.42).

Wilson gives no information about the origin of the term "biophilia". But especially in this meaning and intention, "biophilia" was probably first used and characterized by the philosopher and psychoanalyst, Erich Fromm (1900-1980). *Biophilia* denominates the love of human beings for all life and all lively and vital occurrences and proceedings. "I believe that the man choosing progress can find a new unity through the development of all his human forces, which are produced in three orientations. These can be presented separately or together: biophilia, love for humanity and nature, and independence and freedom" (Fromm, 1997, 101). The relatedness of human beings to their natural and social surroundings is, according to Fromm, one of the eight basic mental needs. The way and the possibility to satisfy these needs are changeable and depend on historical, economic and socio-cultural circumstances. Fromm explained different orientations of relatedness, which he named "character-orientations". In the beginning of his work he distinguished between a "productive and not-productive" effect of character-orientation, then he used the term "biophilic and nekrophilic". Later, in his main work, he denoted the character orientation between "to have or to be". A productive, biophilic or being-oriented character-orientation is always interested in growth and vitality of all, what is well-liked. A biophilic person is attracted to everything that is lively and vital, "and not, because it is big and powerful, but because it is alive" (Fromm, 1994, p.218).

The opposite is "nekrophilic", what means having-oriented, not productive. This orientation represents a destructive character and does not encourage strength and self-reliance.

With reference to nature, the biophilic character-orientation is a prerequisite for relatedness to nature, characterized by love, empathy and responsibility, whereas a nekro-philic orientation leads to emotions and attitudes to nature, characterized by exploitation, domination and destruction (s.a. Funk, 1996).

QUALITIES OF EXPERIENCE OF NATURE

Hågvar and Støen (1996) described a more individual experience-based approach to the experience of nature. This approach can be implicitly connected to the biophilia hypothesis, although the authors were not deeply involved in establishing this connection. Their empirical approach was related to Norwegian people's affiliation, value orientation and more or less bonding to the nature.

Hågvar and Støen's (1996) studies and deliberations have led to a catalogue of different qualities, attributed to the positive experience of nature. On the basis of the question "Why do people go out in nature?" they have tried to explore and analyze the individual value of the experience of nature. Most of their respondents answered very spontaneously that the close contact to nature gives them new energy and a mental boost, which is important to them to survive in everyday life. But the experiences themselves, which give this boost, are various, and different aspects can take effect in different ways. For some, it is silence, for others it is the feeling of freedom, or nature's variety, or the fruits of nature, and, for others, physical challenge. But independent what aspect of nature people are seeking, all are searching for or get at least the same, namely, - a mental renewal. Hågvar and Støen also take into account that experience can have negative or undesirable outcomes. However, they hold the focus on the positive qualities because, in their pedagogical-psychological perspective, they are first and foremost interested in positive experiences as fruitful, joyful, and ways of psyching up. In the book "Green welfare"[1] Hågvar and Støen (1996) described and explained 15 different positive qualities of nature experience as it is shown in Figure 3.

---

[1] The Norwegian title is: "Grønn velferd". Vårt behov for naturkontakt. *(Green welfare. Our need for contact to the nature (translation of the author))*

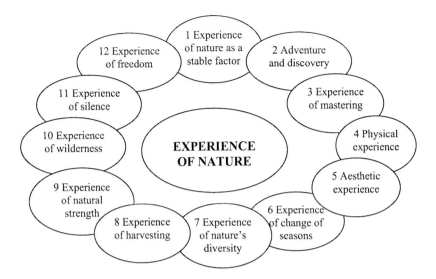

Fig.3: Positive qualities of experience of nature [1] (based on Hågvar & Støen, 1996)

WHAT ARE THE MOST RELEVANT QUALITIES OF EXPERIENCE OF NATURE OF *FRILUFTSLIV* STUDENTS?

In the last six years *Friluftsliv* students at the Finnmark University College in Alta were confronted with Hågvar and Støen"s (1996) catalogue of the qualities of the experience of nature (see Figure 3). They were expected to choose the three qualities that were the most important for them. They had also the option to add a kind of experience that may not have been named in the catalogue, but is very relevant for them. In all years, no new quality was added, suggesting that the catalogue is rather *Friluftsliv* complete and satisfying. On the other hand, three of the qualities, which Hågvar and Støen described, were never chosen or named by the students.

Table 4 shows the summarized results of all six years in absolute numbers.

---

[1] A more extensive and thorough explanation of the qualities of experience of nature is given in Hågvar & Støen (1996, pp.15-26).
Figur 3 shows only 12 qualities, because only these have been relevant in the survey with *friluftsliv* students at the Finnmark University College in Alta. The other three qualities based on Hågvar & Støen are: experience of history, experience of the life circle, and experience of wondering.

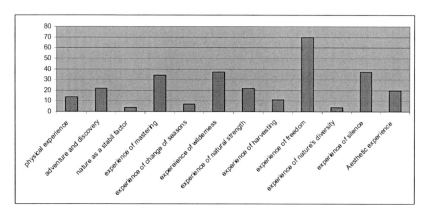

Figure 4: Importance of qualities of experience of nature. *Friluftsliv* students 2006-2011 (N = 94)

According to Hågvar and Støen (1996) and including Nerland and Vikander's (2002), Fisker's (2005) and Haahr's (2005) tighter elaboration and differentiation, the qualities can be summarized and connected to different spheres, levels or realms, which are metonymic with certain approaches to, and understanding and appreciation of the values of the nature. The realms are related to the body, suggesting that the kind of feeling, impression and reflection are mostly engaged with a special experience of nature. In his model of identity development, Fisker (2005) uses the three levels: personal, social and cultural. The "personal level" represents mainly knowledge about the nature, which is acquired by observation, information and experiences with all senses. The "social level" means, above all, the use of nature that is, fighting and mastering the challenges in the nature as well as harvesting the goods and fruits of the nature. The "cultural level" goes more deeply, namely, reflections about vitalism, values of nature and life, the place of the human beings in coming and going.

After students chose, there was a group discussion with the students about their association, understanding and meaning of the qualities. The discussion led to a deeper qualitative analytic understanding of the qualities, which further led to a superordinate categorizing of the qualities. These categories – here called "realms" – are quite close and comparable with the levels of Fisker (2005, pp.98f).

The "cognitive" experience realm

This cognitive realm is represented by the qualities 6, 7, 9 and 10. Nature had caught the meaning of the originality or nativeness, from which human beings have absented themselves, and where they are looking for to get back. Nature is also understood as opposite of urban and, in a way, artificial life. Nature is also attributed with a kind of romantic quality, expressed as qualities like source, sincerity, power, nativeness and immaculateness.

The "physical" experience realm

Qualities 2, 3, 4 and 8 represent the approach that nature can be controlled and dominated. Nature is an arena for doing something, being active. One aspect is to use the nature as an arena for physical, often sport activities, another aspect is harvesting, which includes berry picking, collecting mushrooms, fishing, or hunting. In this tradition nature is experienced as the wild environment, which is in opposition to human beings, who have to fight against it, or use it for their own survival.

The "mental" experience realm

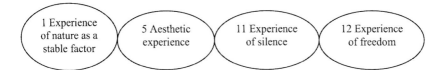

The psychological, affective realm is represented by the qualities 1, 5, 11 and 12. In the main, this realm is connected with deep emotional impressions, which lead to positive feelings. It can, but must not necessarily be connected to certain activities. It is more a state of being; feelings connected with spontaneous reflections, initiated by contact with nature, about life, lifecycles in general and the individual life situation in particular.

It is important to emphasize that the experience of nature is normally not just connected to one aspect, but the combination of several aspects gives a whole value of the experience of nature. And exactly this "total experience" is beneficial mentally, even sometimes a quasi therapeutic effect. Most people suggest that the knowledge about, the feeling, the quasi embodiment of nature is for them very important as existential values. These values are often in relevant everyday life, but in the stress of the working and living situations are hard to find. Perhaps these values are pretty nearly lost, and thus one tries to find again in original nature.

The results of Figure 4, grouped in three realms, described above, are presented in Figure 5. It is clearly visible that the qualities related to the mental realm are chosen most frequently. This result can be denoted as a surprise: young people explain their activities in nature are not first and foremost physical challenges but represents psycho-mental needs. This result requires an explanation, which probably the biophilia hypothesis can give.

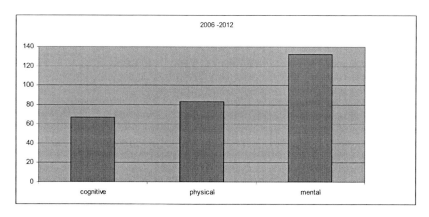

Figure. 5: *Friluftsliv* students experience of nature (academic years 2006-2012; N = 94)

But first the particular results of each year should be presented, in order to determine whether there is recognizable pattern of change over the course of years, and if so, in which direction.

The results are presented diagrammatically, in form of radar diagrams, where the three realms, which were described above, are the peaks of a triangle. The form of the triangle will therefore show the main findings: an equilateral triangle means that all three landscapes received the same value, if the triangle is not equilateral, but has different angles, so is the sharpest angle indicates the highest popularity or importance.

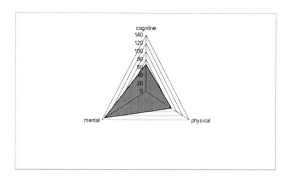

Fig. 6: *Friluftsliv* students experience of nature (academic years 2006-2012; N = 94)

Figure 6 shows the result of Figure 5 in another form. The sharp angle in the mental realm accentuates the importance of these categories. Numerically the cognitive items received 67 votes, the physical items 83 votes, and the mental items 132 votes.

How does it look for the several years of the survey? The following six figures give the special results for the academic years 2006-2007 to 2011-2012:

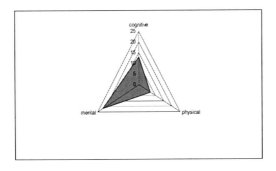

Fig. 7: *Friluftsliv* students experience of nature (academic year 2006-2007; N = 14)

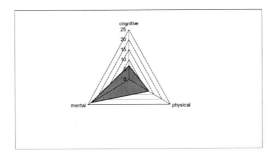

Fig. 8: *Friluftsliv* students experience of nature (academic year 2007-2008; N = 14)

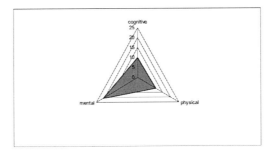

Fig. 9: *Friluftsliv* students experience of nature (academic year 2008-2009; N = 14)

55

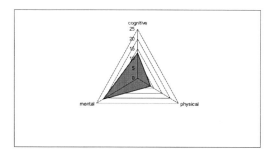

Fig. 10: *Friluftsliv* students experience of nature (academic year 2009-2010; N = 14)

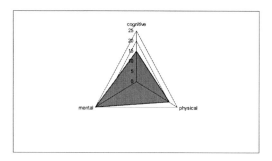

Fig. 11: *Friluftsliv* students experience of nature (academic year 2010-2011; N = 20)

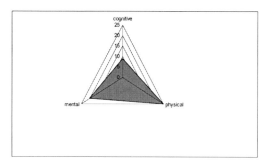

Fig. 12: *Friluftsliv* students experience of nature (academic year 2011-2012; N = 18)

The first interpretation of the results can be had given by looking at the form of the triangle. In the first four years, from 2006 until 2009, the shape is nearly the same, that is, a sharp angle on the mental peak, a more obtuse angle on the other two peaks. This shows exactly that the affective mental reasons are the most important all the time. This finding is mostly influenced, by the students' identification of the experience of freedom, which has consistently a very high value for them followed of the experience of silence (see Table 2).

In the academic year 2010-2011 the triangle starts to show another shape. Even if the tendency is still the same, it is visible that students chose physical related reasons more frequently (nomination: 25 times mental, 20 times physical). This finding can lead to the assumption that nowadays the physical challenges have a higher value in experience of nature. This tendency is confirmed in the students' responses in the following year, and, as well, the whole form of the triangle changed. The experiences of physical challenges in nature have now the greatest importance for these students. Finally, for the academic year 2011-2012, the triangle has changed the centroid, the sharp angle is now on the physical sphere, because the voting has changed: 20 students named mental reasons, 25 students named physical reasons.

This is, in a way, a confirmation of the assumption that Odden (2008) and Waaler (2013) suggested, that is, that the modern *friluftsliv* is more and more based on physical challenges, at least among students. On the other hand, the students' explanations and argumentation for their votes made it clear very often that their three choices were closely connected to each other, for example, physical challenges give them concomitantly an experience of freedom, which they feel when they are going off-piste on ski or are canoeing on wild river or are climbing dangerous mountains.

EXPERIENCE OF NATURE – EXPERIENCE OF OURSELVES?

Preliminary estimates and conclusions, taking into account the biophilia hypothesis

In an evolutionary perspective, human contact with nature and the need of human beings for contact with nature are easily to understand. Human beings are created and develop in and through the nature. Viewed in this light, the *homo sapiens* is a product of several millions of selections and adaptations. Today's type of human being is living on the earth during the last fifty thousand years, during which it is likely that the body, senses, and brain have virtually not changed. Thus, it can be suggested that human beings today are still adaptable and suitable for another kind of life than the one presented to them in the 21st century. The biological heritage has been near-constant from the stone-age, but in the last few centuries people have experienced a fast technological and cultural revolution. But there are still several signs that nature has not disappeared from human thinking, feeling, and development. Nature is still something basic that gives enjoyment to life, vitality, and helps people find mental balance, especially when everyday life is marked of stress and uneasiness. Some may say that life without contact to nature is not healthy for human beings.

To have plants in the house can be seen as a form of nature contact. Research has shown that plants make people more effective and hold them in better balance (Heerwagen & Orians, 1993). Decorating home or office with pictures of nature can also be understood as a sign for searching for contact with nature. This practice should increase the tranquillity of these places (Kaplan, 1983). Contact with nature in *friluftsliv* has also been used with good results in therapy with patients with mental illness (Heerwagen & Orians, 1993; Ingebrigtsen, 1995). The effect of contact with nature for the total health of the person can be attributed to the fact that people come closer to the pristinely way of life (Sjong, 1997). It is possible to say that experiences of nature are connected to something basic in the human being.

Some research suggests that people have an inherent need for contact with nature (Fromm, 1997), that the experience of nature is the core of feeling (Hågvar & Støen, 1996), and early childhood conceptualization in connection to nature has deep importance for the development of personal values and lifestyle[1] (Mayer, 2005). This inherent need is based on biological development and can be described as a genetic factor in human beings' evolutionnary adaption to the life in nature. Contact with nature gives clear and immediate signals about our action and behaviour. Our evolutionary history has created a program that people can receive, reflect and process this feedback, and that will be felt and exercised as satisfying. The biophilia hypothesis gives a heuristic basic for different concepts of the relation of nature and human beings. It suggests that the deep affinity, which the Norwegian people feel to nature, is rooted in their socio-geographic situation. Human dependence on nature is probably still more deeply rooted in the Norwegian people and therefore they are always searching for natural compensation of "unnatural life". On looking for a meaningful and fulfilling human existence Norwegians prefer a biocentric approach, which is interested in a balance of using and saving the nature, based on the understand that human beings are a part of the nature.

Pedagogical implications

At least, the importance of *friluftsliv* in the national curriculum and education in Norway can be reflected based on the biophilia hypothesis. Especially the pedagogical suggestions, which were made by Fromm (1964), and which are principally relevant in the discussion of the questions: wherefore education, what is the aim of education, or what are the methods of education? Even through Fromm made these reflections more than 50 years ago, they are still, or again, contemporary. The question about what are the most important values of a humanistic pedagogy today can be answered in a relevant way with help of the concepts of biophilia and the productive character-orientation. The latter concept (Fromm, 1964; Funk, 1996; 2002) refers to the postmodern ego-orientation. In his pedagogical approach, Fromm was interested in character-orientation, which is, according to him, the background for human behaviour. Fromm explained biophilia as a concept that every live creature has the primary (biophilic) tendency, to preserve life, to perfect oneself, to grow, and to resist the death. According to Fromm (1964) feels simultaneously everybody, who loves the life, attracted by all processes of growth and developing life. Negative tendency and behaviour, however, can be described as necrophilia. Hence the aim of education has to be the promotion of the biophilic or productive abilities. This promotion can happen in the cognitive, emotional and acting adapting process to the natural and social circumstances. Productive handling and dealings are given, when the human being activates his own abilities. Thus will, according to Funk (1996), lead to productive rationality, to productive work and to productive "love", in the meaning of empathy and compassion.

In relation to environmental awareness, Ness (2000, shown in Nerland & Vikander 2002) has provided a model of development and progress (see Figure 13), how to progress from contact with nature to certain attitudes or, in Fromm's terminology, to character orientation. And in the sense of Fromm's pedagogical approach and concept of biophilia is such a learning/development model easily conceivable for a general "education to being".

---

[1] In the end of the last century arose a distinctive research field "significant Life Experience", which was mainly based in research of environmental activist (see e.g. Tanner, 1980; 1998; Palmer, 1993; Payne, 1999)

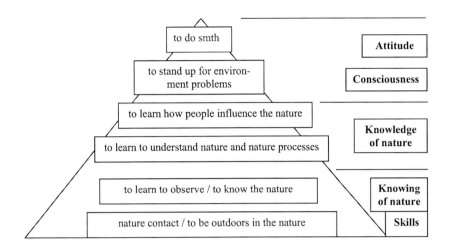

Fig. 13: How to form environmental awareness (source: Nerland & Vikander 2002, p.179)

CONCLUSION

It has been shown in this chapter that the motives for *friluftsliv*, to be outdoors in nature, are for Norwegian students studying *friluftsliv* at the University College in Alta mostly emotionally based. Even when students name physical motives, these are often connected with cognitively oriented reasons. This understanding of *friluftsliv*, based on practical challenges and emotional feeling, thus a connection of practical-physical and practical-mental experience, was described as a biotic understanding of, or a biotic relation, to nature.

Experiences of nature are denoted as the core of *friluftsliv*. The qualities of the experience of nature were described in different approaches. Specifically, the socio-biological approach seems to provide a good explanation for people's need for contact with nature. The biophilia hypothesis describes the dependence of human beings on nature far more than just the material and physical substance. It also holds that human beings depend on nature in their search for contemplative, aesthetic, intellectual and spiritual meaning and satisfaction. Erich Fromm's philosophic-psychological fundamental concept of biophilia when added to the pedagogical approach of the education of character provides the idea of a didactic concept of *friluftsliv*, which, in turn, shows the pedagogical importance and possibilities of *friluftsliv* for learning and development.

REFERENCES

Aas, Ø. & Kaltenborn, B. P. (1995). Consumptive Orientation of Anglers in Engerdal, Norway.*Environmental Management 19, no.5,* 751-761.
Andkjær, S. (ed.). *Friluftsliv under forandring: en antologi om fremtidens friluftsliv.* Slagelse: Bavnebanke.
Berman, W. H. & Sperling, M. B. (1994). *Attachment in Adults, Clinical and Developmental Perspectives.* New York, London: The Guilford Press.

Breivik, G. (1979). *Friluftsliv – noen filosofiske og pedagogiske aspekter.* Kompendiumnr. 50. Oslo: Norges Idrettshøgskole.

Driver, B. L., Tinsley, H. E. A. & Manfredo, M. J. (1992). The paragraphs about leisure and recreation experience scale: Results from two inventories designed to access the breadth of the perceived psychological benefits of leisure. B.L.Driver, P.J.Brown & G.L. Peterson (eds.). *Benefits of leisure.* State college, PA: Venture Publishing, 263-286.

Fisker, H. J. (2005). Unges friluftsliv: en moderne, en traditionel og en post traditionel måde at dyrke friluftsliv som personligt, socialt og kulturelt refleksivt identitetsprojekt. S.Andkjær (ed.). *Friluftsliv under foran-dring: en antologi om fremtidens friluftsliv.* Slagelse: Bavnebanke.

Fromm, E. (1994). *Liebe, Sexualität, Matriarchat. Beiträge zur Geschlechterfrage.* München: dtv.

Fromm, E. (1997). *On Being Human.* London: The Continuum International Publishing Group Ltd.

Funk, R. (1996). Das Biophilie-Konzept Erich Fromms und seine Bedeutung für umweltgerechtes Handeln. M.Zimmer (ed.). *Von der Kunst, umweltgerecht zu planen und zu handeln. Zur Bedeutung der Verhaltenswissenschaften für die Ökologie und für einen konstruktiven Umgang mit unserer Umwelt.* Georgsmarienhütte. Osnabrück: Selbstverlag.

Funk, R. (2002). *Erziehung zwischen Haben und Sein. Nachhaltige Erkenntnisse Erich Fromms.* Typscript: www.erich-fromm.de

Gebhard, U. (2001). *Kind und Natur. Die Bedeutung der Natur für die psychische Entwicklung.* Opladen: West-deutscher Verlag.

Groeben, N., Wahl, D., Schlee, J. & Scheele, B. (1988). *Forschungsprogramm Subjektive Theorien.* Tübingen: A. Franke Verlag

Haahr, J. (2005). Friluftslivet og den levende kulturformidling. S.Andkjær (ed.). *Friluftsliv under forandring: en antologi om fremtidens friluftsliv.* Slagelse: Bavnebanke.

Heerwagen, J. & Orians, G. H. (1993). Humans, habitants and aesthetics. E.O. Wilson & S.R. Kellert (eds.). *The Biophilia Hypothesis.* Washington D.C.: Island Press, 138-172.

Hågvar, S. & Støen, H. A. (1996). *Grønn velferd: Vårt behov for naturkontakt: Fra bymark til villmarks-opplevelse.* Oslo: Kommuneforlaget.

Ingebrigtsen, G. (1995). Ut på tur, aldri sur? Har friluftsliv noen betydning for mental lidelse, DN-notat nr. 7. *Friluftsliv: effekter og goder.* Trondheim: Direktoratet for Naturforvaltning, 85-91.

Kaltenborn, B. P. (1998). The alternate home – motives of recreation home use. *Norsk geografisk Tidsskrift, 52,* 121-134.

Kaltenborn, B. P. & Vorkinn, M. (eds.) (1993). Vårt friluftsliv. Temahefte 3. Trondheim: Norsk institutt for naturforskning.

Kaplan, R. (1983). The role of nature in urbane context. Altman & Wholwill (eds.). *Behavior and natural environment.* New York: Plenum Press.

Kellert, S. R. & Wilson, E. O. (1993). *The Biophilia Hypothesis.* Washington, D.C., Covelo: Island Press

Kleven, J. (1993). *Aktivitetsmønstre i norsk ferie og fritid.* NINA research report 33. Trondheim: Norwegian Institute for Nature Research.

Mayer, J. (1992). *Formenvielfalt im Biologieunterricht. Ein Vorschlag zur Neubewertung der Formenkunde.* IPN-Schriftenreihe 132. Kiel: IPN.

Mayer, J. (2005). Die Natur der Erfahrung und die Erfahrung der Natur. M.Gebauer & U.Gebhard (eds.). *Naturerfahrung. Wege zu einer Hermeneutik der Natur.* Kusterdingen: SFG-Servicecenter Fachverlage.

MD (Miljøverndepartementet) (1987). *Om friluftsliv. St.meld. nr.40* (1986-1987). Oslo.

MD (Miljøverndepartementet) (2001). *Friluftsliv: ein veg til høgare livskvalitet. St.meld. nr.39* (2000-2001). Oslo.

Nerland, J. (2002). *Viten om naturen i forbindelse med friluftsliv – En eksplorerende undersøkelse om: viten om naturen og innvirkende forhold i tilknytning til et friluftsliv der miljø og naturopplevelser er sentrale elementer.* Levanger: Høgskolen i Trøndelag.

Nerland, J. & Vikander, N. (2002). Kunnskap om friluftsliv. FriFo: *Forskning i friluft.* Rapport fra konferansen i Øyer.

Odden, A. (2002). *Hva skjer med norsk friluftsliv?* En studie av utviklingstrekk i norsk friluftsliv 1970-2004. Trondheim: NTNU.

Odden, A. & Aas, Ø. (2002). *Motiver for friluftslivsutøvelse.* Rapport fra konferansen "Forskning i friluftsliv". Oslo: Friluftslivets Fellesorganisasjon.

Odden, A. (2008). *Hva skjer med norsk friluftsliv?* En studie av utviklingstrekk i norsk friluftsliv 1970-2004. Trondheim: University.

Oxford English Dictionary (OED) (1989). Oxford: University Press.

Palmer, J. A. (1993). Development of Concern fort he Significant Influences and Formative Experiences on the Development of Adhults Environmental Awareness in Nine Countries. *EEE, (4), 4,* 445-465.

Payne, P. (1999). The Significant of Experience in SLE Research. *EER, (5), .4,* 365-381.

Pedersen, K. (1999). *Det har bare vært naturlig. Friluftsliv, kjønn og kulturelle brytinger.* Oslo: NIH

Prange, K. (1978). *Pädagogik als Erfahrungsprozess.* Stuttgart: Klett-Cotta.

Roth, H. (1969). *Pädagogische Psychologie des Lehrens und Lernens.* Hannover: Schroedel.

SSB (Statistisk sentralbyrå) (1975). NOS A 732. *Friluftslivsundersøkelsen 1974.* Oslo.

Sjong, M.L. (1993). Friluftsliv som virkemiddel for helse og livskvalitet. Hva sier forskningen? *Kroppsøving (47), 1,* 12-16.

Tanner, T. (1980). Significant Life Experience: a New Research Area in Environmental Education. *JEE, (11), 4,* 20-24.

Tanner, T. (1998). Choosing the Right Subjects in Significant Life Experiences. *EER, (4) 4,* 399-417.

Teigland, J. (2000). *Nordmenns friluftsliv og naturopplevelser.* VF-rapport 7. Sogndal: Vestlandsforskning.

United Nations Development Programme (UNDP) (2011). *Human Development Report 2011: Sustainability and Equity, A better future for all.* New York

Vaagbø, L. (2002). *Den norske turkulturen.* Oslo: Friluftslivets Fellesorganisajon.

Waaler, R. (2013). Friluftsliv in the Norwegian folk high schools – Contents and values. M.Aleksandrovich & H.Zoglowek (eds.). *Psychological and Pedagogical Aspects of Motivation.* Zürich, Berlin, Münster: Lit.

Wilson, E. O. (1984). *Biophilia: The Human Bond with Other Species.* Cambridge: Harvard University Press.

Zoglowek, H. & Rolland, C. G. (2007a). Das Erlebnis – ein brauchbarer didaktischer Begriff in der heutigen Pädagogik? ATEE: Spring University. *Changing Education in a Changing Society.* Klaipeda: University.

Zoglowek, H. & Rolland, C. G: (2007b). Friluftsliv - et emne med de gode opplevelser? *Kroppsøving (57), 3,* 22-25.

Zoglowek, H. & Rolland, C. G. (2009). Bedeutung und Wirkung des Erlebnisses im schulischen Unterricht? ATEE: Spring University. *Changing Education in a Changing Society.* Klaipeda: University.

Zoglowek, H. & Rolland, C. G: (2010): Første gangs, andre gangs – eller hva slags opplevelser finnes i friluftsliv? *Kroppsøving (60), 1,* 10-14

SUMMARY

The article refers to research on motives for *friluftsliv* of the Norwegian people overall and of a student group in *friluftsliv* in particular. Motives for *friluftsliv* are discussed among others on the background of the biophilia hypothesis, which expresses a special biocentric view in the human relation to the nature. With reference to Erich Fromm the author argues that biophila can be consulted for a pedagogical approach in education, which is based on character-orientations. With this understanding, at least, it will be given an attempt to explain a pedagogical based *friluftsliv*.

STRESZCZENIE

W tym artykule autor analizuje motywacje *friluftsliv* wśród norwegów w ogóle, a w szczególności wśród studentów. Motywacja do *friluftsliv* zanalizowana została między innymi na podstawie hipotez o biofilii, które wyrażają szczególny, biocentryczny punkt widzenia na stosunek człowieka do natury. W oparciu o idee Ericha Fromma autor wnioskuje, iż biophila prowadzi do powstania podejścia pedagogicznego w edukacji, które jest osadzone na charakterologicznej orientacji. Z tym nastawieniem dokonana zostanie próba wyjaśnienia pedagogicznie osadzanego *friluftsliv*.

SAMMENDRAG

Artikkelen referer til forskning på motiver for friluftsliv hos den norske befolkning generelt og til en studentgruppe *i friluftsliv* spesielt. Motiver for friluftsliv blir bl.a. drøftet med bakgrunn i biophilia hypothesis som uttrykker et spesielt biosentrisk natursyn. Med referanse til Erich Fromm kan biophilia brukes som pedagogisk tilnærming til dannelse basert på karakterorienteringer. På bakgrunn av denne forståelsen blir det gjort forsøk på å begrunne friluftslivets pedagogisk muligheter.

DR. EWA MURAWSKA, PHD

Pomeranian University
Department of General Pedagogics and Basics of Education
Westerplatte 64
Slupsk 76-200, Poland
E-mail: murawska.szkola@wp.pl

ON THE PROFESSIONAL SUCCESS OF TEACHERS – OPTIMISTIC CONSIDERATIONS

TYPES OF TEACHERS' SUCCESSES

Professional development of teachers and professional promotion related to it, have become an inherent element of professional functioning of both teachers and schools. Accurate management of professional development, conscious facing of new challenges should result in achieving professional success and a sense of satisfaction in a teacher.

In the modern world success has become one of the major values, inseparably connected to work or professional career. It has become the aim, the fulfilment, the determining factor of life investments. „Fluid post-modernity", as Z. Bauman stipulates, is a time of successful people, a time of impressive careers. An important role in promoting this concept is played by the media thanks to/or because of which we often perceive success as a spectacular event with extensive publicity, an event causing admiration, and often envy. However, success is first and foremost a subjective feeling, largely dependent on a personal hierarchy of values. R Łukaszewicz emphasizes that "the connotations of the word success are and have been different. They are changing not only as a result of the historical development of societies, economic and political transformations of particular countries, but they are also conditioned by material and cultural markers of people's living standards, their aspirations and desires, preferences in particular needs and their hierarchy of values and the significance of work in its various dimensions" (Łukaszewicz, 1979, p. 31). The author notices that the first word which reflects a person's professional activity and its effectiveness, was the word „promotion". It meant an "upward movement", and with time it became „an indirect reflection of the results of one's work, and, what is more, a result of a necessity related to the development of hierarchical institutions [...]. By means of professional promotion people not only can, but have to be successful [...]. Promotion can thus be treated only as a necessary element in one of many possible groups of factors that condition professional success" (ibidem, p. 33).

Another concept which appeared in the 1950s was career. At that time personal goals were identified with social ones. When talking about career, one meant results, not people. The third concept reflecting the relations between professional work and its results is definitely success (Dubisz, 2003, p. 1447).

Success is defined as „a positive result of implemented action. Experiencing successes and disappointments constitutes a professional career. Taking into account the essence and regularities of professional career, with regard to a company's functioning, is important for both the organization and its members, since it provides them with an opportunity to feel successful in their professional endeavors. Thus, an emotional engagement of employees in performing their tasks is formed. The sense of being successful is subjective in nature, it depends on the course of a person's career, but it is also conditioned culturally. The conditions of success in an organization are good general and professional qualifications, positive

63

personal features and a realistic level of ambition" (Borkowski, et al. 2001, p. 133). Whereas J. Michalak remarks that „success is not an element of life, but life in its entirety; that it is not so much a state of being pleased, resulting from an achieved goal, as an ability to find happiness in following an aim and being content not only with the result itself, but with everything that leads to achieving that result" (Michalak, 2007, p. 25).

The reasons that man aspires to achieving success could be material gratification, achieving a high social status or prestige and a possibility to exert influence on others. Motivation behind the ambition to succeed can thus be varied, as is the price one pays for being successful. A motivation to succeed means „aspiring to increase or keep one's prowess, at a possibly high level, in all the activities in which one assumes a certain standard, and the performance of which may thus be or not be completed successfully" (ibidem, p. 64).

Success has many faces. It would be hard to deny that. What is the professional success of teachers and what is it related to? K. Czarnecki and S. Karaś believe that the term professional success „comprises all the achievements which concern prowess and effectiveness of purely professional activity in a given work position.[...] Successes are corollaries of an employee's professional development in the working process. The first success in professional life becomes a driving force for the effort in pursuing further successes" (Czarnecki & Karaś, 1996, pp. 171-172).

On the other hand B. Żechowska remarks that" on the grounds of pedagogy, professional success is associated mainly with achievements in educational and didactic work, which can be boiled down to qualitative results in teaching and educating.[...] Professional success of teachers is shown as a mutually connected set of objective and subjective markers, determined by an organized and planned work of a teacher" (Żechowska, 1978, p. 47).

In her research concerning professional success of teachers the author presents the following symptoms of professional success.

1) Measurable symptoms in relation to the working environment, type of school and the level of its organisation:

- Level of didactic-educational results.
- Awards and national distinctions for teachers.
- Professional promotion.
- Recognition by local environment.

2) Symptoms of professional success in teachers' subjective perception:

- Qualitative educational-didactic results.
- Professional satisfaction.
- Acceptance expressed by parents and students.

The mentioned markers are mutually related and may co-exist (see also: Figure 1)

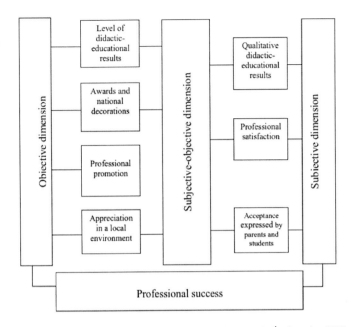

Figure1. Index structure of teacher's professional success (Source: B. Żechowska, 1978, p. 51.)

S.Witek presents subjective markers of teachers' professional success. They comprise:
- Fruition of one's own ideal, professional development plan, vision of the future, awareness of one's own aspirations, desires and needs as well as their fulfillment;
- Considerable and measurable output of one's own teaching work;
- Satisfaction with the course and results of pedagogical activity, achieved mostly due to: using one's high intellectual qualifications in educational practice, identification with the profession, high pedagogical culture, achieving stability in the profession and fulfilling needs, the sense of importance of the performed social mission, correct interpersonal relations at school and its environment;
- Achieving a high, adequate level of personality self-assessment (Witek, 1999, pp. 14-15).

Teachers' professional success comprises many factors. It is conditioned by both subjective/internal factors and external/environmental ones. One might thus say that success is dependent on the teacher's personal predispositions, his level of engagement, axiological preferences, his emotions related to satisfaction with his work, as well as on external factors, i.e.: characteristics and location of the school, working conditions in the classroom, relations with students, relations with superiors, atmosphere at work, leadership, economization of education, intensification of work, social recognition. Such a holistic approach „implies the necessity to consider, through analyses of the conditionings of teacher's professional success various categories of factors without, however, granting any given class of factors a primary position, or neglecting others" (Michalak, 2007, p. 101). Teacher success is therefore a result of numerous factors, as presented by Figure 2.

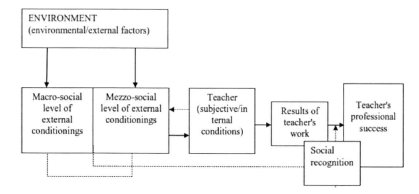

Figure 2. Conditionings of teacher's professional success (Source: J. Michalak, 2007, p. 147)

Teachers' successes are not always noticeable or acknowledged, and their „world" provides them with many pleasant experiences, events and situations, but also – more or less frequently – leaves them facing difficult situations, challenges that belong to the category of (im)possible[1], lack of a sense of control over the course of events, which results in a mixture of achieved successes and bigger or smaller failures that have their price (be it health or psychological problems, related to the "burning out" syndrome etc.).

CAREER SATISFACTION - ON A SUBJECTIVE SENSE OF BEING SUCCESSFUL

The teaching profession, though seemingly stable and steady, undergoes constant changes. It is because teachers function in new, unique situations, and, more importantly, they always act within the framework of dynamic/labile interactions with other people. The work of a teacher, constantly improved and developed, should bring a sense of satisfaction. „Teaching is an activity that consists in constant stimulation, inspires beliefs, orientations and interpretations, which allow students to develop as human beings instead of falling back, while their outlook and range of possibilities expand instead of shrinking. [...]. A person with a vocation acts as a teacher in a better way than a person for whom it is merely a professional occupation, even if there were no differences between them in other respects [...] and has greater ease, in both broad and dynamic manner, with influencing his/her students [...]. When public service, of which teaching is an example, is also a vocation, the person performing it can feel personally fulfilled (Hansen, quoted after: Day, 2008, p. 35). Research into that matter started in the 1930s and it has been carried out ever since. Such a long period has resulted in a variety of definitions of professional satisfaction, as well as in multiple classifications of factors and conditionings that determine its occurrence and power. „The power of our motivation for a particular action determines to what extend, we are ready to undertake that action, and in itself it is also determined by desire to achieve aims that would satisfy our needs. At work the main motivating factor is thus the desire to draw satisfaction from doing one's work" (quoted after: ibidem, p. 97).

---

[1]This issue has been reflected upon in my paper: *Być nauczycielem to znaczy mierzyć się z (nie)wykonalnymi zadaniami zawodowymi [To be a teacher is to face (un)manageable professional challenges].* (Murawska, 2010, pp.123-129)

Satisfaction is related to attitudes towards one's own work, and is defined as satisfaction with work, i.e. „it is an emotional reaction of pleasure or unpleasantness, felt as a result of performing particular tasks, functions and roles" (Strelau, 2000, p. 329). There are different factors determining the feeling of satisfaction. These can be: „a relatively high salary, a fair payment system, actual promotion opportunities, caring and active supervisors, an adequate level of social interaction at work, interesting and varied assignments as well as a high degree of control over the pace of work and working methods" (Armstrong, 2000, p. 121). Those factors are referred to as the factors of professional satisfaction and they are accompanied by the factors of satisfactions with non-professional fields, in other words individual factors such as age, health, work experience, emotional stability, social status, adequacy of work, using one's skills or having a family and a rich social life. Undoubtly, the level of satisfaction is an individual issue, dependent to a large extent on individual needs and expectations. In the course of individual property analysis the authors noticed among others, that the older an employee, the greater his satisfaction, and that professional experience and satisfaction correlate. This indicates that more extensive the experience means a higher level of satisfaction. Cognitive predispositions play an important part here, and people working on assignments below their intellectual potential do not feel satisfaction with their work, whereas those working on tasks exceeding their intelligence may in turn feel frustrated. This relates to adequacy of work, which is a correspondence between one's skills and the requirements in a given job and making use of previously gained skills and experience. Satisfaction grows accordingly to the status of the work performed (cf. Schultz & Schultz, 2002, pp. 300-304).

Professional work is a very complex experience. Therefore, „satisfaction with work can be characterized as a general satisfaction with work or a particular satisfaction" (Strelau, 2000, p. 329). General satisfaction is related to the whole emotional attitude to work, while particular satisfaction is connected with a given element of work. However, „general satisfaction with one's work is not a sum of satisfaction with particular elements of that work. Nevertheless, both general satisfaction with work and particular satisfaction are important factors for in mental health understood as a sense of having a quality life" (ibidem, p. 329).

Another theory is Herzberg's two-factor theory, according to which satisfaction is determined by factors connected with motivation, i.e. achievement, appreciation, responsibility, promotion and the work itself. The other group is comprised of factors related to the working environment, salary, working conditions, equipment, opportunity to super-vise others, or interpersonal relations.

According to B. Żechowska, professional satisfaction of teachers constitutes a subjective manifestation of professional success, and „the level of professional satisfaction depends as much on the quality of achievements in didactic-educational work, as on the material and organizational conditions of school's work, on interpersonal relations, the local environment, and the level represented by students" (Żechowska, 1978, p. 99). However, none of those factors could be perceived as the dominant one.

Having conducted a comparative analysis of professional satisfaction felt by teachers from several countries, W. Wiśniewski argues that satisfaction is „the selection by respondents of such attitudes and behaviors, given in the questionnaire, which enable them to positively solve conflicts in the working environment, and which lead to acceptance of the professional role and currently held school functions" (Wiśniewski, 1990, p. 85). The study singles out factors determining high satisfaction, which are freedom to decide how one's job should be done, clearly delineated professional duties, good atmosphere at work, respect of the milieu.

Z. Kawka assumed that, with respect to teachers satisfaction with work comprises „dimensions of formal rights and obligations, activities, partners, conditions and rewards" (Kawka, 1998, p. 109). The author carried out a study on the relationship between the experienced satisfaction felt and the propensity to normative thinking which she had attributed to teachers. The results of her research revealed a strong discrepancy between the importance of the assumed role, satisfaction with the contact with students and material deprivation which weakens professional satisfaction.

L. Evans distinguishes two factors determining job satisfaction. These are:

- „work comfort – the level of teachers' satisfaction with the working conditions and the atmosphere at work,
- professional fulfillment – the state of mind comprising all the teacher's emotions born as a result of personal success, which s/he attributes to his/her own actions in those fields of professional activity which s/he deems important" (quoted after: Day, 2008, p. 99).

According to A. Wiłkomirska the above mentioned categories of teachers' professional satisfaction could be considered as elements of professional orientation.

1. „Professional development and pedagogical success
- Opportunity to introduce didactic innovations
- Independence in the work performed
- Opportunity to complete one's education
- Student achievements
- Popularity among students
2. Social relations at school
- Relations with superiors
- Relations between teachers at school
- Opportunity to partake in supervising activities
- Co-operation with parents
3. Working conditions (legal and administrative)
- Low risk of job loss
- Evaluation by supervisors
- Salary
- Scope of administrative work to handle" (Wiłkomirska, 2002, p. 119).

Teachers' professional satisfaction constitutes an important aspect of their work, and the manner in which they perceive their work, as well as the level of satisfaction that it provides, influence, in turn, their professional activity – the level of commitment and identification with the profession, creativity, motivation for development. The implications of the sense of professional satisfaction, or the lack thereof, in teachers have greater consequences on the social scale than the results concerning satisfaction in representatives of most other professions. As W.Wiśniewski stipulates „they determine what successors we will have" (Wiśniewski, 1990, p. 91).

AS A CONCLUSION AND A PERSONAL REFLECTION

My long teaching experience[1] leads me to believe that the greatest success lies in direct work with pupils/students, and not in spectacular gratifications for..., or in any formal accolade. I value immensely such things as the expression of admiration (though I'm not entirely sure if I merited it) bestowed upon me by my former student, and a colleague today[2]. This spontaneous gesture of a wise, sensitive young pedagogue is very precious reward, and source of true satisfaction for me. It is worth making the constant effort, to care for the quality of one's work for such moments. Satisfying experiences such as this one enable me to state with absolutely certainty: It is worth being a teacher! Only that and no less than that.

---

[1]This experience isn't limited to my work, but it also involves the atmosphere of the family of teachers I come from. It is an asset which I value more and more with time.
[2]I would like to thank here Monika L., and express my conviction that a beautiful, real teaching career lies ahead of her.

REFERENCES

Armstrong, M. (2000). *Zarządzanie zasobami ludzkimi.[Human resources management]* Kraków.
Borkowski, J., Dyrda, M., Kanarski, L. & Rokicki, B. (2001). *Człowiek w organizacji. Podręczny słownik psychologii zarządzania i dziedzin pokrewnych [Man in organisation. A pocket dictionary of management psychology and related fields]* Warszawa.
Czarnecki, K. & Karaś, S. (1996). *Profesjologia w zarysie.[Outline of professiology]* Radom.
Day, C. (2008). *Nauczyciel z pasją. [Teacher with passion]* Gdańsk.
Dubisz, S. (ed.) (2003). *Uniwersalny słownik języka polskiego, [Universal dictionary of Polish language]* Warszawa.
Kawka, Z. (1998). *Między misją a frustracją. Społeczna rola nauczyciela. [Between mission and frustration. Teacher's social role]* Łódź.
Łukaszewicz, R. (1979). *Wyznaczniki kształtowania sukcesów zawodowych. [Determining factors in forming professional success]* Wrocław, Warszawa, Kraków, Gdańsk.
Michalak, J. (2007). *Uwarunkowania sukcesów zawodowych nauczycieli, [Conditionings of teachers' profes-sional success]* Łódź.
Murawska, E. (2010). Być nauczycielem to znaczy mierzyć się z (nie)wykonalnymi zadaniami zawodowymi. [To be a teacher is to face (un)manageable professional challenges] W. Woronowicz & D. Apanel (eds.). *Opieka – wychowanie – kształcenie. Moduły edukacyjne.* Kraków, 123-129.
Rheinberg ,F. (2006). *Psychologia motywacji. [Psychology of motivation]* Kraków.
Schultz, D. & Schultz, S. E. (2002). *Psychologia a wyzwania dzisiejszej pracy. [Psychology and the challenges of modern work]* Warszawa.
Strelau, J. (ed.) (2000). *Psychologia. Podręcznik akademicki. T.3 [Psychology. Academic textbook, vol. 3]* Gdańsk.
Wiłkomirska, A. (2002). *Zawodowe i społeczno-polityczne orientacje nauczycieli. [Professional and socio-politi-cal orientations of teachers]* Warszawa.
Wiśniewski, W. (1990). Satysfakcja zawodowa nauczycieli – analiza porównawcza. [Teachers' professional satisfaction – comparative analysis] *Kwartalnik Pedagogiczny 3.*
Witek, S. (1999). *Jak osiągnąć sukces zawodowy?* Jelenia Góra.
Żechowska, B. (1978). *Sukces zawodowy nauczyciela i jego uwarunkowania. [Teacher's professional success and its conditionings]* Słupsk.

SUMMARY

The article presents the analysis of the teaching profession and the attempt to answer for the question what is success in teaching profession and what are the conditions of this success? The analysis of the literature and own research show that nowadays the most valued traits of the good teacher is efficiency, professionalism, effectiveness (sometimes even showing off) and achieving the best results possible, preferably spectacular ones which secure a high position in various ratings. Teacher's work entails constant change, new events, incessant dynamism resulting from professional activities; it abounds in difficult situations, but also in joy of well done job and successes.

STRESZCZENIE

Artykuł prezentuje analizę zawodu nauczyciela i jest próbą odpowiedzi na pytanie czym jest powodzenie w zawodzie nauczyciela, i jakie są warunki tego powodzenia? Przeprowadzony przegląd literatury oraz badania własne pokazują, że obecnie najbardziej cenionymi cechami dobrego nauczyciela są profesjonalizm, efektywność (czasem nawet przesadna) i osiąganie najlepszych możliwych wyników oraz widoczna, zapewniona wysoka pozycja w rozmaitych ocenach. Codzienna praca nauczyciela pociąga za sobą ciągłe zmiany, nowe zdarzenia, nieprzerwany dynamizm, wynikający z fachowych czynności. Obfituje w trudne sytuacje, ale przynosi też radość z dobrze wykonanej pracy i sukcesów.

SAMMENDRAG

Artikkelen presenterer en analyse av lærerprofesjon og forsøker å svare på spørsmålet om hva som er suksess i lærerrollen og hva som er betingelser for denne suksessen? Litteratur analyse og egen forskning viser at de mest verdifulle egenskapene for en lærer i dag er yteevne, profesjonalisme, effektivitet (som noen ganger vises frem) og oppnåelse av best mulig resultat, helst noen spektakulært som sikrer en høy posisjon i ulike rangeringer. Lærerens arbeid innebærer stadige forandringer, nye hendelser, og vedvarende endringer på grunn av profesjonsrollen; det er rikelig med vanskelige situasjoner, men også glede ved godt utført jobb og suksess.

DR. SLAWOMIR PASIKOWSKI, PHD

Pomeranian University
Department of Psychology
Westerplatte 64
Slupsk 76-200, Poland
E-mail: pasiks@wp.pl

READINESS TO RESIST AND ITS RELATIONSHIP WITH CREATIVITY

INTRODUCTION

Rebellion, resistance and reactance are terms which describe an individual response to perceived or anticipated frustration of autonomy. Autonomy is regarded as a creative potential (Runco, 2007, pp.288-289). Resistance towards persons or objects may result from a threatened sense of autonomy. Attempts at counteracting the threat lead to the search for alternative ways to fulfill of individual aspirations. These projects can take unconventional forms and depend on the individual person. Moreover, resistance is associated with independence, which is a key feature attributed to creative people (cf. Dowd et al., 1994). For these reasons, many authors imply a direct relationship between resistance, nonconformity and creativity (Apter, 1982; Griffin & McDermott, 1997; Kim, 2010; Madjar, Greenberg & Zheng, 2011; Runco, 2007) and focus on the period of adolescence. The interest in adolescence stems from the fact that during this period resistance is manifested more directly. What is more resistance more often manifests creative properties as well as emancipatory aspects also in the social dimension (cf. Aggleton & Whitty, 1985; Arnow et al., 2003; Balswick & Macrides, 1975; Cowan & Presbury, 2000; Dowd & Sanders, 1994; McDermott, 1988; 2001; Stenner & Marshall, 1995). It is also worth noting that resistance measured as reactance is related to the results obtained in the Openness scale. The scale is part of the NEO PI-R personality questionnaire and measures the personality traits described as readiness to try new experiences and positive rating of novelty (Seemann et al., 2005). Some authors emphasize that the relationship between creativity and resistance depends on birth order and gender (Hertwig, Davis & Sulloway, 2002; Sulloway, 1998). They argue that people born as the second children are more nonconformist and creative, because they occupy a specific place in their family due to this position. However, scientists are not unanimous on this issue – some argue that firstborn children are more creative and rebellious (Baer, Oldham, Hollingshead & Jacobsohn, 2005), while other claim that the relationship between birth order, resistance and creativity is determined by other much more significant variables such as socioeconomic status, family size, gender, age and number of siblings. In the face of these variables the importance of birth order is not as large (Baer, Oldham, Hollingshead & Jacobsohn, 2005; Boling, Boling & Eisenman, 1993; Ernst & Angst, 1983; Zweigenhaften & Ammon, 2000).

It would be reasonable to underline the direct role of gender and sex as factors differentiating the level of creativity (Abra, 1991; Baer, Oldham, Hollingshead & Jacobsohn, 2005), and the level of resistance, autonomy and assertiveness (Sulloway, 1998; Abra, 1991; Hong, 1990; Hong et al., 1994; Joubert, 1990; Seeman et al., 2004). It should be noted, however, that there is data highlighting the importance of other variables which accompany the differentiation of gender in resistance and creativity. These include: the type of tasks performed by a person, different expectations and permissions for boys and for girls, differences in hormonal and neurophysiologic conditions (Abra, 1991; Ai, 1999), gender segregation

71

(Negrey & Rausch, 2009) and the level of education which interacts with gender (Pilar & Grande, 2007).

Resistance is usually associated with expressing anger, aggression, defiance, resentment or courage. Therefore resistance is usually identified with patterns of male reactions rather than female (cf. Ames & Flyn, 2007; Deluty, 1979). Hence, it is assumed that conformism is much more typical for women. However, with regard to readiness to resist men and women do not have to be as differ as it would seem, especially when we treat resistance as a multivariate phenomenon, which is disclosed in different forms. It is probably more adequate to state that men and women differ in terms of these forms.

The frame of the relationship between sex and resistance can be expanded when we take a broader perspective on that letter phenomenon, for instance by taking into account such forms of opposition as seeking confrontation, ingratiation or avoidance. So conceptualized resistance may also look differently in the relationship with creativity. Moreover, from the standpoint of this expanded conceptualization, it would be interesting to study the association between resistance and birth order.

The research presented below was based on two hypotheses. (1) There is a connection between the readiness to resist and creativity, (2) The level of creativity and the level of resistance differ with regard to sex and birth order. More detailed hypotheses were not formulated due to different and often contrary results obtained by others authors. It seems more encouraging, therefore, to consider the shape of the relationship between these variables in a Polish group of late adolescents. The most likely results of the study should indicate a generally higher intensity of resistance in the case of men than in the case of women.

METHOD

Procedure. The study involved 207 undergraduates. Random sampling was use. The sample units were groups of students who earlier received their weekly class schedules. After coming to select groups the researcher ask the students to take part in a study the aim of which was to diagnose the relationship between creativity and reacting to restriction of freedom. Participation in the survey was voluntary, anonymous and was not subject to time pressed. Each respondent who agreed to participate received a set of questionnaires to complete. However, due to incomplete information the final analysis of the data was conducted on 197 individuals (123 women and 74 men). The age of the participants ranged from 19 to 23 years ($M = 20.80$, $SD = 0.93$). The participants included 90 first-born, 61 second-born and 46 individuals born as the third and later child. Birth order and sex were determined by direct answer on the questionnaire sheet.

Measures. The Questionnaire of Readiness to Resist (Pasikowski, 2012) devised by the author, is a the tool based on a multidimensional model of resistance, with the underlying assumption that reactions to social impact may take various forms, from submission to assertive or even aggressive responses. The questionnaire consists of four scales which measure various forms of resistance. These scales have been extracted through factor analysis. The reliability of the scales is in the range of 0.73-0.82 according to Cronbach's alpha. The first scale consists of 6 items which measure retribution (R) as an aspect of resistance. Retribution means expressing anger and resentment, taking action contrary or detrimental to the interests of those exerting pressure or influence. The second scale also consists of 6 items and measures assertive confrontation (Ac) as the next aspect of resistance. Assertive confrontation is expressed by direct statements concerning one's position and by searching for argument in order to change a situation of limitation while at the same time respecting the rights of other people. The third scale relates to creating the impression of submissiveness, while secretly pursuing one's own goals and minimizing potential losses caused by open defiance. This scale consists of 5 items and is called opportunism (O). The fourth scale is designed to measure the readiness to resist in a passive way and is made up of 3 test items. It is called avoidance (Av). The content of all items in the questionnaire describes concrete behaviors in response to external demands and pressures. Possible responses were provided on a seven-point frequency scale. One extreme of the scale was described as "never" and the other extreme as "almost always". The questionnaire was administrated in four stages in order to assess its psychometric properties. Overall 553 undergraduates and graduates took a part in the questionnaire study. Validity and the reliability were confirmed.

The Creativity Checklist proposed by M. Griffin and M.R. McDermott (1998) is designed to measure creativity. This instrument was based on the statement made by D. Hocevar (1981) that in determining the level of creativity of individual people we should refer to the total number of their creative actions and the self-report is relatively the best way to obtain information about creativity. The checklist consists of two sections. The first part is used to measure creative interests undertaken during the previous year. The second part is to measure creative activities also undertaken during the previous year. D. Hocevar claimed that creativity must be analyzed in two aspects: being creative (participating in creative activities) and having an interest in creative acts. Each part of the Creativity Checklist consists of four subscales. The first refers to visual arts (for example painting or photography). The second refers to performing arts such as drama, dancing, playing musical instruments. The third concerns literary arts (writings, either in words or in music, such as poetry, prose and the like). The last subscale relates to domestic arts like making clothes, space design, interior decorations and gardening. Measurement results are obtained for separate subscales and overall. Before the Creativity Checklist was used in the presented research it was modified by the addition of the "creating computer graphics" subscale to the visual arts scale and the "writing computer programs" subscale to the literary arts scale. In addition, the old scale of measurement in the first section was changed from a three-level to a four-level scale of intensity (none, slightly, moderately, very), and in the second section from a three-level to a four-level scale of frequency (never, rarely, sometimes, often). These procedures were designed to complement the scales by taking into account contemporary forms of creative activity using computers and also to improve collected data.

The authors of the Creativity Checklist did not present the results of reliability analysis, however, during modification the tool reliability was observed. During the administration of the tool, one hundred undergraduates (60 females, 38 males, 2 unknown) from stationary and extramural studies, were tested with a new version of the Creativity Checklist. In the case of creative interests scales Cronbach's alpha ranged from 0.72 to 0.82. But only one subscale of creative activities was above 0.70 - "domestic arts". Other subscales did not achieve this level but also did not fall below 0.60. In spite of this it was decided that the new version of the Creativity Checklist would be used, bearing in mind that the results of measurement using the latter scales should be interpreted with special caution.

RESULTS

First an analysis of correlation was performed in order to find answers to the question concerning the relationship between creativity and readiness to resist. It was found that creative interests and creative activities are connected with the readiness for assertive confrontation (Ac) but not in a very strong way. It means that a higher Ac level corresponds with a higher level of creativity. It must be stressed that the reliability of subscales of creative activities, such as visual arts (A.v.a.), performing arts (A.p.a.) and writing (A.w.) was not too high. Hence, the results in scope of the subscales cannot be as certain as the other results. It is worth noting, that none of the other scales of readiness to resist were associated with creativity. The results are shown in Table 1.

Table 1: The relationship between readinesses to resist a creativy

	I.v.a.	I.p.a.	I.w.	I.d.a.	A.v.a.	A.p.a.	A.w.	A.d.a.	total I.	total A.
R	.06	.12	.05	.03	.07	.06	.01	-.05	.09	.03
Ac	.19**	.17*	.23***	.16*	.17*	.13	.23***	.13	.25****	.23***
Av	-.07	.10	.05	.03	-.04	.14	-.04	.00	.04	.01
O	-.03	.03	-.01	-.11	-.02	.04	.00	-.11	-.04	-.04

I.= creative interest, A.= creative acts, v.a.= visual arts, p.a.= performing arts, w.= writing "words", music, and the like, d.a.= domestic arts
*p<.05 **p<.01 ***p<.005 ****p<.001

The next stage was an analysis of variance (MANOVA) based on the following pattern: sex (man, woman) x birth order (first, second, further). The results revealed that sex was the main factor influencing creativity scores (Wilks' lambda = .94, F (8,184) = 5.54, p < .0001; eta^2 = .19). This means that birth order had no influence on the differentiation of creativity. Women displayed a higher intensity of creative interests and creative activity. Detailed results are presented in Table 2.

Table 2: Differences between men and women in terms of creativity

	Women		Men		
	M	SD	M	SD	F (1,195)
I.v.a.	6.30	4.37	5.38	3.61	2.33
I.p.a.	6.22	5.30	4.69	4.75	4.15*
I.w.	4.59	4.78	4.31	4.08	0.17
I.d.a.	6.37	3.88	3.15	2.75	39.18*****
A.v.a.	5.28	3.33	4.92	3.06	0.56
A.p.a.	3.08	2.58	2.81	3.06	0.44
A.w.	3.07	3.28	3.04	3.19	0.00
A.d.a	4.67	3.48	2.84	3.10	13.96****
total I.	23.48	14.02	17.53	11.01	9.72**
total A.	16.11	8.95	13.61	8.85	3.63^

^p=.058 *p<.05 **p<.01 ****p<.001 *****p<.0001

An analysis of variance of resistance scores was also performed (sex x birth order). The main influence factor was sex (Wilks' lambda = .81, F (4.188) = 2.78, p =, 028, eta^2 = .06) and at the level an effect of the interaction between sex and birth order (F (8.376) = 1.79, p = .077, eta^2 = .04) was observed.

With regard to the main effect of gender one-dimensional analysis of variance (ANOVA) showed differences between men and women in Ac- and O- scores. Males proved displayed lower intensity in Ac and higher in O than females. Moreover, differences occurred between men and women in terms of R, but only at a statistical trend level. Men proved dominant in this scope. Detailed results are presented in Table 3.

Table 3: Differences between men and women in terms of readiness to resist

	Women M	SD	Men M	SD	F(1.195)
R	16.98	8.19	19.35	8.80	3.65^
Ac	37.57	7.16	35.59	5.94	3.98*
Av	16.01	5.85	16.53	5.57	0.38
O	18.78	6.41	22.07	6.71	11.74****

^p=.058 *p<.05 ****p<.001

Birth order did not provide the main effect, although one-dimensional analysis indicated a trend toward statistical significance. There were differences in terms of Av (F (2.194) = 2.40, p = .093) and O (F (2.194) = 2.98, p = .053). First-borns displayed lower intensity in Av (M = 15.50, SD = 5.40) than those born as second children (M = 17.51, SD = 6.18). Participants born as the third and later children showed a lower intensity in O (M = 17.98, SD = 6.38) than the first-born (M = 20.89, SD = 6.66) or the second-born children (M = 20.28, SD = 6.77).

Interaction between gender and birth order occurred in one-dimensional analysis, in the case of Av-scores (F (2.194) = 3.91, p <.05) and O-scores (F (2.194) = 4.23, p <.05). The second-born women had a similar level of avoidance (Av) (M = 18.62, SD = 5.91) to that of the first-born men (M = 16.59, SD = 5.03) and the men who were born as the third or later children (M = 17.91, SD = 5.87), but different from the second-born males (M = 15.79, SD = 6.33). The last result did not reach the threshold of statistical significance (p =.056). In addition, the second-born women exhibited a higher intensity of this variable than the women who were born first (M = 14.63, SD = 5.57) and the women born as the third or later children (M = 15.26, SD = 5.43). Males did not differ within their gender group. These results are presented in Figure 1.

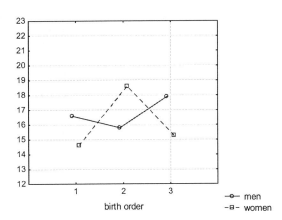

Figure 1. The interaction of gender and birth order in determining the level of avoidance (Av)

In the case of O it was the opposite. Here the males displayed higher results than females. Only the second-born men (M = 19.67, SD = 7.87) and the second-born women (M = 20.68, SD = 6.04) showed similarity. It is particularly interesting in the context of the above data, indicating the lack of differences between groups which were distinguished merely by gender. As for the simple effects, the second-born males proved to be less opportunistic than the first-born males (M = 23.74, SD = 5.93), while the second-born women were more opportunistic than the women born as the third or later children (M = 16.91, SD = 6.41). Other inter-group comparisons revealed no statistically significant differences. These results are illustrated in Figure 2.

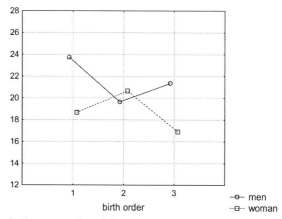

Figure 2. The interaction bewteen gender and birth order in determining the level of opportunism (O)

DISCUSSION

First of all, the results have shown that the relationship between creativity and resistance is not a simple one. Relying on the used tools we can say that in spite of some author's expectations the variables are not firmly connected. Relationship exists only between creativity and the assertive aspect of readiness to resist. This result might indicate the main role of linguistic and communication skills in the connection of the variables. The ability to verbalize may be the basis for performance of mental operations onto real objects. It may also be engaged to communicate attitudes and emotions, without resorting to less socially acceptable forms of expressing disagreement with restrictions. Particulary interesting in this regard is the lack of relationship with retribution (R). It is worth noting that retribution represents the closest equivalent to the properties measured by questionnaires concerning negativity and reactance. (cf. Donnell, Thomas & Buboltz, 2001; Dowd, Milne & Wise, 1991; McDermott, 1988). Of course the results may be mediated by the properties of the tools used in the study.

When it comes to the predominance of women over men in terms of creativity, the result was especially visible in relation to the scales which measure domestic arts and performing arts. The scales relate to activities which may be more associated with femininity, such as dance, painting, sculpture, fashion, clothing design - activities which are sometimes associated with greater sensitivity and aesthetic sense. The predominance of women is confirmed by independent observations (Abra, 1991), which demonstrate the domination of women in terms of performing arts, choreography and literature, but not in music composition and science. Interestingly, the resuluts of the presented research do not confirm the results of other investigations, where birth order was a factor differentiating the level of creativity. Some authors, however, obtained similar results (cf. Boling, Boling & Eisenman, 1993). Generally, the problem of gender differentiation in the context of creativity has not yet been finally resolved. For example, more recent research shows opposite results where males obtained higher scores in the verbal aspects of creativity (Lin, Hsu, Chen & Wang, 2011) or where the difference between males and females does not exist (Stoltzfus, Nibbelink, Vredenburg & Thyrum, 2011). Naturally, this also depends on sample selection and the kind of tool used in the study.

Women's higher scores in the Ac scale can be explained by gender-differentiated language. Women use language intensively for the expression of inner emotions (Gawda, 2008; Maxon, 1991; Strassburger, 1998) and are considered to be more caring about relation-ships, more sensitive towards the feelings of their interlocutors and more conformist than men (Strayer & Roberts, 1997; Cotten-Huston, 1998). Thus, in situations of external pressure they can probably resist in an assertive way using verbal communication to a greater extent than men (Garaigordobil, 2009). In addition, some researches prove that, from their childhood, women care more about relationships (Laireiter & Baumann, 1992; Ptacek, Smith & Dodge, 1994), and this particular feature characterizes the readiness to resist in an assertive way (Ac).

The predominance of men in terms of opportunism may be associated with the conditions of socialization. This means that men are usually expected to be less expressive and more willing to accept efforts and discomfort. On the other hand, the predominance of men may be connected with a less extensive network of relationships. Contrary to men, expressing emotion in the case of women is more accepted and women generally have a more extensive network of social relationships and social support (Bokhorst, et al., 2010). Therefore, they can afford to display more direct opposition. When women behave in this way the consequences, in ther form of possible loss of relationship can be compensated by others relationships.

The higher results of men in terms of resistance as retribution is not surprising. Numerous studies prove that men express direct hostility and aggression towards constraints and pressures more often than women. Moreover, this reaction is more expected of men (cf. Cotten-Huston, 1998; Davidson, 2003; MacGregor & Davidson, 2000).

In the case of birth order, lower intensity of Ac among the firstborns can be explained by the strategy of social functioning which they use, and which is based on the aspiration to dominate and to achieve (Sulloway, 1998).

The same method can be applied to interpret lower readiness to resist in an opportunistic manner (O) in the case of people born as the third or subsequent child. According to F.J. Sulloway (1998), subsequent children use strategies which are related to the expressing sociability, conformity and a tendency to cooperate.

As for the relationship between birth order and gender in shaping the results for resistance, in the case of second-born children, the results of women and men are different. The first comparison was made between women and men, and the second one was made within the same gender group, but between people born in a different order. Second-born women achieved similar scores in the Av scale in comparison to the first-born men, and men born as the third and later children. At the same time these women predominated over the second-born men. In the case of the O scale the results are opposite, with only second-born women and second-born men attaining the same levels in this variable, while first-born males predominate over first-born females, and men born as third children predominate over women born in the same order. This may be interpreted in the context of psychosocial functioning conditions. It is possible that these conditions are associated with one's position in the family. Moreover, they may interact with one's sex and in this way determine the set of features common for second children and gender. In light of this thesis we can claim that women born as second children display readiness to resist by avoidance (Av), and in comparison to other groups they manifest male pattern of such readiness. However, it does not mean that they become similar to males. It is rather a strengthening of gender characteristics - namely an intensification of the tendency to avoid situation of experiencing external pressure.

77

Similar interpretation can be applied to the decrease in the intensity of opportunism (O) in the case of second-born men and the increase of opportunism in the case of the second-born women. For men being the second child favors the reduction of indirect forms of opposition, while for women it fosters such forms. In fact women born as second children had a higher intensity of the Av and O scales than women of different birth order. It is worth noting that if sibling gender had been monitored during the study, the results of women could have been clearer.

After the analysis of the presented results the general conclusion which arises is that resistance and creativity are not determined by birth order alone, but rather by a combination of this variable with others such as gender. Sometimes gender turns out to be much more important in predicting resistance and creativity.

REFERENCES

Abra, J. (1991). Gender differences in creative achievement: A survey of explanations. *Genetic, Social and General Psychology Monographs*, 117(3), 235-250.
Aggleton, P. J. & Whitty, G. (1985). Rebels without a cause? Socialization and subcultural style among the children of the new middle classes. *Sociology of Education*, 58(1), 60-72.
Ai, X. (1999). Creativity and Academic Achievement: An Investigation of Gender Differences. *Creativity Research Journal*, 12(4), 329–337.
Ames, D. R. & Flyn, F. J. (2007). What Breaks a Leader: The Curvilinear Relation between Assertiveness and Leadership. *Journal of Personality and Social Psychology (92), 2,* 307-324.
Apter, M. J. (1982). *The Experience of Motivation. The Theory of Psychological Reversals.* London. New York: Academic Press.
Arnow, B. A., Manber, R., Blasey, Ch., Klein, D. N., Blalock, J. A., Markowitz, J. C., Rothbaum, B. O., Rush, A. J., Thase, M. E., Riso, L. P., Vivian, D., McCullough, J. P. & Keller, M. B. (2003). Therapeutic Reactance as a Predictor of Outcome in the Treatment of Chronic Depression. *Journal of Consulting and Clinical Psychology*, 71(6), 1025-1035.
Baer, M., Oldham, G. R., Hollingshead, A. B. & Jacobsohn, G. C. (2005). Revisiting the Birth Order-Creativity Connection: The Role of Sibling Constellation. *Creativity Research Journal*, 17(1), 67–77.
Balswick, J. O. & Macrides, C. (1975). Parental stimulus for adolescent rebellion. *Adolescence,* 10(38), 253-266.
Bokhorst, C. L., Sumter, S. R. & Westenberg, P. M. (2010). Social Support from Parents, Friends, Classmates, and Teachers in Children and Adolescents Aged 9 to 18 Years: Who Is Perceived as Most Supportive? *Social Development*, 19(2), 417-426.
Boling, S. E., Boling, J. L. & Eisenman, R. (1993). Creativity and birth order/sex differences in children. *Education*, 14(2), 224-226.
Cotten-Huston, A. L. (1998). Anger management and gender differences: from classroom teaching and research to clinical applications. *Journal of Feminist Family Therapy*, 10(3), 15.
Cowan, E. W. & Presbury, J. H. (2000). Meeting Client Resistance and Reactance with Reverence. *Journal of Counseling and Development*, 78 (4), 411-419.
Davidson, I. (2003). Effect of social context on the expression of anger in college men and women. *Dissertation Abstracts International: Section B: The Sciences and Engineering*, 64(4-B), 1939.

Deluty, R. H. (1979). Children's Action Tendency Scale: A Selfreport Measure of Aggressiveness, Assertiveness and Submissiveness. *Journal of Consulting and Cinical Psychology, 47,* 1061-1071.

Donnell, A. J., Thomas, A. & Buboltz, W. C. (2001). Psychological Reactance: Factor Structure and Internal Consistency of the Questionnaire for the Measurement of Psychological Reactance. The Journal of Social Psychology, 141(5), 679-687.

Dowd, E. T., Milne, Ch. R. & Wise, S. L. (1991). The Therapeutic Reactance Scale: A Measure Psychological Reactance. Journal of Counseling and Development, 69 (6), 541-545.

Dowd, E. T. & Sanders, D. (1994). Resistance, reactance, and the difficult client. *Canadian Journal of Coun-selling,* 28(1), 13-24.

Dowd, E. T., Wallbrown, F. M., Sanders, D. & Yesenosky J. M. (1994). Psychological Reactance and Its Relationship to Normal Personality variables. *Cognitive Therapy and Research,* 6 (18), 601-612.

Ernst, C. & Angst, J. (1983). *Birth order its influence on personality.* Berlin and NewYork: Springer-Verlag.

Garaigordobil, M. (2009). A Comparative Analysis of Empathy in Childhood and Adolescence: Gender Diffe-rences and Associated Socio-emotional Variables. International *Journal of Psychology & Psychological Therapy,* 9 (2), 217-235.

Gawda, B. (2008). Gender Differences in the Verbal Expression of Love Schema. *Sex Roles,* 58 (11/12), 814-821.

Griffin, M. & McDermott, M. R. (1998). Exploring a tripartite relationship between rebelliousness, openness to experience and creativity. *Social Behavior and Personality,* 26 (4), 347-356.

Hertwig, R., Davis, N. J. & Sulloway, F. J. (2002). Parental investment: How an equity motive can produce inequality. *Psychological Bulletin,* 128, 728–745.

Hocevar, D. (1981). Measurement of Creativity: Review and Critique. *Journal of Personality Assessment,* 45(5), 450-464.

Hong, S. M. (1990). Effects of sex and church attendance on psychological reactance. *Psychological Reports,* 66(2), 494.

Hong, S. M. & Faedda, S. (1996). Refinement of the Hong Psychological Reactance Scale. Educational and Psychological Measurement, 56 (1), 173–182.

Hong, S. M., Giannakopoulos, E., Laing, D. & Williams, N. A. (1994). Psychological reactance: Effects of age and gender. *The Journal of Social Psychology,* 134(2), 223-228.

Joubert, C. E. (1990). Relationship among self-esteem, psychological reactance, and other personality variables. *Psychological Reports,* 66(3), 1147-1151.

Kim, H. K. (2010). Measurements, Causes, and Effects of Creativity. *Psychology of Aesthetics, Creativity, and the Arts,* Vol. 4(3), 131–135.

Laireiter, A. & Baumann, U. (1992). Network structures and support functions: Theoretical and empirical analyses. H.O.F.Veil & U.Baumann (eds.). *The meaning and measurement of social support,* Washington: Hemisphere, 33-55.

Lin, W., Hsu, K., Chen, H. & Wang, J. (2011). The Relations of Gender and Personality Traits on Different Creativities: A Dual-Process Theory Account. *Psychology of Aesthetics, Creativity, and the Arts,* 1-13.

MacGregor, M. W. & Davidson, K. (2000). Men's and women's hostility is perceived differently. *Journal of Research in Personality,* 34(2), 252-261.

Madjar, N., Greenberg, E. & Zheng, Ch. (2011). Factors for Radical Creativity, Incremental Creativity, and Routine, Noncreative Performance. *Journal of Applied Psychology,* 96 (4), 730–743.

Matud, M. P., Rodríguez, C. & Grande, J. (2007). Gender differences in creative thinking. *Personality & Indivi-dual Differences*, 43(5), 1137-1147.

Maxon, A. B. (1991). Self-Perception of Socialization: The Effects of Hearing Status, Age, and Gender. *Volta Review*, 93(1), 7-18.

McDermott, R. (1988). Measuring Rebelliousness: The Development of the Negativism Dominance Scale. M.J.Apter, J.H. Kerr & M.P. Cowles (eds.), *Progress in Reversal Theory*. Amsterdam: Elsevier.

McDermott, R. (2001). Rebelliousness. M.J.Apter (eds.), *Motivational Styles in Everyday Life*. Washington: American Psychological Association.

Negrey, C. & Rausch, S. D. (2009). Creativity gaps and gender gaps: women, men and place in the United States. *Gender, Place and Culture*, 16(5), 517–533.

Pasikowski, S. (2012). Kwestionariusz do diagnozy gotowości przeciwstawiania się wpływowi społecznemu [Questionnaire for the diagnosis of readiness to resisting social influence]. *Psychologia spoleczna* (In Press)

Ptacek, J. T., Smith, Ronald E., Dodge & Kenneth, L. (1994). Gender differences in coping with stress: When stressor and appraisals do not differ. *Personality and Social Psychology Bulletin*, 20(4), 421-430.

Rhine, W. R. (1968). Birth Order Differences in Conformity and Level of Achievement Arousal. *Child Develop-ment*, 39 (3), 987-986.

Runco, M. (2007). *Creativity Theories and Themes: Research, Development, and Practice*. Burlington, San Diego, London Elsevier Academic Press.

Sampson, E. E. & Hancock, F. T (1967). An Examination of the Relationship Between Ordinal Position, Personality, and Conformity: An Extension, Replication, and Partial Verification. *Journal of Persona-lity and Social Psychology*, 5 (4), 398-407.

Seemann, E. A., Buboltz, W. C., Thomas A., Soper, B. & Wilkinson, L. (2005). Normal Personality Variables and Their Relationship to Psychological Reactance. *Individual Differences Research*, 3(2), 88-98.

Seemann, E. A., Buboltz, W. C., Jenkins, S. M., Soper, B. & Woller, K. (2004). Ethnic and gender differences in psychological reactance: the importance of reactance in multicultural counselling. *Counselling Psychology Quarterly*, 17(2), 167-176.

Stenner, P. & Marshal, H. (1995). A Q methodological study of rebelliousness. *European Journal of Social Psychology*, 25 (6), 621-636.

Stoltzfus, G., Nibbelink, B. L., Vredenburg, D. & Thyrum, E. (2011). Gender, gender role, and creativity. *Social Behavior and Personality*, 39(3), 425-432.

Strassburger, J. R. (1998). Intimacy in couples: Gender, style, and marital satisfaction. *Dissertation Abstracts International: Section B: The Sciences and Engineering*, 59(1-B), 452.

Strayer, J. & Roberts, W. (1997). Facial and verbal measures of children's emotions and empathy. *International Journal of Behavioral Development*, 20(4), 627-649.

Sulloway, F. J. (1998). *Born to Rebel*. London: Abacus.

Zweigenhaften, R. L., von Ammon, J. (2000). Birth Order and Civil Disobedience: A Test of Sulloway's "Born to Rebel" Hypothesis. *The Journal of Social Psychology*, 140(5), 624-627.

SUMMARY

Adolescence is identified as a period of rebellion and resistance. These features correspond with changes and creativity. In own research two questions in relation to this age group were assumed. First whether the creativity of a person and his readiness to resist are related in this age group. Second, whether the level of readiness to resist and the level of creativity actually are changed depending on sex and birth order. The research was carried out on a group of 207 adolescents (19-23 years old) and these have provided predictable but also unexpected results.

STRESZCZENIE

Adolescencja jest utożsamiana z okresem buntu i oporu. Te z kolei z dokonywaniem zmian i kreatywnością. W prezentowanych badaniach postawione zostały dwa pytania, w odniesieniu do tej grupy wiekowej. Pierwsze, czy kreatywność osoby i gotowość do oporu są ze sobą związane w tej grupie wiekowej. Drugie, czy poziom gotowości do oporu oraz poziom kreatywności podlegają zmianom, w zależności od płci oraz kolejności urodzenia. Badanie zostało przeprowadzone na grupie 207 adolescentów (wiek 19-23 lat) i dostarczyło przewidywalne lecz także zaskakujące wyniki.

SAMMENDRAG

Ungdomsalderen er kjent som en periode med opprør og motstand. Disse særegenhetene samsvarer med endringer og kreativitet. I egen forskning er det to spørsmål som ble undersøkt i forhold til denne aldersgruppen. Det første er om en persons kreativitet og vilje til motstand karakteriserer denne aldersgruppen. Det andre er om vilje til motstand og kreativitet endrer seg med kjønn og fødselsrekke. Forskningen blir gjennomført med en gruppe på 207 ungdommer (19-23 år) og har ført til både forventede og uventede resultater.

MGR. EMILIA KARDAŚ

Pomeranian University
Department of Psychology
Westerplatte 64
Slupsk 76-200, Poland
E-mail: emiliakardas@o2.pl

VOLITIONAL CONTROL VS.
STYLES OF COPING WITH STRESS IN OLD AGE

SENILITY - PRELIMINARY NOTES

During the last years, there was a significant increase in the elderly population. In the past only few people had a chance of reaching old age. It is estimated that even until the 18th century probably only 1% of the population lived over 65 years of age, while in the 19th century that indicator rose to almost 4% (Stuart-Hamilton, 2000).

Currently over 15% of the population in industrialised countries has exceeded 60 years of age (Ryn, 2007). We are therefore observing a demographic revolution which consists in changes in the age structure of the world population. There is a constant rise in the number of elderly people and a decline in the population of young people; hence modern societies are referred to as post-retirement societies (Straś-Romanowska, 2007).

On a global scale life expectancy has grown from 45 years in 1955 to 65 years in 1995. Statistics predict that in 2025 it will reach 73 years (Synak, 2003). The fact that world societies are becoming older results from longer life expectancy, a decline in mortality rate, and a decline in birth rate. According to statistics this situation will keep escalating.

Old age is the most diverse phase of human life and a highly individualised one, dependent to a large degree on the course of the previous developmental phases, which differs for every individual. Thus, it is a term which is difficult to define. Reference works provide us with many definitions of ageing and old age, and each definition contributes new information on the topic. According to one theory *"old age is the final stage in human ontogenetic development, preceded by such periods as childhood, youth and maturity"* (Olszewski, 1998, p.855). Old age can also be defined as the final stage in the process of ageing, during which biological, social and mental processes begin to effect each other in a synergetic way, which consequently leads to breaching the human biological and mental balance, without at the same time providing a means of counteracting this process (Zych, 2001).

Ageing can be considered from various perspectives, i.e. the number of years one has lived, biological changes, and mental changes. However, *"the condition for understanding the processes of ageing is an interdisciplinary approach. It allows us to include an entire spectrum of factors conditioning human development"* (Cavanaugh, 1997, p.110). Ageing processes take place constantly throughout our entire lives. Most systems in the human organism begin to indicate an annual depletion rate of 0.8%-1% already at the age of thirty (Hayflick, 1997, after: Stuart-Hamilton, 2000). Biological changes taking place within an ageing human organism contribute to decreased immunity to stress, weaker psychological capacity to adapt, weaker immunological resistance, and decreased efficiency of regulatory mechanisms (Zych, 2005). Psychosomatic disorders, which influence elderly people's life comfort, are an inherent element of the ageing process. According to Wilkins and Adams, 75% of elderly people experience suffering and overall discomfort caused by physical ailments (Stuart-Hamilton,

2000). Bień (2003) introduces results of studies conducted on a group of ageing people, in which only 13% of respondents stated that they do not experience any ailments that would be constant in character. On the other hand 25% of all respondents complained of one or two ailments of this type, whereas 63% complained of three or more.

The biological changes occurring during the ageing period are evidence of the fragility and transience of human life. In order to understand the functioning of an elderly person we need to consider the physical dysfunctions emerging at this stage of an individual's life (Cavanaugh, 1997). Social and psychological factors, alongside the biological ones, play an immensely important role in the ageing process. Mental ageing concerns an individual's self-awareness and his/her capacity to adapt to old age. According to Liliane Israël (1982; after: Zych & Kaleta-Witusiak, 2006) ageing is a process in which time effects a person, whereas psychological ageing consists in the influence of time on one's personality and emotional life.

The psychosocial functioning of an elderly person depends on many factors: state of health, experiences, and the relationship with the environment. An important role is also attributed to stressful situations, social support, activity and the implementation of the social and mental requirements of an ageing person. These factors determine the level of life satisfaction and self-esteem of an individual. What seems to be of great importance is the issue of ageing people's development support, which Leszczyńska-Rejchert (2007) perceives as taking steps on behalf of an individual in order to insure his/her full development.

Szatur-Jaworska (2000) claims that life quality of elderly people is conditioned by their attitude towards themselves and the environment in which they live, as well as by physical and mental health. She emphasises that these factors influence each other on a feedback basis.

There is a dispute in social gerontology concerning the vision of perfect old age. It was started by E. Cumming and W. E. Henry (1961; after: Straś-Romanowska, 2007), who formulated a thesis according to which old age consists in withdrawal from particular life domains. According to this theory elderly people should display passiveness and restrict their activity in order to further develop (Stuart-Hamilton, 2000). On the other, hand the activity theory (Neugarten, Havighurst & Tobin, 1968) (cf. Maddox, 1964), claims that an active life-style guarantees an individual constant development and enables ageing in an optimal manner. Activity allows elderly people to confirm themselves socially, gain a sense of usefulness, and attain personal satisfaction (Wiśniewska-Roszkowska, 1986). In his monograph Olszewski (2003) treats activity in the ageing period as a manifestation of adaptive behaviour. However, he emphasises that the activity must be voluntary, not forced. In reality attitudes towards one's own age and the ability to 'go through life' actively and creatively, acquired long before old age, decide about people's adaptive capabilities (Pufal-Sruzik, 2001). Thus we can say that the past is a prologue to old age, and one's positive adaptation to new conditions will largely depend on the way he/she deals with change. The way in which old age is experienced depends on the ageing person himself/herself, most of all on his/her will power, motivation to act and coping ability. *"For old age is not merely given to people as one of their developmental periods, but it is above all assigned to them, and the way in which they deal with this assignment will constitute their wisdom and maturity"* (Steuden & Marczuk, 2006, p.14).

A successful adjustment to the tasks brought upon by the late adulthood period depends on the scope of adaptive capabilities. Unfortunately, study results show that elderly people exhibit decreased adaptive capabilities, which is connected with a lower energy level and a higher risk of disturbed homeostasis. Thus, it is paradoxical that elderly people show such reluctance towards any forms of changes or novelties, in a life period so abundant in numerous changes (Wiśniewska-Roszkowska, 1989). We can therefore say that the most important task which later life sets for ageing people is to adapt to the difficulties brought upon by old age (Łój, 2007).

There is a group of people fully adapted to old age. However, they constitute less than a fifth of the total elderly population (Olszewski, 2003). The majority of those advanced in years display various indications of defects in the process of adaptation. Factors which can testify to a lack of adaptation are depression, a pretentious attitude, passiveness, egocentrism, hostility, aggression and escape into fantasy (Nowicka, 2006).

AGING BUT STRESS

Despite the fact that old age constitutes the final stage of human life and should provide many various forms of adaptation, it is a period of crisis (Olszewski, 1998). Developmental crises, including old age crisis, are the basis for deliberation in the perspective of life course psychology. Oleś (1992) describes the developmental crisis as one that requires taking new efforts, roles and tasks, connected with specific periods of development. Change gives the individual a possibility to look for completely new adaptive mechanisms. Develop-mental crises are necessary for personality development, acquiring new competences, and their positive solving enables the transition to the next stage of life. They require change in the way people function and in their assessment of themselves and their environment. Situation crises, on the other hand, concern fortuitous events. In these crises the problem lies in coping with a sudden, unexpected, difficult situation and in understanding the sense of the problem. A positive outcome implies working out completely new strategies of coping in difficult situations (Steuden, 2006).

If an ageing person still wants to develop, he/she must make an effort to solve the problems appearing in his/her life. The very emergence of a problem activates the cognitive processes and forces the individual to reformulate the past schemas, and thus to make some changes. Development ensues when a person learns what to do in a crisis situation (Wnuk, 2006). During old age an individual is vulnerable to the effects of numerous stressors, which can become the source of inner strain, stress. The term stress can be regarded from various perspectives. Thus there exist a number of theories and concepts regarding stress and coping with stress. The currently dominating approach is the relational one, according to which stress is regarded as a broad set of biological and psychical states, which arise as a result of stressors perceived as a threat. Stress is a state of an organism which finds itself in a situation subjectively regarded as difficult. *"From the point of view of interaction it is not the situation itself that is stress-inducing. It is the association of a particular situation and specific psychi-cal qualities, personality traits that generates stress reactions"* (Borkowski, 2001, p.16).

The effect of stress depends on numerous factors, such as the perception of a given situation and the ability to cope with it, social support, adaptation capacity, functionality of self-regulatory processes, type of difficult situation, stressor activity extent, personality structure, psycho-physical endurance (Hazon, 1994). Terelak (1995) emphasizes that signify-cant events in an individual's life can be a source of great stress. Studies, using the Life Change Units (LCU) scale, indicate that the most stressful event is the death of a spouse - 100 LCU points. Retirement - 45 pts, changes in living conditions - 25 pts, or moving house - 20 pts - also have significant stress consequences. A high LCU score signifies the risk of harmful effects resulting from stressful events (Borkowski, 2001).

The results of studies presented above indicate that old age is a period in which the accumulation of stressful events has a high probability of occurrence. The most frequent critical events during old age are: loss of close ones, loss of health, loss of economic and social status, loss of prestige and purpose, as well as coping with the perspective of the approaching end of life (Straś-Romanowska, 2007). Faced with so many stress-inducing factors the individual activates various coping mechanisms. Psychologists have shifted their interest from conditions inducing stress to actions taken when faced by a stressful situation (Heszen-Niejodek,

1996). Activity triggered in the face of a difficult situation which is meant to control stress is defined as coping with stress.

The process of coping with stress holds two functions: the instrumental function, the aim of which is to solve the problem constituting the source of stress, and the function of regulating emotions through reducing strain (Lazarus & Folkman, 1984). The 5 most often distinguished methods coping with stress are (Moryś & Jeżewska, 2006):
1. Searching for information – analyzing stressful situation, acquiring knowledge necessary to take required action.
2. Direct action – all actions taken by the subject, apart from cognitive actions, directed at changing the situation or the functioning of one's "ego".
3. Restraining from taking action – sometimes more advantageous than taking action.
4. Intapsychicprocesses – all cognitive processes directed at regulating emotions (e.g. defence mechanisms).
5. Seeking support – asking for help.

Parker and Endler (1992) define coping with stress as a conscious reaction to distressing outside events. Strelau (1996), on the other hand, believes that coping with stress consists in retaining balance between social requirements and one's own capabilities, or in reducing the divergences between them. In his view the subject copes with stress by shifting, changing or investing resources. Oleś (2000) emphasizes the significance of personality maturity for coping with stress. In his view people with low maturity cope through reducing negative emotions or ignoring difficulties, whereas people with high maturity display a tendency to actively cope with difficulties. The most adaptation style of functioning under stress is fluency in shifting from one strategy to another and the ability to use various strategies of coping with stress.

In this part of the article senility was presented as a time of crisis, in which there is a high probability of an accumulation of stressful events. A strong will can make adapting to old age easier and also have influence on the process of coping with difficult situations. The assumption behind the author's studies' (Kardaś, 2009) is that there exists a relationship between the level of volitional control and the preferred style of coping with stress. This connection was studied on a group of elderly people, students of the University of the Third Age. The last part of the article includes the results of own studies, which confirmed the hypothesis of the connection between volitional features and the style of coping with stress.

PSYCHOLOGICAL CHARACTERISTICS OF WILL IN THE CONTEXT OF SENILITY

Each person, regardless of age, wishes to attain happiness and balance in life. The way in which an individual copes with numerous difficult situations occurring at this stage of life depends not only on his/her way of coping with stress, but also on his/her own input, self-discipline and strong will. Nothing in life comes free and attaining a state of satisfaction is not easy and requires individual work, consistency, and perseverance in overcoming obstacles emerging on life's path. The build-up of problems connected with one's physical condition, social and economic situation, occurring in the period of old age, may contribute to the feeling of helplessness. Regardless of age a person has capability of controlling his/her life, as well as designating and implementing goals. An elderly person is able to achieve success and a feeling of happiness if only he/she does not forget that he/she has will power and can exercise it.

Will is a term which has always caused much controversy and has been understood in various ways. Kozielecki (1987) observes that to this day some psychologists do not accept the concept of will and often abstain from using it, introducing substitute terms such as self-regulation system or control system.

One of the first people to investigate the concept of will was Thomas Aquinas. He called will a rational desire and stated that although the intellect is the most important, will has a special place alongside it. According to him people are capable of making decisions regarding their actions and can be responsible for them (Kostkiewicz, 1997).

In the 19th century the will power was perceived as a sort of power, an activity thanks to which people are capable of making decisions and implementing them. Classical psychologists defined will as a *"capacity to consciously, deliberately, and without constraint perform certain actions and abstain from performing others. It is conceiving the pursued goal, combined with activity directed at reaching it"* (Szewczuk, 1979, p.325).

Nowadays the issue of will is a subject of interest to many researchers in Poland and around the world. In the Polish field it is worth to consider the work by Kozielecki (1987) who in his transgressive concept of man showed interest in the issue of will, which he perceives as a functional system, driving the course of intended actions (protective, transgressive). According to his concept will *"performs particularly important functions in such motivational processes as formulating goals, selecting action and controlling their performance"* (Kozielecki, 1987, p.379). The mind is closely related to will and a person who lacks will is not a telic subject.

Kozielecki (1987) mentions that will may undergo certain disturbances on every stage of deliberate action. A person may have problems with making rational decisions (abulia) or with reaching ambitious goals (weakness of will). Disturbances of will may also consist in not implementing action, in spite of earlier planning to do so (restrained will) or in an inability to stop doing what one does not wish to do (explosive will) (Szeluga, Pankiewicz & Szemrowicz, 2008).

In modern psychology will is understood in various ways. Some researchers perceive it as an individual's personality characteristics, others as taking action or a form of inner experience, and others still as a psychological process fulfilling regulatory functions (Trzópek, 2003). Many contemporary researchers, such as Kuhl, concentrate on the signifi-cance of will as a certain hypothetical personality disposition which - especially in the meaning of strong will - can be understood as a constant, relatively stable method of conduct, or as a hypothetical power, which organises certain reaction systems of an individual.

Motivation is an issue widely studied by many scientists. Łoś (2002) made an interesting analysis of the development of motivation throughout the course of human life, according to which a person, in his/her individual development, goes through a phase evolution of motivation and way of thinking. In the first phase of life the individual explores and creates, in the middle phase he/she introduces order and in the final phase collects material goods. Łoś postulates that knowledge of these regularities guarantees effectiveness of action and personal satisfaction.

Nelson (2003), on the other hand, claims that during old age motivation changes its character form personal goals orientation towards providing gratification to others. In his view elderly people need stronger stimulation, greater encouragement and help in taking action. Moreover, they are less enthusiastic. For many years researchers underestimated the signifi-cance of volitional control for motivational processes. However, after a long period of absence, they once again began dealing with the issues concerning will and its mechanisms. In the seventies and eighties many studies were conducted concerning the issue of will, control of action, and the processes mediating between cognition, motivation and taking action. They all remained mutually isolated. An attempt at creating a general and integrating approach was made by Kuhl in his Action Control Theory (Marszał-Wiśniewska & Zalewska, 1992).

Kuhl's Action Control Theory concerns the processes mediating between intention and its implementation, defined as action control or volitional control. According to this concept people differ with respect to the scope of capacity to hold volitional control, popularly called will power. The effectiveness of will power depends mainly on volitional characteristics (Szeluga, Pankiewicz & Szemrowicz, 2008). People who have little action control capacity are state-oriented, whereas people with a large capacity are action-oriented (Kuhl, 1994a).

"In the most general sense the function of will-power (action control) is to reinforce the activating force of the intention and to repress competing action schemes (especially those supported by strong motivational preferences) for as long as it takes the activating force of the first one to outweigh all competing action schemes" (Marszał-Wiśniewska, 2002, p.78). As we probably know, from personal experience as well, simply formulating an intention is not enough to implement it. Both before taking action and during its implementation there emerge many competing motivational tendencies, which may disturb our course of action.

Kuhl (1984; after: Marszał-Wiśniewska, 2002) highlights two types of control: *catastatic* and *metastatic*. The factor activating the metastatic and catastatic type of control is action-orientation and state-orientation. These concepts refer to two distinct motivational states: state orientation, which hinders the implementation of an intention, and action-orientation, which facilitates its implementation.

Kuhl (1994b) stated that the action/state orientation results from an interaction of two factors: personality and situation. He also emphasizes the significance of an individual tendency towards action or state orientation. As a result he differentiates between two types of state-orientation: state-orientation in situations of failure, characterized by thinking about past set-backs, passive action and brooding over suffered failures; state-orientation in decision situations, displayed by indecisiveness, hesitation, procrastination in implementing already formulated intentions. Apart from state-orientation another factor influencing volitional control and hindering implementation of intentions is change-orientation, characterised by inconsistency, elusiveness, inability to continue an action which brings the individual pleasure and satisfaction, as well as premature abandoning of activities and taking up new ones (ibidem).

These two deficits of will (state-orientation and change-orientation) are connected with the two most important functions of strong will: 1) taking action in spite of adversities, 2) sustaining and protecting goal implementation in spite of emerging temptations (Szeluga, Pankiewicz & Szemrowicz, 2008).

According to latest research, power of will can be exercised. Regular and consistent forcing oneself to do things one does not wish to do improves the capacity of self-control (Zajączkowski, 2009). This seems especially important in the old-age period, when there is often a lack of strength and will to take efforts. An excellent form of practicing self-discipline is through forcing oneself to do sports regularly. Raising oneself to any form of activity in old age contributes to the rise of self-control, thus putting one in the right frame of mind. Regular physical exercise facilitates the development of strong will, ambition and motivation (Borkowski, 2001).

The factor which gives sense to our lives, motivates us to taking action, guides us and increases perseverance is a goal. Goals play a very important role in the lives of all people. Hansen and Linkletter (2007) state that having a goal is essential in order to approach life every day with energy and enthusiasm. This goal must be difficult to achieve and should require the individual to overcome his/her own limitations. If a subject has such a goal than neither pain, nor illness, nor old age stress will deter him/her from implementing it. According to Lock et al. (1988; after: Bugajska & Timoszyk-Tomczak, 2006) goals influence concentration, perseverance, help to create optimal strategies of action and improve the level of action performance. People who have no goal in life function in a void, which is usually filled with negative emotions. They collapse into themselves, brooding over their past (Hansen & Linkletter, 2007).

Whether an individual sets himself/herself a goal and functions effectively relates to the locus of control. The way in which we perceive ourselves and the world is largely dependent on where the sense of control is located (Łój, 2007). In the period of old age we can observe a sudden decrease in the sense of control. This is especially true for the sense of inner control. It seems paradoxical that the period of life in which the sense of control constitutes one of the most important dimensions of personality, marks its clear fall (Drwal, 1978).

To summarise, we can state that there is a stereotype of elderly people functioning in society, according to which they are passive, state-oriented, and find it hard to cope with difficult situations. Results of studies conducted by Kardaś (2009) seem to state the contrary. They show a different side of elderly people, seen as individuals actively coping with a difficult situation, setting themselves goals and displaying a directed effort in their aspiration to implement these goals.

In this part of the article the author presents a review of the concepts, which take different perspectives on the issue of will. Since modern concepts question the terms will and will power the author bases her studies on the issue of will in the context of senility, further in the article, on Kuhl's Action Control Theory.

ISSUES REGARDING OWN RESEARCH

The subject of the research conducted by Kardaś (2009) was to determine the volitional characteristics of elderly people. In addition, the question whether will power has influence on the process of coping with old age stress was also investigated. Based on reference works the following theses were formulated:

• Aged people are characterized by state-orientation in decision situations and prefer the avoidant style of coping with stress.

• The volitional control level differentiates the preferred styles of coping with stress in the aged people group.

The studied group was constituted by a specific group of elderly people - 40 students of the University of the Third Age. The respondents' age varied between 60 and 88 years. The average age was 69 years. The control group was comprised of 30 people in the mid-adulthood period. They were all characterized by active lives and involvement in social life. The age of the respondents from the control group varied between 40 and 55 years. The average age was 49 years. Research tools implemented in the study:

• J. Kuhl's Action Control Scale (ACS-90)

• N.S. Endler's and J.D. Parker's Coping Inventory for Stressful Situations (CISS)

Kuhl's Action Control Scale (ACS-90) is used to estimate individual differences with regards to volitional characteristics, which influence the capacity to maintain an intention and put it into effect. It is comprised of 36 test items and three subscales:

1) The AOF subscale
Concerns situations of failure, defeat and unpleasant experiences.

• Action-orientation in situations of failure or unpleasant experiences, displayed through the ability to tear oneself away from an experienced defeat and take another action, or continue with the actions planned beforehand.

• State-orientation in situations of failure or unpleasant experiences, displayed through the lack of ability to tear oneself away from an experienced defeat and take another action, or continue with the actions planned beforehand.

2) The AOD subscale
Concerns initiating previously planned action (difficult, important) and the situation of initiating a boring task, as well as taking up a task in free-time, when one is bored.

- Task-orientation in decision situations, displayed through the ability to initiate a planned action, the ability to plan an intended action and adhering to its implementation, as well as quickly taking action in free time (to break the boredom).
- State-orientation in decision situations (hesitation), displayed through difficulties in initiating planned action (extending the time to initiate action), the inability to create an action plan, long meditation on how to begin an action, long wondering over ways of spending free time, and difficulty with mobilising oneself to do anything.

3) The AOP subscale
Concerns the situation of voluntary taking action, which is interesting and pleasant for the individual.
- Action-orientation while taking action, displayed through the ability to remain with the voluntary taken action, one that brings pleasure and satisfaction; the ability to continue the action taken.
- Change-orientation (state), displayed through premature abandoning of an action in its course, becoming quickly bored with the action taken, considering the value of an action during its course (Marszał-Wiśniewska, 2002).

The Coping Inventory for Stressful Situations (CISS), by N.S. Endler and J.D. Parker, consists of 48 statements, which concern various behaviours displayed by people in difficult situations. The questionnaire measures three styles of coping with stress:

1)   Task-Oriented Coping (TOC) - the respondent who scored high in this scale prefers a directed effort to solve a problem; he/she actively changes a situation, or transforms it cognitively;

2)   Oriented Coping (EOC) - a person who prefers this style concentrates on him/herself and his/her emotional experiences in situations of stress; such people are inclined to fantasies and wishful thinking; the emotional style may temporarily contribute to decreasing emotional tension, however, after some time the feeling of stress increases;

3)   Avoidance-Oriented Coping (AOC) - people who score high in this scale show a tendency to "escape" going through, thinking of, and experiencing situations of stress; it reduces stress temporarily, however, it does not eliminate its source; this style can take on various forms:

- Engaging in Substitute Tasks (ST), e.g. overeating, sleeping;
- Seeking the Company of Others (CO), e.g. visiting, inviting acquaintances and friends (Strelau, Jaworowska, Wrześniewski & Szczepaniak, 2005).

The studies indicate that, in contrast with the "passive old man" stereotype, elderly people are characterised by action-orientation. Based on the data included in table 1 and in table 2 we can state that the research hypothesis describing aged people as state-oriented in decision situations, and as preferring the avoidant coping style, is not confirmed. The respondents from the studied group prefer action-orientation while performing activities and in decision situations. The lowest intensity of action-orientation and the highest intensity of state orientation occur in situations of failure. This means that the students of the University of the Third Age are capable of initiating an intended task, take action quickly in their free time and actively cope with difficult situations. It is certain that they have inner control, they set and persistently implement their goals. However, it should be clear that these results were obtained after a study on a specific group of elderly people, well adapted to old age. It is a population of particularly active people, seeking new knowledge and experiences, open and ready to act. On this basis we can assume that strong will is a factor facilitating positive ageing. With this knowledge every individual can prepare for old age, by earlier shaping his/her will and adaptive methods of coping with difficulties (Kardaś, 2009).

Table 1. Average results in the study and control groups in specific subscales of the Action Control Scale

	Group	N	Mean	SD	Variance	Standard Error of the Mean
AOF	study	40	5,93	2,69	7,25	0,43
	control	30	4,73	2,66	7,10	0,49
AOD	study	40	7,58	2,91	8,46	0,46
	control	30	7,10	2,70	7,27	0,49
AOP	study	40	8,60	2,09	4,35	0,33
	control	30	8,27	2, 42	5,86	0,44

Source: Kardaś E. (2009)

Table 2. Average results for the study and control groups in particular scales of the CISS questionnaire.

	Group	N	Mean	SD	Variance	Standard Error of the Mean	Sten
SSZ	study	40	56,60	8,53	72,71	1,35	6
	control	30	56,50	8,29	68,67	1,51	5
SSE	study	40	44,68	10,21	104,17	1,61	5
	control	30	48,90	9,80	96,02	1,79	6
SSU	study	40	48,65	8,66	75,00	1,37	6
	control	30	44,03	8,06	65,00	1,47	6
ACZ	study	40	22,63	4,76	22,65	0,75	7
	control	30	20,40	5,65	31,97	1,03	6
PKT	study	40	16,85	3,61	13,05	0,57	6
	control	30	15,77	3,08	9,50	0,56	5

Source: Kardaś E. (2009)

In addition, the results of studies conducted by Kardaś (2009) confirm the existence of a relationship between the intensity of will power and the applied styles of coping with stress. There is indication of a positive but weak relationship between the task-oriented coping style and state/action-orientation in decision situations, as shown in table 3. Studies indicate that elderly people characterized by strong will, i.e. action-orientation, more often cope effectively with stress using the task-oriented style. On this basis we can assume that people who actively cope with problems and who display a directed effort aimed at solving a difficult situation, will also have the ability to initiate action and to pursue its implementation. This relationship also appeared in the mid-adulthood group.

Statistical analysis also shows that elderly people characterised by state-orientation, i.e. showing difficulties with implementing their intentions, often use the ineffective emotional-oriented coping style. Based on the results presented in table 3 we can state the occurrence of average negative correlations between the emotional style of coping with stress and state/action-orientation in situations of failure and in decision situations, which means that the greater the intensity of the emotional coping style, the greater the intensity of state-orientation in situations of failure and in decision situations. Hence, we can conclude that people, who concentrate on their emotional experiences in difficult situations, will focus their attention of negative feelings and constantly brood over the suffered set-back in a situation of failure. This relationship is confirmed in the mid-adulthood group (ibidem).

Table 3. The value of correlation coefficients between specific scales in the studied group

		Age	Task oriented	Emotion oriented	Avoidance oriented	Distraction	Social Diversion	AOF	AOD	AOP
		The Studied Group								
Age	Pearson's Correlation	1,00	0,02	0,04	-0,36	-0,35	-0,24	0,18	-0,08	-0,15
	Relevance (two-sided)		0,92	0,82	0,02	0,03	0,13	0,28	0,63	0,35
	N	40,00	40,00	40,00	40,00	40,00	40,00	40,00	40,00	40,00
Task-oriented	Pearson's Correlation	0,02	1,00	-0,10	0,19	-0,03	0,35	0,05	0,31	0,06
	Relevance (two-sided)	0,92		0,55	0,24	0,84	0,03	0,77	0,05	0,73
	N	40,00	40,00	40,00	40,00	40,00	40,00	40,00	40,00	40,00
Emotion oriented	Pearson's Correlation	0,04	-0,10	1,00	0,30	0,48	-0,15	-0,54	-0,37	0,15
	Relevance (two-sided)	0,82	0,55		0,06	0,01	0,36	0,01	0,02	0,35
	N	40,00	40,00	40,00	40,00	40,00	40,00	40,00	40,00	40,00
Avoidance oriented	Pearson's Correlation	-0,36	0,19	0,30	1,00	0,84	0,71	-0,11	0,04	0,20
	Relevance (two-sided)	0,02	0,24	0,06		0,01	0,01	0,49	0,81	0,21
	N	40,00	40,00	40,00	40,00	40,00	40,00	40,00	40,00	40,00
Distraction	Pearson's Correlation	-0,35	-0,03	0,48	0,84	1,00	0,27	-0,29	-0,13	0,14
	Relevance (two-sided)	0,03	0,84	0,01	0,01		0,09	0,07	0,44	0,40
	N	40,00	40,00	40,00	40,00	40,00	40,00	40,00	40,00	40,00
Social Diversion	Pearson's Correlation	-0,24	0,35	-0,15	0,71	0,27	1,00	0,19	0,22	0,09
	Relevance (two-sided)	0,13	0,03	0,36	0,01	0,09		0,23	0,18	0,56
	N	40,00	40,00	40,00	40,00	40,00	40,00	40,00	40,00	40,00
AOF	Pearson's Correlation	0,18	0,05	-0,54	-0,11	-0,29	0,19	1,00	0,52	-0,06
	Relevance (two-sided)	0,28	0,77	0,01	0,49	0,07	0,23		0,01	0,69
	N	40,00	40,00	40,00	40,00	40,00	40,00	40,00	40,00	40,00
AOD	Pearson's Correlation	-0,08	0,31	-0,37	0,04	-0,13	0,22	0,52	1,00	0,22
	Relevance (two-sided)	0,63	0,05	0,02	0,81	0,44	0,18	0,01		0,17
	N	40,00	40,00	40,00	40,00	40,00	40,00	40,00	40,00	40,00
AOP	Pearson's Correlation	-0,15	0,06	0,15	0,20	0,14	0,09	-0,06	0,22	1,00
	Relevance (two-sided)	0,35	0,73	0,35	0,21	0,40	0,56	0,69	0,17	
	N	40,00	40,00	40,00	40,00	40,00	40,00	40,00	40,00	40,00

Source: Kardaś E. (2009)

According to table 3 the following correlations in the studied group were found:

- A positive though weak connection between task-oriented coping and state/action-orientation in decision situations, which means that greater intensity of task-oriented coping causes increased action-orientation in decision situations. The correlation between the TOC and the AOD variables equals $r = 0.31$, $p<0.05$.

- There exist average negative correlations between the emotional coping style and state/action orientation in situations of failure, as well as decision situations, which means that greater intensity of emotional-oriented coping causes increased state-orientation in situations of failure and decision situations. The correlation between the EOC and the AOF variables equals $r=-0.54$, $p<0.01$. The correlation between the EOC and the AOD variables equals $r=-0.37$, $p<0.05$.

Based on table 3 we can state that the research hypothesis, according to which the volitional control level differentiates the preferred coping styles in the group of aged people has been confirmed.

Similar studies, conducted on a group of overweight and average-weight women, were conducted earlier by Chanduszko-Salska & Ogińska-Bulik (2001). The results of these studies indicate that overweight women, who are characterised by action-orientation, after failures and in situations of planning more often prefer the task-oriented coping style in dealing with stress, as opposed to women displaying state-orientation. However, in both groups the women displaying state orientation show a greater tendency towards the emotional style of coping with stress. These conclusions are therefore convergent with results obtained by Kardaś (2009) in the group of elderly people, which means that strong will is conducive to effective coping in difficult situations.

The presented results are only a basis for preliminary conclusions, which require closer verification. In order to achieve a broader scope it would be necessary to study elderly people outside the University of the Third Age.

CONCLUSIONS

Old age is the final stage of human life; however it is a mistake to associate this period with stagnancy and peace. Old age, as presented in this article, is a time of numerous changes, difficult situations requiring elderly people to show resilience and making them pursue further development. Old age does not relieve one from the obligation to constantly develop, on the contrary, it sets new developmental tasks, which can be considered in the categories of old age stress. Both positive and negative changes taking place in the life of an elderly person may cause disturbance of homeostasis. All difficult events influence mood, thinking and functioning of the elderly.

Successful ageing depends on the acceptance of one's own age, the ability to adapt to emerging changes and personal control of one's own life. Unfortunately, the society usually perceives elderly people as senile, requiring constant control and care. This results in depriving elderly people of their independence and inner control, which is the basis for shaping a positive attitude towards oneself and the surrounding world. By depriving elderly people of choice we cause them to develop a state of hopelessness and withdrawal. An elderly person who has no control over his/her life does not take any action, does not aim at implementing it, and does not set himself/herself new goals or challenges. Such a person does not age in an optimal way. In order to prevent this from happening the society should work towards restoring elderly people's sense of causality and control over their lives, through providing them with a possibility to make choices. What is more, we must not forget about the important role of the individual in the process of ageing. It is the individual who has the greatest influence on the way in which he/she goes through his/her old age, and it is his/her attitude, shaped throughout the entire life, that conditions the development of less or more adaptive methods of living through one's old age.

The conclusions from the conducted studies presented in the article show that strong will is conducive to effective coping with stress. Senior citizens displaying strong will, i.e., action-orientation, are more effective in dealing with old age stress, and thus probably adapt better to this period, and age in a positive way. On the other hand, elderly people characterised by lower intensity of strong will, are more likely to use the emotional-oriented coping style. As a consequence these people display a tendency towards greater concentration on the experienced emotions, thus being less effective in coping with difficult situations, emerging in this period of life. Based on this, we can make an assumption that they do not age in an optimal way, and that they may show certain difficulties in adapting to old age.

Despite the crisis, appearing frequently during this period of life, and caused by numerous stressors, one can remain optimistic and effectively cope with changes. A specific group of elderly people, students of the University of the Third Age, provides proof that strong will facilitates proper adaptation to old age, and is one of the conditions of positive ageing. The presented study results indicate that elderly people can control their own lives, set themselves goals and consistently pursue their implementation. They can also effectively cope with old age stress.

Students of the University of the Third Age are a group of people well adjusted to old age. *Life-span* psychology perceives adjustment to old age as taking place throughout our entire life. According to this concept people develop all their lives and constantly work on the shape of their old age. Thus, it is worth to reflect upon it and prepare for it in advance. This gives us a chance to be happy, satisfied grandparents, instead of frustrated, pretentious old men and women.

How, in that case, can one prepare for old age? First of all, one needs to shape positive thinking and optimism in confronting everyday problems. Difficult situations require active searching for alternative ways of solving specific problems, without concentrating on experiencing negative emotions. It is worth to set oneself realistic goals and consistently pursue their implementation. It is also important to induce oneself to take up any form of activity, to consistent effort. This contributes to the increase of self-control, and thus to better well-being. By following these few simple rules we stand a chance for happiness in old age.

REFERENCES

Bień, B. (2003). Stan zdrowia i sprawność ludzi starszych. [State of Health and Efficiency of Elderly People] B. Synak (ed.). *Polska starość. [Polish Old Age]* Gdańsk: Gdańsk University Publishing.

Borkowski, J. (2001). *Radzenie sobie ze stresem a poczucie tożsamości. [Coping with Stress vs. the Sense of Identity]* Warszawa: ELIPSA Publishing House.

Bugajska, B. & Timoszyk-Tomczak, C. (2006). Człowiek stary wobec przyszłości. [Elderly Person Facing the Future]. S. Steuden & M. Marczuk (eds.). *Starzenie się a satysfakcja z życia. [Ageing vs. Satisfaction with Life]* Lublin: KUL Publishing.

Cavanaugh, J. C. (1997). Starzenie się. [Ageing]. P. E. Bryant & A. M. Colman (eds.). *Psychologia rozwojowa. [Developmental Psychology]*. Poznań: Zysk i S-ka Publishing House.

Chanduszko-Salska, J. & Ogińska-Bulik, N. (2001). Kontrola wolicjonalna a radzenie sobie ze stresem kobiet z nadwagą i wagą w normie. [Volitional Control and Coping with Stress Among Overweight and Average Weight Women]. *Zeszyty Naukowe [Scientific Journals]*, 2.

Cumming, E. & Henry, W. E. (1961). *Growing old. The process of disengagement.* New York: Basic Books.

Drwal, R. Ł. (1978). Poczucie kontroli jako wymiar osobowości- podstawy teoretyczne, techniki badawcze i wyniki badań. [Sense of Control as a Dimension of Personality - Theoretical Foundations, Research Techniques and Study Results]. L. Wołoszynowa (ed.): *Materiały do nauczania psychologii. [Materials for Teaching Psychology]* Warszawa: Polish Scientific Publishers PWN.

Hansen, M. V. & Linkletter A. (2007). *Najlepsza reszta życia. [How to Make the Rest of Your Life the Best of Your Life].* Poznań: W Drodze Publishing House.

Hayflick, L. H. (1997). Mortality and immortality at the cellular level. A Review. *Biochemistry.* 62.

Hazon, B. (1994). *Stres.* Warszawa: WWAB.

Heszen-Niejodek, J. (1996). Stres i radzenie sobie- główne kontrowersje. [Stress and Coping with Stress - Main Controversies]. J. Heszen-Niejodek & Z. Ratajczak (eds.). *Człowiek w sytuacji stresu. Problemy teore-tyczne i metodologiczne. [People in Situations of Stress. Theoretical and Methodological Problems]* Katowice: Silesian University Press.

Israël, L. (1982). Le vieillissement psychologique: âge et personnalité. *Gérontologie et Société.* 22.

Kardaś, E. (2009). Siła woli a radzenie sobie ze stresem w okresie starzenia się. Niepublikowana praca magisterska. [Will Power and Coping with Stress in the Period of Ageing. Unpublished M.A. Dissertation]. Gdańsk: University of Gdańsk.

Kostkiewicz, J. (1997). Wola jako kategoria pedagogiczna w kontekście wolności odpowiedzialnej. [Will as a Pedagogical Category in the Context of Responsible Freedom]. J. Kostkiewicz (ed.). *Szkice o kształto-waniu osobowości. [Essays on Personality Shaping].* Rzeszów: Pedagogical University of Rzeszów Publishing.

Kozielecki, J. (1987). *Koncepcja transgresyjna człowieka. Analiza Psychologiczna. [Transgressive Concept of Man. Psychological Analysis]* Warszawa: Polish Scientific Publishers PWN. 379

Kuhl, J. (1984). Volitional aspects of achievement motivation and learned helplessness: Toward a comprehend-sive theory of action control. B.A. Maher (ed.). *Progress in experimental personality research.* New York: Academic Press.

Kuhl, J. (1994a). A theory of action and state orientations. J. Kuhl & J. Beckmann (eds.). *Volition and Persona-lity. Action versus state orientation.* Gottingen: Hogrefe and Huber Publishers.

Kuhl, J. (1994b). Action versus state orientation: Psychometric properties of the Action Control Scale (ASC-90). J. Kuhl & J. Beckmann (eds.). *Volition and Personality. Action versus state orientation.* Gottingen: Hogrefe and Huber Publishers.

Lazarus, R. S. & Folkman S. (1984). *Stress, appriaisal and coping.* New York: Springer.

Leszczyńska-Rejchert, A. (2007). *Człowiek starszy i jego wspomaganie - w stronę pedagogiki starości. [Elderly People and Their Support - Towards Old Age Pedagogy].* Olsztyn: University of Warmia and Mazury Publishing.

Łoś, Z. (2002): Fazowe zmiany motywacji w ujęciu Mariana Mazura a rozwój człowieka dorosłego. [Phase Changes of Motivation According to Marian Mazur in Relation to Adult People's Development]. M. Straś-Romanowska (ed.). *Szkice psychologiczne. Doniesienia z badań. Aplikacje. Refleksje. [Psycholo-gical Essays. Research Reports. Applications. Reflections].* Wrocław: Wrocław University Publishing.

Łój, G. (2007): *Psychologiczne wyznaczniki przeżywanej starości (psychoneuroimmunologia starości). [Psycho-logical Determinants of Experienced Old Age - Psychoneuroimmunology of Old Age].* Mysłowice: Górnośląska Wyższa Szkoła Pedagogiczna Publishing.

Maddox, G. L. (1964). Disengagement theory: A Critical Evaluation, *The Gerontologist*. 4.

Marszał-Wiśniewska, M. & Zalewska, A. (1992). „Siła woli" we współczesnym ujęciu. ["Will-Power" in Con-temporary Perspective]. A. Eliasz & M. Marszał-Wiśniewska (eds.). *Temperament a rozwój młodzieży. [Temperament in Relation to Adolescent Development]*. Warszawa: Institute of Psychology, Polish Academy of Sciences PAN.

Marszał-Wiśniewska, M. (2002). Adaptacja Skali Kontroli Działania J. Kuhla [Adaptation of J. Kuhl's Action Control Scale] (ACS-90). *Studia Psychologiczne. [Psychological Studies]*. 78

Moryś, J. & Jeżewska, M. (2006). Historyczne, społeczne i medyczne aspekty problematyki stresu. [Historical, Social and Medical Aspects of the Issue of Stress]. B. Borys & M. Majkowicz (eds.). *Psychologia w medycynie. [Psychology in Medicine]*. Gdańsk: Medical University of Gdańsk.

Nelson, T. D. (2003). *Psychologia uprzedzeń. [The Psychology of Prejudice]*. Gdańsk: GWP Publishing.

Neugarten, B. L. & Havinghurst, R .J. & Tobin, S. S. (1968). Personality and pattern of aging. B.L. Neugarten (ed.). *Middle Age and Aging*. Chicago: Chicago University Press.

Nowicka, A. (2006). Starość jako faza życia człowieka. [Old Age as a phase of Human life]. A. Nowicka (ed.). *Wybrane problemy osób starszych. [Selected Problems of Elderly People]*. Kraków: Impuls Publishing Houses.

Oleś, P. (1992). Zjawisko kryzysu psychicznego. [The Psychological Crisis Phenomenon]. A. Januszewski, P. Oleś & T. Witkowski (eds). *Wykłady z psychologii w KUL. [Lectures on Psychology in the Catholic University of Lublin]* 6, Lublin: Editorial Staff, KUL Publishing.

Oleś, P. K. (2000). *Psychologia przełomu połowy życia. [Psychology at the Half-Tun of Life]*. Lublin: Scientific Society of the Catholic University of Lublin.

Olszewski, H. (1998). Starość i starzenie się. [Old age and ageing]. W. Szewczuk (ed.). *Encyklopedia psycho-logii. [Encyclopedia of Psychology]*. Warszawa: Innovation Foundation. 855

Olszewski, H. (2003). *Starość i witaukt psychologiczny: atrybucja rozwoju. [Old Age and Positive Attribution of Development]*. Gdańsk: Gdańsk University Publishing.

Parker, J. D. A. & Endler, N. S. (1992). Coping with coping assessment. *European Jpournal of Personality, 6 (5)*, 321-344.

Pufal-Sruzik, I. (2001). Możliwości twórcze osób w różnym wieku. [Creative Capabilities of People in Various Age]. A. A. Zych (ed.). *Demograficzne i indywidualne starzenie się. [Demographic and Individual Ageing]*. Kielce: Swietokrzyska Academy Publishing House.

Ryn, Z. J. (2007). Starość nam otwiera drzwi. [Old Age Opens the Door for Us]. *Charaktery*. 7.

Strelau, J. (1996). Temperament a stres: Temperament jako czynnik moderujący stresory, stan i skutki stresu oraz radzenie sobie ze stresem. [Temperament vs. Stress: Temperament as a Factor Moderating Stressors, State and Results of Stress as well as Coping with Stress]. J. Heszen-Niejodek & Z. Ratajczak (eds.). *Człowiek w sytuacji stresu. [People in Situations of Stress]*. Katowice: Silesian University Press.

Strelau, J., Jaworowska, A., Wrześniewski, K. & Szczepaniak, P. (2005): *Kwestionariusz Radzenia Sobie w Sytuacjach Stresowych CISS. Podręcznik*. (The CISS Questionnaire. Textbook). Warsaw: Psychological Test Workshop, Polish Psychological Association.

Steuden, S. (2006). Rozważania o godności z perspektywy człowieka w okresie starzenia się. [Considering Dignity from the Perspective of a Person in the Period of Old Age]. S. Steuden & M. Marczuk (eds.). *Starzenie się a satysfakcja z życia. [Ageing in Relation to Life Satisfaction]*. Lublin: KUL Publishing.

Steuden, S. & Marczuk, M. (eds.) (2006). *Starzenie się a satysfakcja z życia*. Lublin: KUL Publishing. 14.

Straś-Romanowska, M. (2007). Późna dorosłość. Wiek starzenia się. [Late Adulthood. The Ageing Period]. B. Harwas-Napierała & J. Trempała (eds.). *Psychologia rozwoju człowieka. Charakterystyka okresów życia człowieka. Tom 2. [Psychology of Human Development. Characteristics of Human Life Periods. Vol. 2].* Warszawa: Polish Scientific Publishers PWN.

Stuart-Hamilton, I. (2000). *Psychologia starzenia się. [Psychology of Ageing].* Poznań: Zysk i S-ka Publishing House.

Synak, B. (2003). Problematyka badawcza i charakterystyka badań. [Research Issues and Characteristics of Studies]. B. Synak (ed.). *Polska Starość. [Polish Old Age].* Gdańsk: Gdańsk University Publishing.

Szatur-Jaworska, B. (2000). *Ludzie starzy i starość w polityce społecznej. [Elderly People and Old Age in Social Policy].* Warszawa: ASPRA-JR Publishing.

Szewczuk, W. (1979). *Słownik psychologiczny. [Dictionary of Psychology].* Warszawa: Wiedza Powszechna Publishing. 325

Terelak, J. F. (1995). *Stres Psychologiczny. [Psychological stress].* Bydgoszcz: Branta.

Trzópek, J. (2003). *Problem woli. Między antropologią filozoficzną a psychologią mechanizmów regulacyjnych. [The Issue of Will. Between Philosophical Anthropology and the Psychology of Regulatory Mechanisms].* Kraków: Societas Vistulana Publishing House.

Wiśniewska-Roszkowska, K. (1986). *Nowe życie po sześćdziesiątce. [New Life After Turning Sixty].* Warszawa: PAX Publishing Institute.

Wiśniewska-Roszkowska, K. (1989). *Starość jako zadanie. [Old Age as a Task].* Warszawa: PAX Publishing Institute.

Wnuk, W. (2006). Sytuacje trudne osób starszych w perspektywie geragogiki. [Difficult Situations of Elderly People in the Perspective of Geragogics]. S. Steuden & M. Marczuk (eds.): *Starzenie się a satysfakcja z życia. [Ageing in Relation to Life Satisfaction].* Lublin: KUL Publishing.

Zych, A. A. (2001). *Słownik gerontologii społecznej. [Dictionary of Social Gerontology].* Warszawa: ŻAK Academic Publishing.

Zych, A. A. (2005). Pierwszy siwy włos... Szczególne cechy starzenia się osób z niepełnosprawnością intelek-tualną. [First Grey Hair ... Particular Ageing Features of Intellectually Disabled People]. *Bardziej Kochani. (Loved More)* 1.

Zych, A. A. & Kaleta-Witusiak, M. (2006). Geragogika specjalna- moralnym obowiązkiem naszych czasów. [Special Geragogics - A Moral Obligation of Our Times]. A. Nowicka (ed.). *Wybrane problemy osób starszych. [Selected Problems of Elderly People].* Kraków: Impuls Publishing House.

Internet sources:

http://www.drszeluga.republika.pl/silna.doc.; Szeluga J., Pankiewicz P. & Szemrowicz D., *Silna i słaba wola a alkoholizm. [Strong and Weak Will in Relation to Alcoholism].* 22 Feb. 2008. Web.

http://zajaczkowski.org/2008/04/07/gdy-zabraknie-silnej-woli/; Zajączkowski B. *Gdy zabraknie silnej woli... [When There Is a Lack of Strong Will...].* 2 Mar. 2009. Web.

SUMMARY

The aim of the article is to bring the reader closer to the psychological issue of will in the perspective of ageing. The article presents a view that it exists a connection between the volitional control level and the preferred style of coping with old-age stress. The results obtained by the author suggest that there is a relationship between task-oriented coping and state or action orientation behavior in decision situations: aged people characterized by strong will. i.e. action orientation, often cope with stress more effectively, while aged people characterized by state-orientation often use the ineffective emotional coping style.

STRESZCZENIE

Celem artykułu jest przybliżenie czytelnikowi psychologicznej problematyki woli w perspektywie starzenia się. W artykule zaprezentowano pogląd, że istnieje związek między poziomem kontroli wolicjonalnej a preferowanym stylem radzenia sobie ze stresem starości. Uzyskane przez autorkę wyniki sugerują, iż istnieje związek między zadaniowym stylem radzenia sobie ze stresem a orientacją na stan lub działanie w sytuacjach decyzyjnych. Osoby stare, charakteryzujące się silną wolą, częściej radzą sobie ze stresem w sposób efektywny, podczas gdy osoby stare charakteryzujące się orientacją na stan częściej stosują nieefektywny, emocjonalny styl radzenia sobie ze stresem.

SAMMENDRAG

Målsetning med artikkelen er å bringe leseren nærmere vilje som psykologisk spørsmål i et aldringsperspektiv. Synspunktet i artikkelen er at det finnes en sammenheng mellom viljekraft og den foretrukne måten å mestre stress i alderdommen på. Forfatterens funn antyder at det er en sammenheng mellom oppgaveorientert mestring og handlingsorientert/ikke-handlingsorientert atferd i beslutningssituasjoner: Eldre mennesker med sterk vilje, d.v.s. oppgaveorienterte, mestrer oftere stress mer effektivt, mens eldre mennesker som ikke er handlingsorienterte, oftere bruker lite effektive emosjonelle mestringsstrategier.

DR. MARIA ALEKSANDROVICH, PHD

Pomeranian University
Department of Psychology
Westerplatte 64
Slupsk 76-200, Poland
E-mail: maria.aleksandrovich@gmail.com

BALLET DANCERS:
EXAMINATION OF THE COMPONENTS OF PROFESSIONAL SUCCESS

I intend to work for this dance of the future.
I do not know whether I have the necessary qualities;
I may have neither genius nor talent nor temperament.
But I know I have a Will; and will and energy
Sometimes prove greater than
either genius or talent or temperament.
Isadora Duncan

INTRODUCTION

People have been dancing for thousands of years to express emotions, feelings, and ideas through movement, as well as to communicate without words. Most people like to dance and for most people dancing is nothing more than a hobby. Professional career in dance, especially ballet, it is constant dedication and commitment. Young people who are aspiring to go into dance, especially a ballet career, must love dance and classical ballet enough to put years of hard training and everyday study during their childhood and youth, in other words, they must be strongly motivated.

Motivation in general can be described as an internal energy force that determines all aspects of our behaviour and as the ability to initiate and persist at a task thanks to one's numerous efforts and energy or drive. Motivation in ballet (Taylor and Taylor, 1995) is a will to work hard in the face of fatigue, boredom, pain, and the desire to do other things. Motivation will impact everything that influences the dancer's performance: physical conditioning, technical and tactical training, mental preparation, and general lifestyle including sleep, diet, school or work, and relationships. At the same time in the field of dance motivation it is the only factor related to performance that dancers can control. While the abilities and task difficulty stay fairly constant during the performance season, the only thing dancers have control over is their motivation. The performance formula indicates that three factors contribute to the quality of a performance: motivation, ability, task difficulty (Figure 1):

Motivation + (Ability - Task difficulty) = Performance

Figure 1. Performance formula (Taylor & Taylor, 1995).

Recent research conducted in the field of dance psychology (Aleksandrovich, 2004; Barrell & Terry, 2003; Burt, 1995; Carr & Wyon, 2003; Doumenc, Sudres & Sztulman, 2005; Fetisova, 1991; Nieminen, 1998; Quested, Duda, 2009, Urena, 2004) shows that successful learning experiences in dance not only depend on how much motivation the dancer brings to the studio, but also on what motivates individuals to dance. Some motivational theories can be successfully applied in dance. One of them it is Self-Determination Theory, SDT (Deci & Ryan, 1991), which is a macro theory of human motivation and personality, concerning people's inherent growth tendencies and their innate, natural or intrinsic tendencies to behave in effective and healthy ways. This theory emphasizes the reasons why people are engaged in certain activities, and the extent to which human behavior is self-endorsed as opposed to externally regulated.

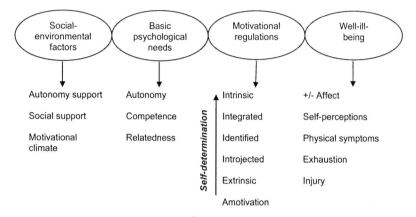

Figure 2. Schematic representation of Self-Determination Theory (Quested & Duda, 2009, p. 37)

Another motivational theory, Achievement Goal Theory, AGT (Diener & Dweck 1978; Dweck & Elliott, 1983 Harackiewicz et al., 2002) studies how individuals define success and competence. Success and failure are not absolute events but based on a perception of achieving or not achieving one's goals. Competence moderated attitudes and behaviours are more prevalent in ego-involved activities than task-involved ones. Achievement does not moderate intrinsic motivation in task-involving conditions, in which people of all levels of ability can learn to improve. In ego-involving conditions, intrinsic motivation was higher among high achievers who demonstrated superior ability than in low achievers who did not demonstrate such ability (Butler, 1999).

Motivational Process Model (Dweck, 1996) includes following components:
- Implicit theory of intelligence
- Seeking and evaluation of information
- Motivational orientation
- Overt behaviour
- Outcome evaluation (Figure 3).

In the frames of our research the most important component of the model is behaviour. Dweck (1996) differentiated between two types of behaviours in achievement contexts:
- Mastery oriented behaviour pattern
- Helpless behaviour pattern.

Mastery oriented behaviour pattern is a characteristic of the learner, who wants to acquire new competencies and who wants to be able to have command of new situations. The information processing of this learner focused on the surveillance of learning process and the search for new strategies that were useful in attaining this learning goal (Dweck & Leggett, 1988; Heyman & Dweck, 1992).

While helpless behaviour pattern is a characteristic of the learner, who shows various maladaptive behaviours. They did not attribute their successes to action taken, but rather explained them predominantly through uncontrollable causes (for example luck or task difficulty). Meeting the failure, they reduced their aspiration, experienced negative emotions, demonstrated lower levels of persistence, and gave up the task easily (Heyman & Dweck, 1998; Kamins & Dweck, 1999; Abd-El-Fattah, 2006).

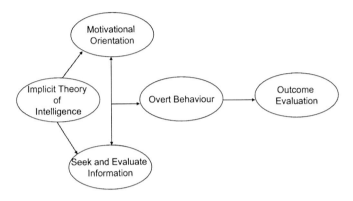

Figure 3. Motivational Process Model (Abd-El-Fattah, 2006, p. 548)

Quested and Duda (2009, 2010) make a case for enhancing dancers' intrinsic motivation and task-involvement towards dance. They studied how the quality of a dancer's motivation can impact persistence in training, satisfaction of learning experiences, emotions, and self-esteem. According to their research, intrinsically motivated dancers participate in dance because they want to, and love dancing simply for the sake of dancing. While extrinsically motivated dancers dance for external reasons such as avoiding feelings of guilt, demonstrating their ability to others, or receiving praise. A dancer's sense of competence and personal goals depend on whether he or she is task-involved or ego-involved. Task-involved dancers consider competence to be based on the self, in other words, self-referent.

The task-involved dancer is:
- Primarily driven to dance for reasons of self-improvement
- More likely to persist and enjoy learning experiences

The ego-involved dancer is:
- Involved in dance to show supremacy over others or to reap some kind of external reward (e.g. get a specific part in a show)
- Is likely to have favorable learning experiences when achieving supremacy/reward

The risk for the ego-involved dancer comes when supremacy/reward is not achieved. This can happen when a dancer moves from a local dance school (big fish, little pond) and take up a place at a vocational dance school (little fish, big pond). After years of feeling like "the best" in the class, a dancer may suddenly feel distinctly "average" compared to others in the class. In these circumstances an ego-involved dancer is likely to feel their sense of self threatened and experience heightened anxiety and, as a result, decrease is effort towards dance exercises.

The career of a ballet dancer makes special demands on the physical and mental qualities of the dancer and consists of years of everyday hard training. It is difficult to evaluate the minimum number of hours and years of training required to develop expertise in ballet dance, but there is no doubt that hard training is crucial for dancers (Urena, 2004). There is also no doubt that early training is necessary for classical ballet dancers to adapt their hip joints for maximal turnout (Miller, Callander, Lawhon, & Sammarco, 1984, Sosnina, 1997, Soboleva, 2005). At the same time Schnitt and Schnitt (1987) theorized that in order to produce an elite dancer, 10-15 years of training, starting at an early age, are required to refine the requisite movement skills of ballet. Quested and Duda on the basis of Epstein's (1989) TARGET acronym created a framework for supporting dancers' intrinsic motivation and task-involvement:

- Task – dancers have a selection of diverse and challenging exercises
- Authority – dancers are given a degree of choice and volition over learning
- Recognition – individual progress is valued
- Grouping – co-operative learning in small, collaborative groups
- Evaluation – dancer self-referenced achievement judgments supported
- Timing – allow sufficient time for practice and improvement

Ballet dancers are performers, and performing for people can be stressful, demanding on personal lives, and on emotions. Dancers also have to contend with the fleetingness of the profession – one injury, and their career as a performer can be over. But to be professionally successful requires having appropriate cognitive abilities and achievement motivation (Atkinson & Feather, 1966; Schuler & Prochaska, 2011). If the behaviour of a certain profession is not focused on an achievement as a main goal, achievement motivation plays an even more important part (Schuler & Prochaska, 2011).

A basic construct of competence motivation is the degree of approval or disapproval attached to the result of the child's mastery attempts which relates directly to one's sense of competence. The theory of achievement motivation is based on a person's feelings of personal competence. According to the theory, competence motivation increases when a person successfully masters a task (Harter, 1978). Achievement motivation depends on self-consciousness, the tendency for emotional conflict between expectations of success and fear of failing, aspects of the activity, difficulty of the tasks, mastering objects or humans, and experiencing pride for one's achievements (Atkinson & Feather, 1966; McClelland, 1985; Murray, 1938; Weiner, 1985).

Characteristics of people with high achievement motivation

- Want to succeed
- Require constant feedback
- Avoid low risk and high risk jobs. Undertake medium risk
- Self-motivated, self-directed
- Self challenging but realistic goals
- Prefer to work alone or with high achievers
- Goal is accomplishment or challenge itself
- Assume personal responsibility for problem solving
- Sequence tasks in relation to goals
- Prioritize tasks to attain goals
- Evaluate by monitoring results and establishing check points
- Non-traditional
- Independent at earlier age.

Ballet as an artistic performance can be a nice example of such professional achievements. In our research we decided to examine the components of the professional success, conducting the research on a group of dance students who are to become professional dancers, as well as successful adult ballet dancers.

METHODS AND TECHNIQUES

Participants and Procedure. For the period 2004-2009, a group of young ballet dancers from the following ballet groups took part in this research: the Comprehensive Ballet School in Gdansk (CBS), Gdansk, Poland (105 dancers); the Belarusian Ballet College (BBC), Minsk, Belarus (59 dancers); the Belarusian National Theatre of Opera and Ballet (BNTOB), Minsk, Belarus (2 dancers); the Polish Dance Theatre (PDT), Poznan, Poland (10 dancers); the Ejfman Ballet Group (EBG), St. Petersburg, Russia (15 dancers); and the Dance Group Berezka (DGB), Moscow, Russia (7 dancers). The total sample is 198 dancers (Table 1).

Table 1. Representation of the participants

Nationality / Ballet groups		Number of the participants			Median age
		Women, N = 110	Men, N = 88	Together, N = 198	
Russian	DGB	6	1	7	23,7
	EDG	7	8	15	22,3
	BBC	39	20	59	16,6
	BNTOB	1	1	2	25,5
Polish	CBS	50	55	105	14
	PDT	7	3	10	32,3

All the participants had been studying in their respective ballet school for at least one year. The questionnaires were administered individually or in small groups. Participation in the study was voluntary and anonymous.

Instruments. For the purposes of this study, a questionnaire was created to assess the level of dance expertise and professional success (Aleksandrovich, 2004). This self-report questionnaire consists of 24 questions in sections. Question 12-18 are based on transformed data from Urena (2004). For to study the personality traits the NEO-Five Factor Inventory, NEO-FFI, (Costa, McCare, 1990) was used. For the assessment of interpersonal behaviour, the questionnaire by Senko (1998) was used. The statistical analysis of the data was done by using STATISTICA 6.0.

RESULTS

The results of the analysis of the self-reports collected during our research show that 48.3 % of the sample believe their career development is successful, while 51.7 % think they are unsuccessful in their development as professional ballet dancers. But when we look at the objective evaluation of success, giving by other professionals (high marks on classical dance, participation in professional workshops, first place at the competitions and festivals, first roles and professional awards), we notice 75.2% can be considered as unsuccessful and only 24.8 as successful. The results of the factor analysis are presented in the Table 2.:

Table 2. The results of factor analysis

Variable	Weight	%
Nationality	1	65,2
Neuroticism	2	61,5
Extraversion	3	60,1
Positive Dominate and Sub-dominate forms of personal behaviour	4	56,3
Conscientiousness	5	52,1
Openness	6	47,1
Task orientation	7	42,4
Positive Dominate forms of personal behaviour	8	40,6
Talk orientation	9	40,3
Negative Sub-dominate forms of personal behaviour	10	37,6
Gender	11	35,4
Emotional forms of personal behaviour	12	32,4
At what age you have started professional dance training?	13	31,4
Dancing for more then 10 years	14	28,5
Negative Dominate and Sub-dominate forms of personal behaviour	15	25,6
Positive Sub-dominate forms of personal behaviour	16	25,2
At what age you have started dancing?	17	24,3
At what age you have started ballet school?	18	23,2
Professionally doing modern dance	19	20,2
Professionally doing choreography	20	19,4
Negative Dominate forms of personal behaviour	21	17,3
Participating in professional workshops	22	17,2
At what age you have started your participation in professional workshops?	23	17,1
Professional doing classical ballet	24	12,2
Agreeableness	25	8,7
Dancing for 5-10 years	26	4,3
Dancing for 1-5 years	27	2,2
Rational of personal behaviour	28	1,0

As can be seen in table 3, the values of the factors 1-6 in professional success in ballet are similarly high (47,1-65,2 %). In this group of the participants the highest value has factor *Nationality* (65,2 %), personality trait *Neuroticism* is on the second place (61,5 %), personality trait *Extraversion* is on the third place (60,1 %), *Positive Dominate and Sub-dominate forms of personal behaviour* are on the fourth place (56,3 %), personality trait *Conscientiousness* is on the fifth place (52,1 %) and personality trait *Openness* is on the sixth places (47,1 %). The results of factor analysis show unexpected position for the personality trait *Agreeableness*. Its value is 8,7 % and it is on the twenty-fifth. Surprisingly *Rational forms of personal behaviour* landed in the last of twenty-eight positions (1 %).

DISCUSSION

In our research group most of the participants started dancing at the age of 6-7 years. During 5-10 years of everyday training they had to develop technical and artistic skills, because the scenic activity of ballet dancers demands. In this group the analysis of the importance of all the variables for success in ballet showed an interesting hierarchy. In our sample, the five most impor-

tant variables for professional success were *Nationality, Neuroticism, Extraversion, Positive Dominate* and *Sub-dominate Forms of Personal Behaviour*, and *Conscientiousness.*
The importance of the *Nationality* factor leads us the idea about the differences in the approaches to the ballet education and theatre everyday life of Polish, Belarusian and Russian ballet groups. Ilin (2003) found out, that special *psychological difficulties* for ballet dancers are such as:

• discrepancy of expectations: ballet dancing is not a "leisure activity" but "hard work", especially when you do not want or you are not able to work, to dance;

• necessity to prove yourself positive from the first lesson, even if you have no any professional training before;

• fears, such as: "fear of the teacher", "fear of professional examinations", "fear to be considered as unpromising", "fear of injury".

All these fears as well as high sensibility of the dancers could be the reasons for the high rate of the *Neuroticism.* In our research more than the half of the sample of ballet dancers showed high neuroticism and this result corresponds with the study conducted by Fetisova (1994). In this connection it is also interesting that in the Vysotskaya's (1976) study of ballet dance students the low level of neuroticism was significantly correlated with bad emotional expressiveness and average level of neuroticism with high emotional expressiveness. Here we also have a partial explanation why in our study *Extraversion* is on the third place. For ballet dancers it is important to be active, friendly, assertive and emotional. These characteristics of extraversion especially important for young ballet school dancers. The young dancers with high emotional reactivity have developed the main characteristics of successful ballet dancing better than their colleagues with low emotional reactivity (Vysotskaya, 1976) table 3.:

Table 3. Development of main characteristics of successful ballet dancing (in points)

Characteristics	High emotional reactivity	Low emotional reactivity	p-level
Emotional expressiveness	4.25	3.70	$p < 0.01$
Artistry	4.12	3.60	$p < 0.05$
Ability to dance	3.99	3.60	-
Classical dance	3.84	3.51	-
Characteristic dance	4.02	3.50	$p < 0.05$
Actor's skills	4.20	3.72	$p < 0.05$

Specialists in dance education (Zaharov, 1976; Blok, 1987 & Fetisova, 1991) underline such psychological features which are necessary for ballet dancers to achieve success and efficiency in ballet:

• Close cooperation with the ballet master

• Respect for the canons of classical dance

• Complex of physical and spiritual qualities: body constitution, musicality, artistry, memory and diligence

• Bright individuality

• Internal ability to operate the thoughts and feelings and to express them in movements, gestures and poses

• Strong regime to be always health and in a good shape.

It is not so easy to fulfill all these demands. That is why *Conscientiousness* is also high in our research. It helps dancers to be strong in goal orientation, to be organized, reliable and self-disciplined. *Positive Dominate* and *Sub-dominate Forms of Personal Behaviour* help dancers to adapt to the new situations, to accept teacher's / choreographer's demands and to agree with the rules of the group.

CONCLUSION

On the basis of our own research and research of other authors we tried to show the physical, emotional and social complexity of the *professional success in ballet*. Without doubts, professional success in ballet dance has many sides and components. The results of the present research, on the one hand, show the empirical importance of such factors of professional success in ballet as *Nationality*, *Neuroticism*, *Extraversion*, *Positive Dominate* and *Sub-dominate Forms of Personal Behaviour*, and *Conscientiousness*, and, on the other hand, help to enrich a colourful portrait of professional ballet dancers, whose career development requires deep experience and high achievements in relatively young age.

REFERENCES

Abd-El-Fattah, S.M. (2006). The implicit theories of intelligence: A review of Carol Dweck's motivation process model. *International Education Journal*, 7(4), 547-553.

Aleksandrovich, M. (2004). *Uwarunkowania osobowościowe poziomu sukcesu członków grupy baletowej.* Badanie realizowane na Uniwersytecie Gdańskim podczas stażu naukowego w ramach Specjalnego Stypendium Rządu RP 2003–2004.

Aleksandrovich, M. (2010). Professional success in ballet: ballet teacher's role evaluation. In: Janik, T. & Knecht, P. (eds.). *Pathways in the Professional Development of Teachers* (246-251). Wien: Lit.

Ames, C. (1992). Achievement goals, motivational climate and motivational processes'. In G. C. Roberts (ed.), *Motivation in Sport and Exercise* (pp. 161–176). Champaign, IL: Human Kinetics.

Atkinson, J. W., Feather, N. T. (Eds.) (1964). *A theory of achievement motivation.* New York: Wiley.

Barrell, G., Terry, P. (2003). Trait anxiety and coping strategies among ballet dancers. *Medical Problems of Performing Artists*, 18, 59-64.

Burt, R. (1995). *The male dancer: Bodies, spectacle, sexualities.* London: Routledge.

Carr, S. (2006). An examination of multiple goals in children's physical education: motivational effects of goal profiles and the role of perceived climate in multiple goal development. *Journal of Sports Sciences*, 24, 281-297.

Carr, S., Wyon, M. (2003). The Impact of Motivational Climate on Dance Students' Achievement Goals, Trait Anxiety, and Perfectionism Source. *Journal of Dance Medicine and Science*, 7 (4), 105-114.

Conroy, D., Elliot, A., & Hofer, S. (2003). A 2 X 2 achievement goals questionnaire for sport: evidence for factorial invariance, temporal stability, and external validity. *Journal of Sport and Exercise Psychology*, 25, 225-256.

Costa, P. T., Jr., & McCrae, R. R. (1992). Four ways five factors are basic. *Personality and Individual Differences*, 13, 861-865.

Cumming, J., & Hall, C. (2004). The relationship between goal orientation and self-efficacy for exercise. *Journal of Applied Social Psychology*, 34, 747-763.

Deci E, Ryan R (1985) Intrinsic Motivation and Self-determination in Human Behavior, New York: Plenum

Doumenc, A., Sudres, J., & Sztulman, H. (2005). Approach of the ponderal and body dimensions of professional young ballet dancers vs. young amateur. Neuropsychiatry of Childhood and Adolescence, 53, 299-308.

Duda, J. & Nicholls, J. (1992). Dimensions of achievement motivation in schoolwork and sport. *Journal of Educational Psychology*, 84, 290-299.

Duda, J. L. (1993). Goals: A social cognitive approach to the study of achievement motivation in sport. In R. N. Singer, M. Murphey and L. K. Tennant (eds.), *Handbook of Research on Sport Psychology*, pp. 421–436, New York: Macmillan.

Dweck, C. S. & Elliott, E. S. (1983). Achievement motivation. In P. Mussen (Ed.), *Handbook of Child Psychology: Socialization, personality, and social development* (Vol. 4, pp. 643-691). NY: Wiley.

Dweck, C. S. (1984). Motivational processes affecting learning. *American Psychologist*, 41 (10), 1040-1048.

Dweck, C.S. (1992). The study of goals in psychology. *Psychological Science*, 3 (3), 165-167.

Dweck, C. S. (1996). Implicit theories as organizers of goals and behaviour. In P. M. G. J. A. Bargh (Ed.), *The Psychology of action. Linking cognition and motivation to behaviour* (pp. 69-90). New York: Guildford Press.

Elliot, A. J. (1999). Approach and avoidance motivation and achievement goals. *Educational Psychologist*, 34, 169-189.

Elliot, A. J. & Harackiewicz, J. M. (1996). Approach and avoidance achievement goals and intrinsic motivation: A mediational analysis. *Journal of Personality and Social Psychology*, 70, 416-475.

Fetisova, Y. V. (1991). The psychological portrait of a ballet dancer. *Soviet Journal of Psychology*, 12 (3), 63-73.

Harter, S., (1978). Effectance motivation reconsidered: Toward a developmental model. *Human Development*, 1, 34-64.

Hodge, K. & Petlichkoff, L. (2000). Goal profiles in sport motivation: A cluster analysis. *Journal of Sport and Exercise Psychology*, 22, 256-272.

Lacaille, N., Koestner, R., & Gaudreau, P. (2007). On the value of intrinsic rather than traditional achievement goals for performing artists: a short-term prospective study. *International Journal of Music Education*, 25, 245-257.

McCrae, R. R., & Costa, P. T., Jr. (1997). Conceptions and correlates of Openness to Experience. In R. Hogan, J. A. Johnson & S. R. Briggs (Eds.), *Handbook of personality psychology* (pp. 825-847). San Diego: Academic Press.

Miller, A. (1991). Personality types, learning styles and educational goals. *Educational Psychology*, 11 (3,4), 217-238.

Miller, E. H., Callander, J. N., Lawhon, S. M., & Sammarco, G. J. (1984). Orthopedics and the ballet dancer. *Contemporary Orthopedics*, 8, 72-97.

Motivation: A question of quality not just quantity (2012). From http://www.dancewisdom.com/motivation-is-a-question-of-quality-not-just-quantity/ Date: 20.08.12

Nicholls, J. G. (1984). Achievement motivation: conceptions of ability, subjective experience, task choice, and performance. Psychological Review, 9, 328-346.

Niemenen, P., Varstala, V., & Manninen, M. (2001). Goal orientation and perceived purposes of dance among finnish dance students: a pilot study. *Research in Dance Education*, 2, 176-193.

Nieminen, P. (1998). Motives for Dancing Among Finnish Folk Dancers, Competitive Ballroom Dancers, Ballet Dancers and Modern Dancers. *European Journal of Physical Education*, 3 (1), 22-34.

Pintrich, P.R. & Schrauben, B. (1992). Students' motivational beliefs and their cognitive engagement in classroom academic tasks. In D. Schunk & J. Meece (Eds.), *Students perceptions in the classroom: Causes and consequences* (pp. 149-183). Hillsdale, NJ: Erlbaum.

Quested, E. & Duda, J. L. (2009). Setting the stage: Social-environmental and motivational predictors of optimal training engagement. Performance Research: A Journal of the Performing Arts, 14, 36-45.

107

Ravaldi, C., Vannacci, A., Bolognesi, E., Mancini, S., Faravelli, C., & Ricca, V. (2006). Gender role, eating disorder symptoms, and body image concern in ballet dancers. *Journal of Psychosomatic Research*, 61, 529-535.

Schnitt, J. M., & Schnitt, D. (1987). *Psychological issues in a dancer's career.* In A. J. Ryan and R. E. Stephens (Eds.), Dance medicine: A comprehensive guide (pp. 334-349). Chicago, IL: Pluribus Press.

Smith, R., Smoll, F., Cumming, S., & Grossbard, J. (2006). *Measurement of multidimensional sport performance anxiety in children and adults: The sport anxiety scale-2.* Journal of Sport and Exercise Psychology, 28, 397-398.

Tiggemann, M., & Slater, A. (2001). A test of objectification theory in former dancers and non-dancers. *Psychology of Women Quarterly*, 25, 57-64.

Urena, A. C. (2004). *Skill acquisition in ballet dancers: the relationship between deliberate practice and expertise.* Dissertation submitted to the Department of Educational Psychology and Learning Systems in partial fulfillment of the requirements for the degree of Doctor of Philosophy The Florida State University, College Of Education. Retrieved July 22th, 2007, from http://etd.lib.fsu.edu/theses/available/etd-07122004170955/unrestricted/ revisedcurena dissertation.pdf]

Valentini, N., & Rudisill, M. (2006). Goal orientation and mastery climate: a review of contemporary research and insights to intervention. *Studies of Psychology*, 23, 159-171.

Van Yperen, N. W. (2006). A novel approach to assessing achievement goals in the context of the 2X2 framework: identifying distinct profiles of individuals with different dominant achievement goals. *Personality and Social Psychology Bulletin*, 32, 1432-1445.

Блок, Л.Д. / Blok (1987). Классический танец. История и современность. – М.: Искусство.

Васильев В.В. / Vasilev (1983). Путь к мастерству / Художественное творчество. – Л.: Наука, – 226-229.

Высотская Н.Е. / Vysotskaya (1976). *Изучение индивидуальных качеств, влияющих на успешность овладения профессией артиста балета*: автореферат дис. ... кандидата психологических наук. Ленинград

Гройсман, А. Л. / Grojsman (2004). Комплексная коррекция психических состояний артистов балета. *Психологический журнал.* 25, № 1. – Р. 83-89.

Захаров, Р. / Zaharov (1976). Записки балетмейстера. – М.: Искусство.

Ильин, Е.П / Ilin (2003). Дифференциальная психология профессиональной деятельности. – Питер.

Сенько, Т.В. / Senko (1998). Психология взаимодействия: Часть вторая: Диагностика и коррекция личностного поведения. – Мн.: Карандашев.

Соболева, О. С. / Soboleva (2005). *Продуктивность творческой деятельности артистов балета*: автореферат дис. ... кандидата психологических наук : 19.00.13 / Рос. акад. гос. службы при Президенте РФ Москва.

Соснина, И. Г. / Sosnina (1997) *Специальные способности артиста балета: Природа, структура, диагностика*: диссертация ... кандидата психологических наук : 19.00.01 Пермь.

Фетисова, Е. В. / Fetisova (1994). Эмоциональный слух в комплексе психологических характеристик личности артиста балета // Художественнный тип человека. Комплексные исследования / Под ред. В. П. Морозова и А. С. Соколова. – М., 1994.

http://mikebarnesanth.wordpress.com/2012/03/25/ballet-dancers-and-motivation/ Date: 20.08.12

http://www.danceclass.com/dance-teachers.html Date: 22.08.12

http://www.networkdance.com/dance-ballet-articles/Importance-of-motivation-for-dancers/7 Date: 22.08.12

SUMMARY

This article explores the components of the professional success of ballet dancers, as well as the motivation of successful adult ballet dancers to find out what is the pushing point to start ballet dance training and what the significance of dance performance is to the dancers themselves. The results of the research are based on quantitative research on the components of professional success of ballet dancers, conducted in the group of ballet students as well as young professional ballet dancers.

STRESZCZENIE

Ten artykuł przedstawia wyniki badania składników fachowego powodzenia tancerzy baletowych, jak i motywacji spełnionych dorosłych tancerzy baletowych dla wyjaśnienia tego, co kieruje młodych ludzi do rozpoczęcia zajęć tanecznych oraz jakie jest znaczenie tańca dla tancerza. Wyniki badania są wynikami analizy ilościowej opartej na badaniu składników fachowego sukcesu tancerzy baletowych, zrealizowanym na grupie tancerzy studentów szkół baletowych oraz grupie młodych ale znanych tancerzy baletowych.

SAMMENDRAG

Artikkel forklarer de viktigste komponentene for profesjonell suksess til ballettdansere. Dessuten beskrives voksne suksessrike ballettdansere sin motivasjon. Målet er å finne den utløsende faktoren for å begynne å trene ballet, samt hvilken betydning dansens utførelse har for danseren. Resultatene er basert på et kvantitativ undersøkelse av komponenter for profesjonell suksess til ballettdansere. Deltakere har vært både ballettdans elver og unge utdannete profesjonelle ballettdansere.

MGR. RUNE WAALER

Finnmark University College
Department for Sports and Science
Follumsvei 31
9509 Alta, Norway
E-mail: Rune.Waaler@hifm.no

FRILUFTSLIV IN THE NORWEGIAN FOLK HIGH SCHOOLS – CONTENTS AND VALUES

INTRODUCTION

After completing upper secondary school about 11% of students in Norway choose to spend one year studying their favourite subject of interest at folk high schools (Netland, 2011).

The folk high school was started in Denmark in 1844 and in Norway in 1864 (Mikkelsen, 2002). The Danish pastor Nikolai F. S. Gruntvig (1783-1872) is considered the founder of the folk high school (Arne, 1964; Torjusson, 1997; Mikkelsen, 2002). Gruntvig was inspired by English university campuses – where students and teachers lived together on the campus grounds. But the folk high school was intended to be an alternative to the schools characterized by memorization and examinations. Gruntvig envisioned a school for the people without Latin or exams, a school in which the mother tongue, the history and the living word were the best means of giving youth a general education and develop their manners (Akerli, 2001). Living together, students and teachers became an important aspect.

In the 1970s, the study of friluftsliv as a subject gradually made its way into the folk high school. Friluftsliv had by then been part of the Norwegian culture for a long time. Friluftsliv in Norway is more than outdoor-life or backpacking. Friluftsliv is a term in the Norwegian culture. Its tradition communicates values of great importance for the Norwegian identity – values such as a sense of national community, contemplation, nature experience and a social environment with family and friends (Skirbekk, 1981; Faarlund, 1986; 2009; Nedrelid, 1993; Goksøyr, 1994; Odden, 2008). In recent decades, values such as self realization, personal achievement and excitement have become increasingly common within friluftsliv, especially among the younger generation (Odden, 2008).

The earliest friluftsliv course of study in Norway was probably created at Aust-Agder folk high school in 1973 (Tordsson, 2003). Øytun folk high school in Alta, Finnmark was the first to base all their course offerings on friluftsliv, in 1992. Since then, the number of courses in friluftsliv has slowly increased and continues to do so today. Ten to fifteen years ago, the courses were called "Friluftsliv" or "Sports and friluftsliv". Today, course names are usually along the lines of "Friluftsliv-adventure" and "Mountaineering-guide."

This article reflects on changes in the course offerings in friluftsliv over the last ten years and relates them to results from a survey of student values pertaining to friluftsliv carried out in the autumn and spring. The main question is whether there are motivation changes from between autumn and spring, what that can tell us about the teaching in folk high schools, and what consequences the value orientation of students may have for folk high school teaching in the future.

ANALYSIS OF FRILUFTSLIV COURSE OFFERINGS

I have categorized the friluftsliv study programmes offered at the folk high schools into three major classes:
1. Traditional friluftsliv
2. Classical friluftsliv
3. Activity-oriented specialization

The first two concepts are well established through the work of Gunnar Breivik (1978), who described the dichotomy of the Norwegian friluftsliv in 1978.

1. *Traditional friluftsliv* includes activities such as hunting, fishing, berry picking and gathering of other renewable resources in the rural tradition. The main point is to have an errand in nature.

2. *Classical friluftsliv* is a tradition that developed among townspeople. Here the outdoor trip is a goal by itself and does not need any further justification. Hiking and skiing trips at a relaxed pace are the most common activities. New activities such as windsurfing, climbing and river kayaking slowly broke their way into the classical friluftsliv tradition in the 1970s (Breivik 1998).

3. *Activity-oriented specialization.* According to Odden (2008), the new, modern activities did not seriously win ground until 1985. Concurrently, the growth of traditional and classical types of friluftsliv stagnates (Odden, ibid). The modern activities are highly specialized and require both specialized skills and -equipment (Odden, 2008, p.181). Not only do the activities themselves change, but the motivation also becomes more oriented toward mastering challenges and experiencing action and excitement. These changes in friluftsliv have been described by several authors (Pedersen, 1999; Skogen, 1999; Breivik, 2001; Bischoff & Odden, 1999; 2008). To classify the course offerings in the folk high schools the past ten years it is necessary to either define this third category, or better define the nuances between and within the existing categories. Kleven (1993) uses four categories of friluftsliv: *"Classical friluftsliv" "Use of nature" "Action-oriented youth and sports culture"* and *"A quiet walk"* (Kleven, 1993). Pedersen (1999) uses the categories *"wanderers" "gatherers"* and *"specialists,"* where the specialists represent modern friluftsliv. In this article the term *"Activity-oriented specialization"* will be used. The content of courses falling into this category is oriented toward one or more activities emphasizing the elements of speed, specialized equipment and specific knowledge and skills. Examples of such activities are: various forms of climbing, kiting, off-road bicycling, or off-piste skiing. The category of activity-oriented specialization is then further divided into two subcategories: *general with several activities* or *focused on one or two activities.*

CLASSIFICATION OF THE COURSES

The classification of the courses was based on information gathered from the folk high school course catalogue and school web pages and by speaking with teachers at several schools. An in depth discussion would deal with whether it is appropriate to apply the term *friluftsliv* to many of these outdoors activities. Table 1 gives an indication of the changes occurring in the courses offered between 1998 and 2008.

The number of folk high schools and the number of folk high schools offering courses in friluftsliv decrease between 1998 and 2008. Despite this, the number of courses in friluftsliv increased from 80 to 109. According to observations from the folk high school catalogues (IF and IKF, 1998-2008) and personal communication with folk high school employees (Michaelsen, 2009 and Solem, 2009), it seems that folk high schools are narrowing in and specializing in their subject profile. Earlier, folk high school typically had one or two courses in friluftsliv, while the schools that offer friluftsliv in 2007/08 build a broader friluftsliv community around three or more courses.

Courses with a clear conservation theme are declining in number. They are not found at all among the specialization courses. Conservation-theme courses offered in the classical and traditional categories make up only 4% of all courses offered in 2008, down from 25% in 1998. In 1998/99, the terms conservation or ecology were used in course names or course descriptions: "experience friluftsliv and learn ecology at sea, on the mountain plateau and in the mountains" (Fana folk high school (fhs)), "contemplate our relation to nature" (Hallingdal fhs) or "naturalist knowledge and valuing nature is part of the program" (Bakketun fhs), (folkehøgskolekontoret, 1998). These formulations disappear around the year 2000. Based on this, one may easily think the folk high schools have removed conservation from their programmes, but that is probably not the case.

Table 1: Friluftsliv courses offered between 1998 and 2008 in Norwegian folk high schools

Number of friluftsliv courses, by type, between 1998/99 and 2007/2008				
	1998/99	2001/02	2004/05	2007/08
1 Traditional friluftsliv	**12(15%)**	**18**	**8**	**10(9%)**
General, nature and wilderness	2	7		
Hunting and fishing	8	8	6	7
Conservation	2	3	2	3
2 Classical friluftsliv	**51(64%)**	**43**	**29**	**26(24%)**
General	29	32	24	21
Conservation	18	6		1
Guiding	3	3	3	2
KRIK (Christian youth sports group)	1	2	2	2
3 Activity-oriented specialization	**17(21%)**	**39**	**55**	**73(67%)**
General with several activities	8	24	40	52 (48%)
Focused on one or two activities	9	15	15	21 (19%)
Sailing	3	2	2	3
Snowboarding and/or skiing		3	3	8
Dogmushing	3	4	3	3
Horses	1	1	2	2
Climbing				2
Surfing			1	1
Air sports and/or scuba diving	2	2	2	2
Search and rescue		3	2	2
Total number of friluftsliv courses	**80**	**100**	**92**	**109**
Number of schools with friluftsliv course(s)	50	48	45	46
Total number of folk high schools in Norway	83	81	78	77

Sources: Informasjonskontoret for folkehøyskolen (IF) and Informasjonskontoret for Kristen folkehøyskole (IKF), 1988, 2001, 2004 and 2007

Courses in the traditional and classical tradition more than halved in number during the period. At the same time, activity-oriented specialization courses tripled, and now make up 67% of the courses. The general level of participation in modern activities in Norway for youth age 16-24 was 36% in 2004 (Odden, 2008, p.96). The folk high school offer of modern activities is therefore twice as large as the phenomenon would warrant.

Friluftsliv activities offered in the folk high school appear to be changing, potentially faster than in the society at large. While traditional activities such as skiing, hiking, fishing and picking berries experience a downturn, more activity-oriented forms of friluftsliv such as off-piste skiing and snowboarding, climbing, off-road biking, telemark skiing and kayaking are growing in popularity. And the greatest increase is in courses that include several active-ties. In 2007/2008, activity-oriented specialization with several activities made up 48% of all courses offered. Among courses focusing on only one or two activities, ski and snowboard courses increase the most, and make up more than 7% of the courses in 2007/2008.

According to Odden (2008, p.65), 4% of the Norwegian population went off-piste in the mountains in 2004. It is unlikely that the corresponding value for youth for 2008 is as much as 7%, the percentage in folk high schools. Courses that include off-piste as one among many activities come in addition to this. The actual percentage of students participating in off-piste activities is probably above 10%. The offer of mountain off-piste activities in folk high schools is seemingly much more extensive than what the prevailing level of activity among Norwegian youth.

Trends in courses offered agree with Odden's conclusion (2008) that "*Outdoor recreation is becoming more varied and specialized*". Traditional activities like hiking, skiing, picking berries and fishing diminish among youth age 16-24 years. At the same time, snowboarding, off-piste skiing, off-road biking, ski sailing, rafting, mountain climbing and caving increase.

Odden (2008, p.94) points out that overall participation in friluftsliv activities among young people is in decline. A decrease in classical and traditional trip- and harvesting activities among youth can account for this reduction. The folk high schools are going against the current of our time when they increase the number of friluftsliv courses. But they are following the flow if you consider their change to more modern and specialized activities. And in a sense they are going faster than the current: the number of specialized courses offered has more than tripled since 1998. This increase is far greater than expected based on the change in outdoor recreation of youth.

STUDENTS' MOTIVATION FOR FRILUFTSLIV

The school year 2007/2008, 1333 students attended friluftsliv courses in Norwegian folk high schools. Each student received, through their teacher, two identical questionnaires about their motivation for friluftsliv. The first survey was done 2-3 weeks after school started in the autumn, the second 2-3 weeks before school ended for the summer. 707 students returned their answers in the autumn of 2007, a response rate of 53%. In the spring of 2008 there were 473 student responses, which is 67% of the autumn responses and 35% of the population. I asked the students: "*What do you wish to experience by taking this programme?*" The question went on to relate this to their favourite friluftsliv activity at the folk high school. A measure of 90% for the value *social environment* means that 9 out of 10 students rated this value as "Very important". In this paper, motivation is understood as synonymous with the term "value" which I use in the remainder of the text. The motivational factors social environment, personal development, etc. are operationalizations that have been used in several Norwegian surveys on friluftsliv over the last twenty years (Aasetre et al., 1994; Odden & Aas, 2002; Odden, 2008; Skår et al., 2008). For all students, these were the most important values they sought:

Table 2. Students' motivation for friluftsliv during the school year 2007/2008 (percent responding "Very important").

VALUE	AUTUMN 2007	SPRING 2008	CHANGE
Social environment	90 %	86 %	-4 %
Personal development	81 %	74 %	-7 %
Improve one's skills	75 %	70 %	-5 %
Speed and action (excitement)	73 %	69 %	-4 %
Nature experience	68 %	71 %	+3 %
Risk	37 %	30 %	-7 %
The tranquillity of nature	28 %	26 %	-2 %
Hunting and harvesting	10 %	10 %	No change

Sources: Authors own, 2010

114

The students may seem to answer with less zeal in the spring compared to the autumn. Nearly all of the values decrease in their importance. It may reflect that students are nearing the end of the course and hold fewer expectations. Answers in the fall are based on expectations while the answers in the spring are based both on their experiences so far and their expectations of the last 2-3 weeks at the folk high school. Because of this, the answers provided to the different values should be analyzed relative to each other.

The *social environment* is the most important value for folk high school students. Many folk high school alumni and proponents would be pleased that there is plenty of room for a good social environment in the modern friluftsliv. An immediate question is rather; are students paying more attention to each other than to nature?

The values *personal development* and *improve one's skills* can be interpreted as forms of self realization. Their importance decreases slightly more than average. Today's youth face a globalized and individualized youth culture that promotes new activities and sets of attitudes that contrast starkly with traditional friluftsliv (Odden, 2008, p.19). Self realization values such as personal development and improving one's skills are gaining ground in general. They are strongly planted in the folk high schools, yet they lose ground during the year.

The values *speed and action* and *risk* also decrease in importance. *Nature experience* is ranked as far down as fifth place in the autumn and third place in the spring. These ranks do not imply that nature experience is not an important value. Almost 70% of the students answered that it is very important to them. Nonetheless, four other values are more important in the autumn, and two in the spring. Nature experience is the only value that is given more weight by students in spring compared to autumn. Social environment, the self realization values, speed and action and risk decrease in importance, while nature experience becomes more important.

Risk is top ranked among the less important values, and shows a clear reduction. One would think course names such as "Friluftsliv Extreme" or "Backpacker/Extreme sports" appealed to risk motivated students. But no courses could have been categorized as risky friluftsliv. Eleven courses had the term "extreme", or phrases like "adrenalin kick" or "de-fying your boundaries" in their name or description in 2007/2008. After reading the detailed description of the courses and speaking to course coordinators I have found no signs that these courses are oriented toward objective or subjective risk[1] in either the content or organization of the course. Therefore, they are placed in the category *activity-oriented specialization*. The values expressed by the students confirm this. They seek speed, action and self realization through improving their activity-specific skills, but are relatively unwilling to take risks.

According to Odden (2008), nature experience and contemplation is one of the most valued aspects of friluftsliv, also among young off-piste skiers and snowboarders. We have reason to believe that nature experience still is strongly represented among the youth doing modern activities. In the folk high school, we see that the self realization values hold a stronger position than nature experience. These values are equally strong when spring comes.

Judging from the statistics from autumn, values related to nature experience may seem to have a weak position in the folk high schools. There are several possible reasons for this. We meet the students at a specific point in time, characterized by the stage of the course. For a course including skiing on steep slopes, it is only natural that during the first skiing days in fall, the first priority is managing and mastering the activity. As skills improve, one is able to direct more attention towards nature. In addition, "*nature experience*" is a term with several possible dimensions of meaning. An essential part of the experience for some may be sharing

---

[1] *Objective risk*, i.e. external events, refers to dangers outside of one's control, for instance, falling rocks, water temperature, our equipment or a change in weather. *Subjective risk* refers to decisions made by the individuals, regarding use of equipment, interpreting the weather, skills and awareness. The terms are well established and used by Tronstad (2005) in the context of climbing and applied by Horgen (2009) to the teaching of canoe paddling.

it with someone. Some integrate feelings such as physical exertion and sense of achievement, while others tend to think of it as quietly observing nature around them. It is interesting to note that Børge Ousland makes a distinction between nature experience and the sense of one's own skills and abilities, when writing about his polar expeditions in the magazine Friluftsliv nr. 6 - 2008 (Valle, 2008). On the other hand, Marit Holm in Friluftsliv nr 5 - 2009 includes physical exertion as a large part of her nature experience (Valle, 2009).

Aside from the value of a good social environment, the modern activity-based values decrease during the year at folk high school, and this is matched by an increase in the traditional values. This is peculiar, given that the course offerings seem not to focus on con-veying nature experience, but rather action and self realization. However, the end result is the opposite. During the year, the students concern themselves more with nature, and less with self realization, action and risk. What is the explanation?

Could it be the case that teachers and folk high schools actually prefer the traditional and classical friluftsliv? Most of the teachers had their introduction to friluftsliv in the 60s, 70s or 80s, and were educated in the 70s, 80s and 90s. At that time, most socialization to friluftsliv took place at home and college education in friluftsliv was oriented towards traditional and classical activities and values. Odden supports the idea that these values and preferences are sustained today. He argues that a person who grew up in a community where friluftsliv was a common activity acquires a lifelong relationship to the activities (Odden, 2008).

Could it be the case that courses being offered at folk high school don't express their values accurately? Do schools possibly advertise their friluftsliv activities with action and self realization, but actually teach nature experience because that is where their preferences lie? Or are they making a conscious choice of the values being promoted? Perhaps the folk high school wishes to teach the value of nature experience. They then might market their courses in the way they think will attract the most students, adapting the course content as well to recruit students? I believe that many teachers and schools hold values of the traditional and classical friluftsliv, but are intentionally making use of modern friluftsliv in their recruitment and teaching.

LARGEST CHANGE IN THE SPECIALIZATIONS

To better understand the nuances of how student values develop through the year, the answers were broken down into three groups according to which course category the respondent belonged to:

Table 3: Students' motivation for friluftsliv during the school year 2007/2008, by course category (percent responding "Very important"). [1]

Value	Classical friluftsliv			Activity-oriented specialization – general			Activity-oriented specialization - focused		
	Autumn n; 149	Spring n; 102	Change	Autumn n; 372	Spring n; 240	Change	Autumn n; 142	Spring n; 119	Change
Social environment	93	89	-4	91	88	-3	87	81	-6
Personal development	77	71	-6	81	72	-9	86	81	-5
Improve one's skills	67	65	-2	72	66	-6	90	81	-9
Speed and action (excitement)	60	58	-2	78	71	-7	80	77	-3

[1] The traditional friluftsliv category is not included in the table, since there were only 35 responses in autumn and 12 in spring, too few to analyze.

116

Nature experi-ence	76	83	+7	68	68	None	63	65	+2
Risk	25	17	-8	41	34	-7	45	35	-10
The tranquil-lity of nature	44	49	+4	39	35	-4	27	33	+6
Hunting and harvesting	9	9	None	8	7	-1	5	9	+4

Sources: Authors own, 2010

The clearest difference between autumn and spring is the decrease in the value of *risk* in all course categories. The change is largest within the activity-oriented specializations that focus on one or two activities. The self realization value *improving one's skills* also decreases. Counter to this, *nature experience* and *the tranquillity of nature* increase.

Almost 19% of the courses are specializations focusing on one or two activities. These are popular courses with full classes. The number of students is often higher for these classes than other friluftsliv courses. The proportion of folk high school students in these highly focused courses is probably above 20%. This group of students is the most highly specialized. Students have chosen to use a year of their life to concentrate on one or two activities. These students have likely thought through which course to attend quite thoroughly, and they are very motivated to acquire knowledge, experience and attitudes pertaining to their activity of choice.

According to Bjørn Michaelsen (pers.comm., Michaelsen, 2009), who teaches the course "Mountaineering – Off piste" at Øytun folk high school, and Arne Myksvoll (pers. comm, Myksvoll, 2009), who teaches the course "Friluftsliv" at Hallingdal folk high school, these students are both willing to take risks and eager to improve their own skills. Many of them are young skiers and snowboarders who regularly take high risks in the mountains because they lack knowledge and skills when it comes to assessing avalanche conditions and safety. These youth, who would otherwise be unlikely folk high school candidates, are targeted when folk high schools market courses with an off-piste focus. Through the year, students devote themselves to skiing or snowboarding and gain the knowledge, skills and attitudes necessary to evaluate risk and consequence. Torkjel Solem (pers. comm. Solem, 2009), principal of Torshus folk high school, believes that the principles of ecology, conservation and safe back country travel are still present in folk high school teaching. However, this material is not visible in the schools' outward representation. We can presume that the instruction the students received during their year at folk high school was at least in part responsible for the observed reduction in risk motivation, the decreased importance of improving skills and the increased importance of nature experience.

Among the *specializations* with a more general approach, the clearest trend is a decrease in values related to self realization, *speed and action* and *risk. Nature experience* does not increase as it did for specializations with a focus. The regression of the first set of values could likely be explained by the true values of the schools and teachers and the course instruction through the year. But for this group of students, representing almost half of the responses, *nature experience* has not become more highly prioritized.

Among the students of *classical friluftsliv* the value *nature experience* is becoming more widespread. Concurrently, less weight is placed on personal development. This could likely be explained by the same mechanisms at work for the students of specialization courses; that the teachers' own preferences tend toward traditional friluftsliv, where nature experience is the core value.

Overall, the collected material shows a decrease in the self realization values and a corresponding increase in the nature experience value. But the change is strongest for specializations focusing on one or two activities. Nature experience is still not the most important motivation among students, but is considerably strengthened through the school year. It is within the specializations that we find the highest importance placed on self realization, speed and action, and risk at the start of the school year. And it is for this group of students the instruction/teaching of the folk high schools seems to have the greatest impact on values.

CONCLUSION

Young people's participation in traditional friluftsliv activities such as skiing trips and hiking trips has been declining since 1970 and this trend is expected to continue (Odden, 2008, p.96). It is through friluftsliv as a family activity in childhood and youth that the traditional values nature experience, tranquillity, and the joy of being tired from a physical activity is shared and becomes a lasting part of that individual's identity. A high age at first introduction to friluftsliv could potentially mean that the self realization values are the first values youth associate with friluftsliv.

Folk high school thus has been given a new mandate, a task that used to be the domain of parents and family. Previously, folk high schools were concerned with sustaining and developing the values youth already associated with nature experience. Today, to a much greater degree, they have to introduce their students to the value of nature experience. Many folk high schools appear to have chosen course form and content that appeals to young and modern students. At the same time, the value-changing process that occurs during the school year shows that they have taken the new mandate seriously.

I am glad to say that folk high schools still teach about nature experience and awaken traditional values in their students, despite the superficial impression that the entire year is centred on speed, action, developing one's skills and self realization. It is also a pleasant discovery that students in the highly specialized and action-oriented courses are the ones who develop their appreciation of nature experience the most.

REFERENCES

Akerlie, O. (2001). *Frilynt folkehøyskole 1864-2001.* Norsk folkehøgskolelag.

Arne, E. (1964). *Norsk folkehøyskole i 100 år.* Oslo: Noregs Boklag.

Bischoff, A. & Odden, A. (1999). *Ungdom og friluftsliv – endring i lys av modernitetsprosesser.* Meeting notes from the conference Naturforvaltning og samfunnsforskning II in Oslo 12th-13th October 1999. *DN- notat 1996-6.* Trondheim: Directorate for Nature Management.

Breivik, G. (1978). To tradisjoner i norsk friluftsliv. G. Breivik & H. Løvmo (eds.). *Friluftsliv fra Fridtjof Nansen til våre dager.* Oslo: Universitetsforlaget.

Breivik, G. (1998). *Jakten på spenning,* Skrifter i utvalg, bind 10. Oslo: Norwegian School of Sport Sciences, Institutt for samfunnsfag.

Breivik, G. (2001). Risikoatferd og jakten på spenning. S.D. Thelle (ed.). *På den usikre siden. Risiko som fore-stilling, atferd og rettesnor.* Oslo: Cappelens forlag a.s.

Folkehøgskolekontoret (1998). *Folkehøgskolen i Norge, FIN-katalogen blant vener.* Informasjonskontoret for folkehøgskolen, Informasjonskontoret for kristen folkehøgskole.

Folkehøyskolerådet, 1988, 2001, 2004 and 2007.

Faarlund, N. (1986). Askeladden. *Om gripe fjellet- og ble grepet av fjellet,* Hemsedal: Nordisk forum for vegledning i Natur og Friluftsliv.

Faarlund, N. (2009). Levendegjør Norsk friluftstradisjon! *Ute 3.*

Frenning, I. (2004). *Friluftsliv in one Norwegian Primary school – a sign of success.* Tromsø: University.

Goksøyr, M. (1994). Nasjonal identitetsbygging rundt 1900 gjennom friluftsliv og idrett. *Nytt Norsk Tidsskrift 2.*

Horgen, A. (2009). *Kano på vann og vassdrag. Kanopadling og friluftslivsveiledning.* Kristiansand: Høyskole-forlaget.

Informasjonskontoret for folkehøyskolen (IF) and Informasjonskontoret for Kristen folkehøyskole (IKF), 1988, 2001, 2004 and 2007. *Katalog for folkehøyskolene 1988-1999, 2001-2002, 2004-2005 and 2007-2008.*

Kleven, J. (1993). *Aktivitetsmønstre i norsk ferie og fritid.* NINA research report 33. Trondheim: Norwegian Institute for Nature Research.

Mikkelsen, A. (2002). *Gruntvig for begynnere... og oss andre.* Norsk folkehøgskolelag and Informasjonskon-toret for folkehøyskolen.

Nedrelid, T. (1993). Friluftslivets år 1993 – nødvendig vedlikehold av et identitetsskapende kulturtrekk? *Dugnad, 4.*

Netland, O. A. (2011). *Statistics of students at Norwegian Folk High School.* Folkehøyskolerådet for folkehøy-skolen, Oslo

Odden, A. & Aas, Ø. (2002). *Motiver for friluftslivsutøvelse. Teori, metoder og resultater fra norske under-søkelser i perioden 1974-2001.* Rapport fra konferansen Forskning i friluft, Øyer 19.-20. November. Oslo: Friluftslivets fellesorganisasjon.

Odden, A. (2008). *Hva skjer med norsk friluftsliv? En studie av utviklingstrekk i norsk friluftsliv 1970-2004.* Trondheim: University.

Pedersen, K. (1999). *Det har bare vært naturlig friluftsliv, kjønn og kulturelle brytninger.* Oslo: NIH.

Skirbekk, G. (1981). *Filosofihistorie 2. utg.* Oslo: Universitetsforlaget.

Skogen, K. (2001). Friluftsliv som seismograf for sosial endring: Jegere og snowboardere i det senmoderne. K. Heggen, J.O. Myklebust & T. Øia, *Ungdom. I spenninga mellom det lokale og det globale,* 56-67. Oslo: Det Norske Samlaget.

Skår, M., Odden, A. & Vistad, O.I. (2008). Motivation for mountain biking in Norway: Change and stability in late-modern outdoor recreation. *Norsk geografisk tidsskrift, 62,* 36-45.

Tordson, B. (2003). *Å svare på naturens åpne tiltale. En undersøkelse av meningsdimensjoner i norsk friluftsliv på 1900 tallet og en drøftelse av friluftsliv som sosiokulturelt fenomen.* Oslo: NIH.

Torjusson, A. (1997). *Den norske folkehøgskulen.* Oslo: Det Norske Samlaget.

Tronstad, S. (2005). *Innføring i klatring.* Oslo: Akilles.

Valle, R. (2008). Friluftsprofilen Børge Ousland I Nansens forspor. *Friluftsliv, 6.*

Valle, R. (2009). Friluftsprofilen Marit Holm. *Friluftsliv, 5.*

Aasetre, J., Kleiven, J. & Kaltenborn, B.P. (1994). *Friluftsliv i Norge: Motivasjon og adferd.* NINA Oppdrags-melding; no. 309. Trondheim: Norwegian Institute of Nature Research

Oral sources:
Michaelsen, B. (2009). Teacher ("Mountaineering – Off piste") at Øytun folk high school

Myksvoll, A. (2010). Teacher ("Friluftsliv") at Hallingdal folk high school

Solem, T. (2009). Principal of Torshus folk high school

SUMMARY

Folk high school programmes in *friluftsliv* in Norway are largely oriented toward high-speed modern and specialized activities. At the start of the school year, students value social activities, personal development, achievement, action and excitement most highly. Never-theless, during the year they develop values related to of nature experience and the more modern values regress. Teaching of *friluftsliv* in folk high schools is based more on nature experience than on achievement and risk, but this is hardly evident in the course descriptions.

STRESZCZENIE

Programy nauczania kierunku *friluftsliv* w Otwartych szkołach wyższych (Folk Universities) w Norwegii głównie zorientowane są na współczesne wysoko-szybkościowe oraz wyspecjalizowane czynności. Na początku roku szkolnego studenci bardzo wysoko oceniają społeczne formy aktywności, rozwój osobisty, osiągnięcia, czynności oraz ogólne zainteresowanie. Jednak, w toku roku akademickiego rozwijają oni wartości, wynikające z doświadczeń związanych z naturą, więc występuje regres w dziedzinie wartości współczesnych. Nauczanie *friluftsliv* w Otwartych szkołach bazuje w większym stopniu na doświadczeniach związanych z natura, niż na osiągnięciach i ryzyku, ale nie wynika to z opisów kursu.

SAMMENDRAG

Folkehøyskolens tilbud i friluftsliv i Norge er i stor grad rettet mot moderne fartsfylte og spesialiserte aktiviteter. De viktigste verdiene for elevene ved skolestart er sosialt samvær, personlig utvikling, prestasjoner og fart og spenning. Likevel utvikler elevene naturopplevelsesverdier igjennom året, og de moderne verdiene går tilbake. Formidlingen av friluftsliv i folkehøgskolens er i stor grad basert på naturopplevelse og i mindre grad prestasjoner og risiko, men dette uttrykkes nesten ikke i skolenes fagbeskrivelser.

PROF. IRYNA SURINA, PHD, D.SC.

Pomeranian University
Department of Sociology
Westerplatte 64
Slupsk 76-200, Poland
E-mail: isurina@wp.eu

THE RESULTS OF THE CREATIVE YOUTH'S
SOCIALIZATION PROCESS

In the context of modern society's transformation, the problem of youth's personality development is one to which special attention is devoted. Particularly if it comes to the youth dealing with creative (cultural) activity on a professional level (hereinafter referred to as: creative youth).

The mutual relations of society and personality do not limit themselves to the society's influence upon personality. Another aspect is of substantial importance: that of personality's influence upon society. When considering this assumption as the foundation, personality is simultaneously an object and a subject of social relations.

Numerous researchers are of the opinion that the socialization is a process of individual's integration with society – over the course of creating various types of social communities (groups, social institutions and organisations etc.) through the internalisation of fragments of culture, social norms and values on the basis of which socially meaningful personality traits are formed.

In the process of socialization two stages might be differentiated: social adaptation and interiorisation. Social adaptation signifies the individual's becoming conformed to socio-economic conditions, accepting functions and roles, social norms as well as respecting ecological norms (the life environment). Interiorisation is a process of absorbing social norms and values into man's internal world, the process consisting in the transformation of external activities into internal mental ones.

In the process of socializing what is being subjected to forming and transforming is this social structure of personality. The social structure of personality is understood as the whole of objective and subjective individual traits, created and appearing in the process of man's diverse activity, under the influence of social groups into which one is accepted as well as that of social processes.

In the social structure of personality the following elements can be differentiated (Осипова, 1996; Андреева, 1994):

1) The manner in which traits (qualities) are realised in social activities, manifesting itself in the life-style and such types of activities as the working, socio-political, culture-cognitive, family-existential ones etc.

2) Objective social needs of personality. At the foundation of personality's structure lie social needs. In other words: personality's structure is determined by objective regularities which define man's development as a social entity. Personality itself may or may not be aware of the existence of those needs, but they do exist independently from this awareness and do not cease to exist and influence the ways (styles) of behaviour.

3) Innate abilities for creative activity, knowledge, habits. It is precisely those creative abilities that set apart an individual undergoing the process of personality forming from the fully-shaped personality. In a word, creativity is a fundamental characteristic trait of a human being as a personality.

4) The degree of immersion into society's cultural values, i.e. personality's spiritual world. Alexei N. Leont'ev wrote that the fundamental question concerning the process of forming (establishing) of personality – is the transformation of motives (tendencies) into the steady whole, something which characterizes personality. The author classified three factors pertaining to the question of personality forming: "...the extensiveness of the man-world relations, their hierarchy and general structure" (Леонтьев, 1975, p.127).

5) Moral norms and rules by which personality is guided. What is essential in this approach is the conviction that the most basic rules establish the main line (style) of human actions. The conviction related to the realization on the part of personality of its objective (existing regardless of awareness) needs which form the centre of personality's structure.

Let us consider the fact that all the above-mentioned structural elements apply – to an extent – virtually to all personality types. Each personality – in its own way – participates in society's life, possesses knowledge, guiding lines.

Personality's social structure is in a state of permanent transformation in accordance with the changing social environment. Personality receives new information, new knowledge which is transformed into convictions. The convictions, in turn, define the character of man's actions. Hence the process of socialization might be interpreted as a process of personality's social structure's transformation in accordance with society's expectations.

Undoubtedly, the elements of personality's structure influence social roles that are being realised. Fulfilling social roles is meaningful in personality's life, in its ability to function effectively within society's constraints. According to Erich Fromm, "man not only sells products, but he sells himself as well and perceives himself as a product (...) And as with all the products it is the market that determines the value of these or those traits and even determines their very existence. If the traits a human being is offering do not result from the demand, he is devoid of any traits whatsoever..." (Фромм, 1995, pp.106-107). This is precisely why the activity needs to be perceived from the social standpoint, apparent in human's endeavour to realise himself as personality in accordance with the social status and role.

An important factor in the process of socialization is the choice and processing of information in the information-related dimension of personality; those depend on the chosen strategy. If, for instance, one chooses a defensive, survival-cantered strategy, then the solution of all the essential problems and corresponding answers may be accompanied by the so-called boomerang (rebound) effect in the functioning of socialization's institution. Thus, the choice of a strategy and accepting solutions is fully dependant on the socio-cultural environment of the institution.

Personality's socialization manifests itself in the roles showed through a given personality's actions. As noted in the field literature, actions determined by the roles in essence consist in unconscious role-fulfilment, but in certain cases such actions are fully conscious. Consequently, through such behaviour a given person still learns and creates a desired image of "I" (Осипова & Москвичева, 1996).

Ervin Goffman, an American researcher, devised a concept of playing a dramatic role consisting in putting a conscious effort into this role-playing in such a way as to elicit a desirable impression from others. The actions are regulated through negotiating not only the required expectations of the played roles, but also the expectations of a given social environment. According to this concept, each of us is an actor in front of an audience (Гоффман, 2004).

The role-learning has at least two aspects:
1) One needs to learn to fulfill duties and realize the rules in accordance with the role played;
2) One also needs to obtain (acquire) orientations, feelings and expectations suitable for the given role. The second aspect is thought to be of a greater importance.

Certain people are unable to successfully fulfil their role if in the process of socialization it has not been accepted by them as one of value, satisfying a certain need, matching their internal world. The process of learning the majority of essential roles typically starts at an early stage of childhood together with the emergence of abilities related to defining the roles and statuses. Considerable part of this stage of learning is undergone unconsciously and without many difficulties.

While discussing the youth's personality forming one needs to keep in mind that a given stage is preceded by the problem of psychological maturity of personality. Lidia Bozhovich suggests that psychologically mature personality is possessed by a man who has achieved a specific, quite high level of mental development. The basic trait of this development is the emergence in the man of abilities to behave independently from the direct influence of circumstances around him instead being guided by his own, consciously set goals (Божович, 1992, pp.192-193).

The emergence of such ability is conditioned by an active character of man's actions. This very context influences the fact that personality is superior to the circumstances. Generally speaking, socialization places an emphasis over the fact in what scope the social, cultural or economic processes and structures shape man's personality.

Personality shaping is the main goal of socialization. Jan Szczepanski defines social-lization as "this part of whole environment's influence which introduces the individual to participation in social life, teaches him to act in accordance with accepted rules, to understand the culture and makes him competent to earn a living and fulfil specific social roles" (Miller, 1981, p.21).

One could therefore conclude that socialization is understood as a process of making an individual a part of the human community and its life and it demonstrates the manner in which one should participate in social life in a commonly accepted way.

Galina M. Andreeva states that socialization presents a mutual process which includes: an individual's adaptation of social experience by the way of inclusion into a given social environment, a system of social relations; a process of active shaping on the part of an individual of the system of social relations at the price of the individual's inclusion into the social environment (Андреева, 1994). Man does not accept social experience in a direct way, but also transforms it into his own values, aspirations and orientations.

As Zbigniew Skorny points out: "an influence of socialization upon an individual may be positive or negative depending on the content of norms, role models, codes of behaviour and hierarchy of values accepted by a given group" (Skorny, 1976, p.11).

The youth professionally dealing with creative/cultural activities is characterised by certain peculiarities which make them stand apart from the rest of the youth. This is why this group is sometimes referred to as "different" from the remaining youth; the term "abnormality" is tended to be used. This type of abnormality, however, finds a perfect ground in reality. Among characteristic traits of such abnormality one can find a specific vision and style of life.

This type of abnormality is conditioned by the mode of life of the creative youth in a modern society. Abnormality is a certain limit of acceptable behaviour in typical situations which constitutes a norm for a given social group of creative youth. From the viewpoint of participants of other groups of youth, this norm appears to be abnormal since it does not conform to established patterns, concepts and stereotypes of behaviour in such a situation.

In this context the author wishes to make a reference to the words of Viktor Frankl, who claims that "the more specific the man is, the less he conforms to the norm – both in the sense of the average norm and the ideal one. People pay for their individuality with the departure from the normality and – what happens – from the ideal. The importance of this individuality, however, sense and value of human personality are always related to the community in which it exists (Франкл, 1990).

An age-temporal index has a significant influence upon the development of creative youth. Swetlana N. Ikonnikova believes that "the comprehension of time's importance is connected with the growth of self-consciousness of personality happens when a man perceives time as a development perspective and unfolding his potential, when he reclaims the feeling of time's value, when a psychological feeling of its "flow" is born, the irreversible loss of time passed, the pressure of the ever-increasing rhythm of life" (Иконникова, 1974, pp.13-14).

The factors influencing the development of creative personality include socio-cultural orientations which are dependent on personality consciousness, its social experience and a system of values. As psychologists and philosophers point out, socio-cultural orientations are shaped from two sides – through the influence of absorbed in the process of socialization knowledge, norms, values meaningful for the society and compiling its common, generalised and rational experience; and through the individual's participation in social life, adaptation in it of specific forms and ways of life activity. If those both sides are not contradictory, a specific uniformity is created of forming socio-cultural orientations; conversely, a conflict between personality and society may result.

The shaping of socio-cultural orientations "...corresponds to the social needs of personality in the self-development and self-expression, in particular of social, historically specified forms of life activity characteristic for the mode of living of society and social groups to which an individual belongs and identifies itself through" (Сурина, 1999, p.72). Consequently, one can define a considerable role of socio-cultural orientations in the social regulating and directing of creative youth's actions.

It should be noted that youth's orientations towards social values are the combining component of socio-cultural orientations and are created under the influence of territorial, ethnic, cultural, geopolitical and socio-economic factors.

We shall perceive socio-cultural orientations as youth's orientations towards various elements of society's culture. In addition, they manifest themselves in youth's social behaviour, and so we may analyse them as youth's dispositions which greatly influence the process of socialization. Socialization contributes to the constant personality growth. It is a complex and dynamic process accompanied most often by age-related crises. This is why the direction of socialization may be both along an ascending or descending line.

Primarily the process of personality-shaping of a young person, aspiring to deal with culture on a professional basis is connected with groups of reference, values and norms which it represents. And as long as this group (or one similar to it according to axionormative system) does not become real, this young person will undertake behavioural imitation, i.e. he or she will consciously copy the behavioural model appropriate for it - although Neil Smelser believes that imitation and identification are positive mechanisms since they enhance the development of specific behavioural pattern.

In the process of socialization many modes of communication exist. Two different ways of communication are classified generally: external and internal. The external communication is a contact with people unfamiliar to us. Internal communications consist of statements and questions, in general, within a family circle (Смелзер, 1994, p.119). Communication contributes to the development of self-consciousness, abilities and self-realisation of a young person.

"Failure" or "success" of socialization may depend on the methods applied for its realisation. Sociologists have proved that the methods used in the process of socialization influence the readiness of people to absorb the commonly accepted values. Society is unable to survive if its values and norms are not accepted by the new members. Socialization, however, can never be 100 percent effective. The commonness of socialization's failure within the whole generation may be the foundation for social changes in the life of the future generations (ibidem, pp.125-126).

As the criteria of personality's socialization Antanina I. Kovaleva classified the following:
1) Holding formed dispositions, stereotypes, values, "perceptions of the world" of the man;
2) Personality's adaptation, its normotypical behaviour;

124

3) Social identity. The main criterion of socialization, however, is not the degree to which an individual conforms to the circumstances, but the degree of its autonomy, self-confidence, inventiveness, lack of inferiority complexes (Ковалева, 1996, p.111).

While discussing the personality development of a young theatre and cinema actor one may conclude that acting as a form of professional venture influences the process of personality's socialization in an ambiguous way. M. Andreeva believes that while acting an actor develops a double personality, simultaneously remaining the same person and becoming 'the other' (Андреева, 2002, p.30). There appear simultaneously identical and non-identical image of "I", implementing two different souls out of which one emerges in the foreground while the other – "temporarily goes into hiding, but never quite vanishes without trace since its the proper soul of the actor" (ibidem, p.30).

This is exactly where the essence of the process of creative youth's socialization becomes fully apparent, especially in the case of acting. It is impossible to separate oneself from bipolarity, since otherwise an actor stops being one. This circumstance further complicates the socialization process. In this particular case within the structure of personality different types of identification cross each other – the identification with oneself as a person and the identification with one's acting role. Not uncommonly, this process results in the change of the influence of various socialization factors on a young actor's personality development.

Identity is a subjective indicator of personality's socialization. As A. Kovaleva suggests, a successful socialization is conditioned by a successful identification. Social identity develops in a normal way if within a man social environment's demands are practically realized. The negative side of identification prevails if an individual strives to be what he or she should not (Ковалева, 1996, p.111).

The identity's shaping is a dynamic process of self-perception plays. Sudden realization of the existing identity's inadequateness leads to confusion and the necessity of the search for another identity. The breakthrough which takes place in self-realization is a crisis of identity; however, this crisis acts as a shock stage in the personality development.

Particularly in the case of the creative youth a characteristic trait is to realise their individuality, and the introduction to common human values happens through the expression of their originality. This group is characterised to a greater exchange by "closing" within a professional community than by "departure" from this level of identity. This kind of closing, however, is not synonymous with individual's arrested development, any kind of limits to possibilities of one's individuality's expression. For the remaining youth rebound tendencies are characteristic – closing within mid-level communities, which respectively leads to individual's arrested development, limiting of the possibilities to express individuality. Communities of the mid-level are not homogenous. The core of the professional creative communities is the fact that socio-cultural foundation is prevalent in which essential diversity of social relations is reflected. Closing within the discussed communities and the introduction to them is conditioned by the fact that a young person is a voluntary subject in this community, he or she develops themselves and the community as well.

Vladimir A. Jadov shows that social identification is conditioned by the deep personality need for acceptance by the others, for the group defence as well as the need for self-realization, expectation of a positive response from "the inner circle" – groups of reference and communities. Identification with groups, communities is the result of inter-personal, inter-group co-operation. Identifying oneself with specific groups and communities, one puts to a test a need to explain the causes and conclusions of his or her group solidarity.

Presenting the theatre as an institution of identification we shall establish that the identification process in it transpires through the mastering of role. In accordance with the concept of Konstantin S. Stanislavski, an actor should inhabit the played character to an extreme extent, be able to see it in a profound and complete way. The main aspect in a drama is the action in progress. It is this action that has a peculiar pedigree: it does not limit itself to external events transpiring on the scene. "...Coming to the agreement some time in the future and once for all understanding by the word 'action' not actor's play, is not an actor's performance, not external, but internal, not physical, but spiritual action... (…). Creativity is effective and active above all in a spiritual sense (…). Only this kind of creativity, consisting of the internal action, scenic. This is why we shall establish that in the theatre only the efficient, spiritually active is scenic" (Станиславский, 1989, p.99.)

According to K. Stanislavski, an actor's work over a role should undergo three phases: one of learning, one of experiencing, and one of embodiment.

In the phase of learning an actor is to meticulously get to know everything about the character to be played obtaining the common memory and sensations. The phase of experiencing (the main one) – here an actor constructs the image of the character upon the foundations of his or her emotions. Those very emotions create the internal and external world of an actor. However, in order to make the stage wishes come alive, one must make them creative wishes and actions of the actor himself, related to his 'organic environment'. "In a word, one can only live his or her own, living, original emotions" (ibidem, p.101). The phase of embodiment solidifies the internal readiness of an actor to live the spiritual world of a character connected with the technique of external expressiveness, but an actor himself is not lost or destroyed in the character's image since he does not forget about himself.

In practice, the three completed phases of role mastering constitute the mechanism of socialization in theatre. Those phases reflect other characteristics of socialization since an actor should not only learn, experience and embody "the other" entity – axionormative system of character's personality, but refer the said entity to one's own. Successful and positive correlation of this kind is transmitted to successful socialization or is favourable to it. In other cases it leads to disturbed socialization, elsewhere called the diverting socialization. This may lead to a situation where an actor inhabits character's image to such an extent that the image itself will become the core of his personality. And this is where a correction of actor's axionormative system takes place, which will be fully responsible for the influence on his personality development. One of the common symptoms of this kind of diversions is the rushed socialization. It is related to a premature acquisition by the youth of social roles and a forced identity.

Among negative moments of theatrical socialization one can put, in the words of I. Andreeva, a direct relation between staginess and suicidal moods, sadomasochism and other types of diverting behaviour (Андреева, 2002, p.180). It is for this category of people that the theatre becomes an organic form and sometimes provokes and encourages such phenomena as cruelty, submissive humility or suicides. In such cases we may refer to the disturbed or diverting socialization.

Consequently, two sides of the theatrical socialization – positive and negative – are not barred from each other. In reality, they commonly transgress into the other's territory, subtly becoming one and it is not always possible to tell them apart. However, in each particular case we are able to find this measure, this border after all together with the norms that define staginess in the real life world.

Diversions in socialization, shown as the result of mastering the role by an actor, may be treated through the correction of the socialization process. The correction's content is established on the basis of what is not done or is done in a diverted way in the socialization norm, of what the extent of diversion is and in what this diversion manifests – or may manifest – itself. The correction is put into practice in the managing of the theatrical socialization of creative youth.

Let us now consider the theatre as the institution of socialization. Theatre possesses its own system of values and norms. Through the theatre a free "inscrutable (or abnormative)" behaviour is imitated. In essence, the theatre is a specific part of society's cultural life and, simultaneously, one of many levels of human reality. One might talk about correlation of the real life and the theatre (although theatre *is* a part of real life), when the theatre transgresses from the stage into the real life, or when life bursts onto the stage. Thus, staginess is a characteristic trait of embodying scenic roles in the real life. This whole phenomenon happens through "the socialization prism".

Staginess in life is defined as "constructing one's life according to theatre-cantered models, active presence in the commonness of performance and artistic order, pageantry. It is also the transgression into the everyday world of specific theatre terminology, the functioning of the theatrical thesaurus in the everyday speech" (ibidem, p.55). Through this process, the socialization prism of acting for young people transforms into the norm of life's staginess. The degree of this staginess, however, consists in the correlation in young actor's life of the theatrical sphere and the real life, although for them the staginess is the normal, and the lack of it – abnormal state.

Drawing upon the above assumption, we might say that the shaping of the young actor's personality takes place through the acquisition of staginess of life. Staginess, in turn, combines within itself social and personal affairs of the youth professionally invested in acting. The degree of staginess peculiar to a young actor reflects his or her degree of self-expression and personality development.

The society is interested in the cooperation of social and personal affairs. This cooperation, in essence, manifests itself in the degree of actor's professionalism on the one hand, and from the other – in the degree of staginess in real life, which to a large extent suggests an accelerated socialization of young actors.

In conclusion, the preoccupation of the youth with acting is an essential existential need expressed in the drive for perfection and creativity (Афанасьева, 1998, p.276). The foundation of creative youth's socialization is the creativity expressed through the staginess. The real creativity always manifests itself in the physical and mental energy, diverse abilities, the consciousness, will, complex mental, emotional feelings of man, i.e. in the young man's personality development. Therefore, the effects of the socialization process are the acquired, defined personality traits, a specific style and quality of life.

REFERENCES

Miller, R. (1981). *Socjalizacja, wychowanie, psychoterapia.* Warszawa: Państwowe Wydawnictwo Naukowe.

Skorny, Z. (1976). *Proces socjalizacji dzieci i młodzieży.* Warszawa: Wydawnictwo Szkolne i Pedagogiczne.

Андреева, И. М. (2002). *Театральность в культуре.* Ростов-на-Дону: Южно-Российск. гос.ун-т.

Андреева, Г. М. (1994). *Социальная психология.* Москва: Изд-во МГУ.

Афанасьева, О. В. (1998). *Творчество как саморазвитие личности.* Москва: Луч.

Божович, Л. И. (1992). Этапы формирования личности в онтогенезе. *Возрастная и педагогическая психология.* Москва: Изд-во МГУ, 1992, с.192-193.

Гофман, Э. (2004). *Анализ фреймов. Эссе об организации повседневного опыта.* Москва: Ин-т социологии РАН.

Иконникова, С. Н. (1974). *Молодежь: социологический и социально-психологический анализ.* Ленинград: ЛГУ.

Ковалева, А. И. (1996). *Социализация личности: норма и отклонение.* Москва: ИМ.

Леонтьев, А. Н. (1975). *Деятельность. Сознание. Личность.* Москва: Политиздат.

Смелзер, Н. (1994). *Социология.* Москва: Феникс.

Осипова, Г. В. (ред.) (1996). *Социология.* Москва: Аспект-Пресс.

Станиславский, К. С. (1989). Работа актера над ролью. *Собр.соч. в 9-ти томах, т.4.* Москва: Искусство.

Сурина, И. А. (1999). *Ценности. Ценностные ориентации. Ценностное пространство.* Москва: Социум.

Франкл, В. (1990). *Человек в поисках смысла.* Москва: Прогресс.

Фромм, Э. (1995). *Бегство от свободы.* Москва: Прогресс.

SUMMARY

In this article the author attempted to present the nature of the process of socialization, as well as to show characteristic traits of the creative youth's socialization. In addition, the author described the stages of the role mastering as the mechanism of socialization in theatre with the results of young actors' socialization.

STRESZCZENIE

W niniejszym artykule ukazano istotę procesu socjalizacji, przedstawiono cechy charakterystyczne procesu socjalizacji twórczej młodzieży, opisano stadia opanowania roli jako mechanizm socjalizacji w teatrze, a także efekty socjalizacji młodych aktorów.

SAMMENDRAG

I denne artikkelen forsøker forfatteren å presentere sosialiseringsprosessens vesen, og samtidig vise karakteristiske trekk ved kreativ ungdoms sosialisering. I tillegg beskriver forfatteren stadier i rollemestring som en mekanisme av sosialisering i teater der effekten er unge skuespilleres sosialisering.

DR. PIOTR PRÓCHNIAK, PHD

Pomeranian University
Department of Psychology
Westerplatte 64
Slupsk 76-200, Poland
E-mail: piotrprochniak@wp.pl

MOTIVES OF POLICEMEN PREPARING FOR THE PEACEKEEPING MISSION IN KOSOVO

INTRODUCTION

UN resolution 1244 from June, 10th 1999 authorized a Peacekeeping Mission in Kosovo, as a result of the wars in the Balkans in the final decade of 20th century. Many countres, including Poland, have sent their soldiers and police officers to Kosovo. The base of the Polish policemen is located in Kosovska Mitrovica. Their task is to maintain public order in Kosovo. Kosovo is an area inhabited by many national and ethnic groups: Serbs, Bosnians, Gypsies and Albanian. The tensions arising between these groups make participation in the mission very risky. Police officers must isolate violent individuals within different ethnic groups, escort dangerous criminals out of these groups, disarm bombs remaining after the Balkan conflicts and to eliminate drug routes from Asia to Europe. Participation in the mission is voluntary. The aim of this research was to investigate the motives of the Polish policemen during the peace mission in Kosovo in the Balkans (Próchniak, 2009). There is a lack of systematic research on motives of policemen who are taking part in peace missions. (Policemen rather rarely participated in peace missions.)

The motivation to become a police officer can be an expression of the sensation seeking personality trait (Zuckerman, 1994). This trait has been defined as "seeking varied, novel, complex and intense sensations and experiences and the willingness to take physical, social, legal, and financial risks for the sake of such experience" (Zuckerman, 1994, p.27). Sensation seeking includes such aspects as: thrill and sensation seeking (TAS); experience seeking (ES); disinhibition (DIS); boredom susceptibility (BS) and total sensation seeking (Total).

The above aspects of sensation seeking have shown its associated with the police officer's job. Carlson and Lester (1980) compared police officers working in urban and suburban areas. Police officers from the suburbs had a higher score on the adventure seeking scale (TAS) (which was designed especially for policemen) than the urban police officers. Homant, Kennedy and Howton (1993) found that sensation seeking among policemen correlated significantly with the tendencies to participate in a high-speed vehicular pursuits. Goma-i-Freixanet and Wismeijer (2002) compared Spanish police bodyguards with a control group avoiding risky activities and people practicing risky sports. The results showed that police bodyguards scored higher on the TAS scale and lower on the BS scale than the control group avoiding risky activities. They also had lower scores on the ES, BS and the Total scale in comparison to the people practicing high risk sports. Levin and Brown (1975) compared a group of policemen and prisoners. It was found that prisoners got higher results only on the BS scale, while there were no differences among the participants on other scales.

Studies on motives of policemen not only involved sensation seeking. Most research in this area was conducted on the process of selecting the carrier of a police officer. Earlier studies indicated that Power was the basic motive for choosing this profession. In fact, according to later research, the motives of policemen can be more complex. In a study conducted by Lester (1983) policemen were motivated by the financial expectation and a perspective of stable employment. These resulte were similar to the onessobtained of Hopper (1977). In his study about 70% of police recruits were motivated by financial benefits. These results contrast with the ones obtained by Meagher and Yentes (1986). Their study suggested that new policemen were motivated by a broad range of thrill-seeking activities that would provide new experience and enable them to help others. In conclusion - it is hard to explain policemen's motivation if we take into account only one motive.

The above research was conducted in the United States where there is a strong stereotype of policemen:; a lonely sheriff who takes extreme risks to help others. Contrary to the sheriff stereotype in the USA, in Taiwan helping others and doing an exciting job are not motives characteristic of police officers. Family tradition and agood salary are the predictors of choosing a carrier in the police (Tarng, Hsieh & Deng, 2001).

Research conducting on possible differences between women and men in their motives to join the police provided inconclusive results. Some studies suggested that such differences occurred. In these studies women were more interested in helping others than men, others revealed such differences (Meagher & Yentes, 1986; Ragnella & White, 2004),

There is a lack of research concerning police officers participating in peace missions. The purpose of this article is to study the motives of policemen preparing for the peace mission in the Balkan region of Kosovo. As discussed earlier, findings in this area indicate specific motives of police officers (Hopper, 1977; Tarng, Hsieh & Deng, 2001). According to these studies, a hypothesis was formulated that policemen preparing for the peace mission in the Balkans would score higher on the stimulation motive.

METHOD

Participants. The respondents were a group of policemen who participated in a special training preparing them for the peace mission in Kosovo. The group consists of 86 policemen, male only (M = 32.9; SD = 4.5). The policemen had an average of 9 years of experience. The special course took place at the Police School in Slupsk, Poland. Among the participants were antiterrorists, pyrotechnicians and detectives. Participation in the course was voluntary.

Procedure. The policemen were informed about the goals of the study. After receiving information about the aim and the instructions to the questionnaire, the policemen individually filled in the answers. The study was conducted during the training at the Police School in Slupsk. Participants filled in the questionnaire in groups of 20 to 30 people.

Questionnaire. In the present study oo motive measurement, a questionnaire of own authorship was used. Each policeman first had to answer several questions regarding age, sex, and the years of job experience. The questionnaire included 10 factors that might potentially influence a policeman's decision to participation in a peace mission. These factors are: Maintenance of social order, Financial benefits, Maintenance of peace in the world, Social recognition and prestige, Need for change in one's life, Battle with injustice, Looking for risk, Helping others, Discovering new places, Achieving ambitious goals

The policemen were asked to rate the degree of influence of each factor on a 1 (no influence) to 7 (great influence) point Likert rating scale.

RESULTS

Firstly, means and standard deviations were calculated for each of the 10 motives. The results are presented in the table 1.

Table 1: Motives of policemen preparing to peace mission in Kosovo, mediums and standard deviations

Motives	M	SD
1. Maintenance of social order	4.05	1.56
2. Financial benefits	4.48	1.51
3. Maintaince of peace in the world	4.43	1.49
4. Social recognition and prestige	4.01	1.71
5. Need for change in one's life	4.52	1.59
6. Battle with injustice	4.61	1.51
7. Looking for risk	4.43	1.55
8. Helping others	4.60	1.27
9. Discovering new places	4.72	1.30
10. Achieving ambitious goals	4.33	1.46

The most important motive for policemen participating in a peace mission was *discovering new places* (M = 4.72; SD = 1.30). *Battle with injustice* was also important (M = 4.61; SD = 1.51). On the other hand *social recognition and prestige* was a rather weak motive for participation in a peace mission.

A statistical correlation between the policemen's motives was conducted in order to find possible intercorrelations. The results are presented in Table 2.

Table 2: Correlation matrix of motives of policemen preparing for the peace mission in Kosovo, r Pearson

Number of motive	1	2	3	4	5	6	7	8	9	10
1	1	.10	.43	.12	.09	.54*	.22*	.30*	.01	.08
2	.10	1	.20	.19	.44*	.13	.39*	.26*	.36*	.43*
3	.43*	.20	1	.21	.31*	.60*	.37*	.42*	.27	.26*
4	.12	.19	.21	1	.27*	.18	.32*	.23	.15	.35*
5	.09	.44*	.31*	.27*	1	.31*	.55*	.20	.26*	.23*
6	.54*	.13	.60*	.18	.31*	1	.45*	.34*	.24*	.19
7	.22	.39*	.37*	.32*	.55*	.45*	1	.12	.26*	.39*
8	.30*	.26*	.42*	.23*	.20	.34*	.12	1	.28*	.31*
9	.01	.36*	.27*	.15	.26*	.24*	.26*	.28*	1	.44*
10	.08	.43*	.26*	.35*	.23*	.19	.39*	.31*	.44*	1

*p<,05

Most motives of policemen intercorrelate. Correlation between motives suggests the existence of a deeper, unexplained structure of motives of policemen participating in peace missions. The next step was to conduct a factor analysis to discover the basic and main motives of Polish policemen. The factor analysis results are presented in Table 3.

Table 3: Motives of policemen preparing for the peace mission in Kosovo, factor analysis Varimax

Motives	Factor 1	Factor 2
1. Maintenance of social order	-.07	.80
2. Financial benefits	.74	.02
3. Maintaince of peace in the world	.26	.76
4. Social recognition and prestige	.48	.17
5. Need for change in one's life	.64	.21
6. Battle with injustice	.18	.83
7. Looking for risk	.62	.34
8. Helping others	.31	.50
9. Discovering new places	.63	.08
10. Achieving ambitious goals	.73	.08
Total variance (%)	36.17	15.27

Factor analysis indicated that two main factors explained about 51.5% of variance. First factor explains about 36.17% of variance and includes such motives as financial benefits, need for change of one's life, looking for risk, discovering new places, achieving ambitious goals. This factor grouped the motives concentrated on the Self. The second factor explains 15.27% of variance and includes the following motives: maintenance of social order, maintenance of peace in the world, battle with injustice, helping others. This factor describes motives concentrated on the others.

DISCUSSION

The main goal of the study was to analyze the motives of Polish policemen participating in peace mission in the Balkan region of Kosovo. The policemen individually filled in the Motives for the Peacekeeping Mission Survey questionnaire. The results of this study indicate that policemen attained the highest scores on motives concentrated on the Self. The hypothesis behind this study were supported in this paper. The current findings are consistent with the results of Meagher and Yentes (1986) and Ragnella and White (2004). In the studies by these researchers new police officers were motivated by a broad range of thrill-seeking activities. The policemen preparing for the peacekeeping mission are people who appreciate challenges, prefer unforeseeable situations and adventure. They are interested in a broad range of thrill-seeking activities and difficult tasks in Kosovo. Surprisingly, the financial motive does not dominate among policemen (this motive is significant, but not the most important). It is a curious result because the salary on a peacekeeping mission is higher in comparison to regular police salary.

A higher level of thrill motives also can have negative consequences. In literature of risk taking behavior thrill motives correlate with underestimating risk (Trimpop, 1994). As a consequence, underestimating risk on a mission can lead to daring behavior on the part of the policemen.

Motivation to participate in the risky mission in Kosovo involves not only individualistic motives. The present study reveals prosocial motivation of policemen: helping others and maintenance of social order. These motives are characteristic not only of policemen on a mission but also of many police officers around the world. The results are similar to those which were obtained by Ragnella and White (2004). World peace is an important motive for policemen but it does not have the highest rating. This motive is probably specific only for policemen on peacekeeping missions because in daily police work world peace is of little significance. However, we must remember that altruistic motives are not dominate among policemen participating in the peacekeeping mission in Kosovo. Factor analysis revealed that individualistic motivation explains more of variance. It means that the basic motivation of policemen's participating in a peacekeeping mission is their own needs. The presented results have substantial limitations concerning the explanation of policemen's motives. They were obtained on a relatively small group of policemen, with the highest occupational competences, hence they are not representative of all policemen. The results have practical consequences for the process of recruitment and selection for the mission. Personal motives can be a variable involved in selecting a police officer for a peacekeeping mission. Of course, not only the motives of policemen should be assessed in the selection process for the peacekeeping missions. Earlier research indicated that other features of personality such as low Neuroticism, high Assertiveness or respect for social norms are important in the selection for police work (Eber, 1991).

Future studies on policemen preparing for peacekeeping missions should not concentrate only on the personal motives. Further research could have focus on the personal structure of values of the policemen preparing for missions (e.g. using Schwartz's model). Studies on personal values can broaden the knowledge about policemen who risk their lives for others. Other research on the motives of police officers can be conducted from the Point of view of the Self Determination Theory. Intrinsic and extrinsic motives can play an important role in becoming policemen on a peacekeeping mission. Finally, it would be interesting to study the connections between the motives of police officers and their well being as well as other psychological variables.

REFERENCES

Carlson, L. D. & Lester, D. (1980). Thrill seeking in police officers. *Psychological Reports, 47*, 1102.

Eber, H. W. (1991). *Good cop includes bad cop: A supplementary concept of police brutality.* Paper presented at the annual meeting of the Society of Multivariate Experimental Psychology, Albuquerque, N M. (cited in Lorr, Strack).

Goma-i-Freixanet, M., & Wismeijer, A. A. J. (2002). Applying personality theory to a group of police body-guards: A physically risky prosocial prototype? *Psicothema, 14*, 387-392.

Homant, J. R., Kennedy, D. B. & Howton, J. D. (1993). Sensation seeking as a factor in police pursuit. *Criminal Justice and Behavior, 20, (3)*, 293-305.

Hopper, M. (1977). Becoming a policeman: Socialization of cadets in a police academy. *Urban Life, 6*, 149-168.

Lester, D. (1983). Why do people become police officers: A study of reasons and their predictions of success. *Journal of Police Science and Administration, 11*, 170-174.

Levin, B. H., & Brown, W. E. (1975). Susceptibility to boredom of jailers and low enforcement officers. *Psycho-logical Reports, 36*, 190.

Meagher, S. & Yentes, N. (1986). Choosing a career in policing: A comparison of male and female perceptions. *Journal of Police Science and Administration, 14*, 320-327.

Próchniak, P. (2009). Polish Police Officers: Risk taking and Personality. *Journal of Police and Criminal Perso-nality, 24 (2)*, 104-109

Ragnella, A. J. & White, M. D. (2004). Race, gender, and motivation for becoming a police officer: Implica-tions for building a representative police department. *Journal of Criminal Justice, 32 (6)*, 501-513.

Tarng, M., Hsieh C. & Deng T. (2001). Personal background and reasons for choosing a career in policing: An empirical study of police students in Taiwan. *Journal of Criminal Justice, 29*, 45-56.

Trimpop, R. M. (1994). *The psychology of risk taking behavior.* Amsterdam: Elsevier Science.

Zuckerman, M. (1994). *Behavioral expressions and biosocial bases of sensation seeking.* New York, Cambridge: University Press.

SUMMARY

The aim of the present study was to identify the motives of policemen preparing for the peacekeeping mission in Kosovo. The sample consisted of 86 policemen in the preparing period (*M* age = 32.9, *SD* = 4.5). (For example: antiterrorists, pyrotechechnians, detectives.) The Motives for the Peacekeeping Mission Survey was used as a method of the study. It was found that policeman scored higher on motives concentrated on the personal needs: financial benefits, sensation seeking, achieving ambitious goals and discovering new places.

STRESZCZENIE

Celem badania było poznanie motywów udziału w misji pokojowej w Kosowie polskich policjantów z Jednostki Specjalnej Polskiej Policji. W badaniu wzięło udział 86 policjantów (*M* age = 32.9, *SD* = 4.5) (na przykład: antyterroryści, pirotechnicy i detektywi). Policjanci wypełnili Kwestionariusz Motywów udziału w Misji Pokojowej. Rezultaty badań wskazują na to, że policjanci przy wyjeździe na misję kierują się przede wszystkim własnymi potrzebami: korzyściami finansowymi, poszukiwaniem ryzyka, poszukiwaniem ambitnych celów czy poznawaniem nowych miejsc.

SAMMENDRAG

Undersøkelsen har hatt som målsetning å identifisere motivene til politifolk som forbereder seg til fredsbevarende oppdrag i Kosovo. Undersøkelsesgruppen besto av 86 politifolk i forberedelsesfasen (*M* alder = 32.9, *SD* = 4.5). (F.eks.: antiterrorister, pyroteknikere og etterforskere.) Undersøkelses-gruppen fikk utdelt spørreskjema om sine motiv for fredsbevarende oppdrag. Resultatene viste at politifolk skåret høyest på motiv som er konsentrert rundt selvet: økonomiske fordeler, spenningssøken, ute etter avanserte mål og kjennskap til nye steder.

DR. BEATA PAWLIK, PHD

Gdańsk University
Department of Economical and
Business Organizations' Psychology
ul. Bażyńskiego 4
Gdańsk80-952, Poland
E-mail: bpopielarska@wp.pl

THE MOTIVATIONAL ROLE OF THERAPY WITH THE USE OF A DOG IN THE PROCESS OF SUPPORTING CHILDREN'S DEVELOPMENT

'SUPPORTING DEVELOPMENT' IN THE ASPECT OF THERAPY WITH THE USE OF A DOG

Both in everyday language and in the scientific literature in relation to various developmental disturbances, we use the term "supportive development". This concept is composed of two terms: development and support. The word "development" occurs most often in the context of a particular biological or social system – an individual's development, understood as a holistic psychophysical system, but also a particular social group, nation or civilization.

Psychological development is understood as a process that increasing quantitative changes lead to qualitative changes, enabling the achievement of higher stages of development. Developmental changes are always progressive in nature. Both, traditional (Szuman, 1955) as well as modern concepts of development, stress the importance of individuality and individual activities in the process of progressive change. Tyszkowa (1988) recognizes the individual psychological development as a process of restructurisation and structurisation of an experience, whose driving force is the activity of the person.

The concept of helping/supporting the development implicitly assumes that the development does not proceed properly; it is disturbed and requires support. Supporting someone can be understood as giving reliance or support. Assisting and supporting means also coming to the rescue. Helping someone is related to a pro-social or even altruistic attitude of a human being (Feldman, 1985, p.252). Helping raises specific 'interpersonal interaction', consisting of "influencing": "Influence can be intentional and non-intentional, professional or not, positive or negative according to accepted values, etc. Therefore support is not possible without influence" (Kaja, 2002, p.13). In case of an abnormal development, the support is based on enabling the unit to achieve the optimum that will facilitate the adaptation processes of the individual with reference to its surroundings.

Therapy with a dog is a popular method of supporting treatment for people with disabilities, especially children. This method was also applied to healthy children, affected by discrete forms of developmental disorders, as well as the elderly, who suffer from old age and loneliness.

The views of some well-known therapists and the representatives of science greatly influenced the idea of using dogs in people's healing processes. In 1937, Sigmund Freud's daughter Anna noticed that the human-dog relationship is heavily laced emotionally and sentimentally. S. Freud and C.G. Jung, while working with the mentally ill, also found that associating with animals triggers certain projection mechanisms and positive emotions in patients. In Jungian therapy animals and animal symbols were the pretext for the interpretation of the archetypal content. In 1942, Kris and Bellac, creating the Children's Apperception Test, found that children more easily build an emotional bond with animals rather than with adult men (Masgutova, 2004).

One of the first people who described the psychotherapeutic value of animal rehabilitation, psychiatrist B. Levinson, who noticed that the contact of one of his patients with a dog, not only facilitated communication with the patient, but also improved and accelerated the healing process of the child. Levinson also made interesting observations on the progress of children with autism who have been in contact with their dogs. These children, playing with their pets, were more eager to establish relationships with people. Levinson called the therapy with the use of animals *Pet Therapy*. He believed that human contact with animals, contributes to achieving emotional balance, and also allows an individual to meet the primary needs of sensual contact (Levinson & Mallon, 1996). At this point, it becomes a legitimate question: Why a dog? A number of factors speak in favour of a dog in the role of a therapist: first of all, a dog is an easily accessible animal; it does not require great effort in its maintenance. Secondly, the dog is inextricably linked with the fate of man in socio-historical terms. Over the centuries, dogs have been used by people for various jobs, which contributed to the process of domestication of the dog. A dog, living forever in the human herd, has reached such a level of social development that mutual communication between it and a man is accurate, simple and direct. Choosing a dog for the role of a therapist is also based on its psychophysical conditions. A dog is an animal with a high level of intelligence, learns quickly and eagerly, and perceives the cooperation with a man as a natural aspect of its life and a value in itself. Moreover, it has a well-developed capacity for empathy and emotional expression, is socialized and easily interacts with a man. A dog also meets the contact and communicative conditions: it is one of the few animals that can establish long-term relation-ships with people, as the only animal in the world is able to establish eye contact with humans, and effectively communicate with humans using non-verbal communication (Knabit, 2005). It is a faithful and patient man's companion. Touching a dog gives birth to a positive sensory-emotional experience due to the type of coating (soft fur), and also because of the friendly behaviour of the dog. Thanks to these "properties" the dog is able to adopt a "phenomenological attitude" - being a part of nature itself; it treats "its" patient as a nature's component. Such an attitude allows full acceptance and tolerance towards the child. It also facilitates the socio-emotional "distance". Dogs are very keen observers. Nothing escapes their attention. They "seize" contact with humans with each and every of their senses. They are extremely sensitive to the "active reception" of human behaviour. They do not only listen carefully but also emphatically "absorb" the messages coming from a man (Śpiewakowska, 2009).

Therapy with a dog, as an innovative form of work with the sick man or child, is not classified as a direction associated with a specific therapeutic school or psychotherapy. At this point, it should be considered whether the mentioned form of development takes the form of therapy or whether it bears the hallmarks of the psychotherapeutic process. The word therapy comes from Greek *therapeia* and means care, treatment, but also care and support, and even refers to the behaviour associated with the worship. In the colloquial sense therapy equals treatment, referring to both the physical and mental aspect, using various methods and means. Psychotherapy, in the broadest sense, is understood as the impact and therapeutic agents, both psychological and environmental. In a narrower sense it includes the planned and systematic psychological impact, which aims to improve human mental functioning and to achieve its higher level of social adaptation. The word therapy in comparison to the concept of psychotherapy has a much wider significance, however, in relation to working in the system: dog-human/therapist-patient does not fully emphasize the psychological benefits of this form of cooperation. Using the word 'therapy' often draws attention to the biological effects associated with a particular form of treatment, not seeing the issues closely related to psychological problems, such as: motivation, self-esteem and self-evaluation associated with it, the state of emotional-affective processes, mental balance, etc. Therapy with a dog can become a source of positive psychological effect not only for the participant, who is the direct recipient, but also for their family. Illness of a child, especially one that is a permanent disability, is one of the factors that may destructively affect the entire family system. Family recognized as an interpersonal system is being harmed when one of its elements "does not work efficiently", causing an imbalance in the entire system. Care for a disabled child requires increased investment not only in the material sphere, but primarily in the psychological sphere, requiring from healthy family members constant endurance, patience, cheerfulness and positive attitude. For many parents having a disabled child is a source of personal unhappiness, interpreted in terms of life's failure. Many marriages that have a permanently sick child, goes through difficult crises and falls apart. Traditional psychotherapy tries to "change players" in the family system. Therapy with a dog is based on the belief that the "players" cannot be changed, but you can modify their attitudes and course of action in a situation which they found themselves in. Parents can be integrated towards a sick child by taking steps in that system: child-dog-parents (also included in the roles of therapists). Changing the attitudes of parents is difficult and requires long-term modeling and group interaction.

Returning to the main stream of the considerations, it can be noted that the ideas related to the form of therapy described in this article are close to the assumptions of humanistic psychotherapy, referring to the phenomenological philosophy of existential thought of Kierkegaard, Husserl, Heidegger, Jaspers, Binswanger, Sartre and Buber. For those involved in therapeutic work with a dog, as well as for psychologists representing the humanistic orientation, the subject of this therapy – the patient – is a value in itself. The measures taken are individual and are closely linked with the possibilities and values of the individual patient and their family system. The chief value guiding the undertaken work is to enable participants to achieve not only the ability to self-fulfill themselves, but also join the path of self-realization. Therapeutic tasks, consisting of carrying out a psychological contact are determined in accordance with the principle of updating and customizing the experience, "the processes are happening now."

The importance of contact in human development is emphasized by the authors who represent the humanistic orientation in psychology. Bugental (1978), in his excellent essay devoted to the assumptions of humanistic psychology notes that "the peculiar nature of man is expressed through his continuous remaining in relationships with other people. Humanistic psychology is always a man in his interpersonal systems" (Bugental, 1978).

The problem of human contact with the outside world was also one of the main topics of prof. Antoni Kepinski's considerations, who believed that relations with the world are the foundation of human personality: "As far as a human being is concerned, the matter of emotional contact with the environment, especially in the first years of life, undoubtedly plays a major role in the development of personality and in the further events of life" (Kepinski, 1985). People suffering from various forms of disability are often characterized by weak relationship with the surrounding reality. The use of 'contact' therapy (such a role is assigned to sessions with dogs) helps to establish communication with the environment. Sensual contact – a 'more elementary and primitive means of emotional communication than a word' can, however, meet basic human needs (Kratochvil, 1988).

There are two basic forms of therapeutic trainings with use of dogs. The first form is the "therapeutic play", which aims for the participant in the session to establish a touch and emotional contact with the dog-therapist. The second type of class is called "effective cooperation" and is the patient's realization of exercises involving a dog, which help to improve or regain health by a sick person (Kulisiewicz, 2009; 2011).

In classes with the use of dogs the following persons can participate:

- with developmental disorders
- mentally disabled
- after diseases or injuries leaving permanent traces in the psychophysical condition
- with visual or hearing impairments
- socially unadjusted
- single people living in nursing homes or hospices

Properly developed and implemented program of therapy with a dog may be favourable to the following results:
- reduction of muscle strain
- increasing the locomotive ability
- stimulation of motor skills
- improvement in the emotional-affective functioning
- stimulation of the mental development
- expanding the verbal skills and correcting speech defects
- development of social skills
- formation of character by taking responsibility for other class participants and for a dog
- increasing the motivation to perform rehabilitation exercises
- strengthening self-esteem
- enabling contact with the animal and the other participants
- integrating the family environment with a person participating in activities
- creating opportunities for fun
- establishing a natural relationship with the world.

Observations on the motivational role of therapy involving a dog in this article are the result of many years of work with disabled children attending the environmental day-room in Tczew, kindergartens and special schools in Sopot; and the cooperation with children with retarded motoric development as well as those emotionally impaired, in two kindergartens in Gdansk.

THE SITUATION OF A CHILD ENGAGED IN THE LONG-TERM THERAPY SUPPORTING DEVELOPMENT

Even for an adult who does not manifest any restrictions related to the understanding of their situation, the need to participate in long-term therapy is perceived as a serious difficulty. A child, especially the intellectually and physically disabled, is a particularly diffi-cult subject of a rehabilitation conduct. The exercises, which it should perform, give visible results when they are done carefully and systematically (Allen, 1972). Some exercises are related to overcoming the "guarding" reaction, e.g. before the physical pain, associated with stretching muscles, with the tiring exercises in suspended belts on the track, etc.

In particular, it is difficult to encourage children with intellectual disabilities, whose insight into their own is limited, to work systematically. These children often defend themselves against enhancing exercises because they do not understand their significance in relation to their own efficiency. What is more, children with normal mental development level are reluctant to take part in the process of rehabilitation. Exercises supporting the development of a child, as intellectual as motoric, are difficult and require patience, attention and commitment of the young patient.

By joining the therapeutic work with children, one must, first and foremost, take into account the properties of developmental period in which the child is located, a disorder that is the cause of taking the therapy up, as well as the type and nature of emotional-social relations, through which the child is associated with the immediate environment, primarily with his mother, father, siblings and other family members, peers, teachers, etc. Firstly, one must also make sure that the child is not afraid of contact with animals, especially with a dog. Many children are afraid of dogs, because their parents taught them to fear.

"Reversing" this nature by dog the therapist requires patience and gentleness. A child who is afraid of dogs is initially merely an observer of other children's play with the animals and its guides. It should only be included into activities after gaining confidence towards the pet and expressing their willingness to participate.

Anxiety and fear are strong demotivating factors in taking up therapeutic tasks. It is possible to observe that children participating in the classes do not only manifest fear but also anxiety. Fear can be tamed. It is associated mainly with the lack of experience with dogs or defectively formed attitude towards dogs, in which taking care has been confused with hostility towards these animals. Long-term and non-invasive establishing relationships with a dog, favors gaining trust towards and changing attitude towards it. It is much harder to overcome anxiety, which manifests itself by strong physiological reactions of the organism, as well as panic attacks. Both an adult and a child do not understand the sources of experienced anxiety. Many children, who took part in a therapy that was carried out with a dog, have been "rejected" by their parents because of illness. Parents, of course, deny such a thing, but the child's behavior exposes the actual state of family relationships. Horney (1982) sees the sources of fear in the fundamental psychological needs from early childhood, and especially in the state of deprivation of the need of love. Unconscious anxiety, in an emergency, usually causes excessive reaction which is strongly and negatively emotionally marked. Anxiety combines with hostility: "The relationship between anxiety and hostility is limited not only to the fact that hostility leads to fear. This process occurs in the opposite direction: when fear comes from a sense of danger, a defensive reaction in the form of hostility is formed" (Horney, 1982, p.63). Hostility and anxiety towards the world makes it impossible to take any form of therapy, in order to change behaviour. It requires a very consistent and patient-oriented procedure in order to reduce a negative emotional attitude. In the process of therapy with a dog, often quite a defensive attitude can be seen. The strongest form of this kind of destructive behavior could be observed in the case of a three-year old blind boy who was diagnosed with mental retardation. The boy has not left his playpen since he was born. He would fill the time by eating corn crisps and playing a musical box. His life was very monotonous and was brought to sleeping and two other routine habits: eating and pressing the music box. When he was three years old his mother, who was a single mom, decided, due to her professional situation, to give it to a specialist center for eight hours a day. The new situation was traumatic for the child. His crying was interrupted only by his crunching or by the sound of music. Moreover, it appeared that the child feels relatively safe only in the playpen, because, in a way, it became familiar only with its sensory properties. The child had never touched the other surfaces than the ones of the playpen. It did not experience in cognitive nor sensual manner all the "contact" areas which a healthy child experiences: flooring, carpeting, wall and various objects. All of these "obvious" stimuli evoked in him first state of panic, then a deep despair. The mother "detained" the boy in the playpen, as she was guided by fear, loneliness and feelings of helplessness, arising from having a disabled child. Instead of taking action in order to support the development of his son, in a way, that led to his unconscious secondary regression. Unknown world, the world "outside the playpens," was threatening to the boy and he responded to it with hostility and fear. Changing the situation of the child required, first of all, the psychological co-operation with the mother, in order to change her attitude towards herself and other people, and above all, to his own son. The next step was a slow introduction of the child to a "richer," cognitive world and gradual depriving it of the "routine" security tools: crisps and music box. First, off went the music a music box, because it's sound, and especially the frequency of the sound was unbearable for the other children, teachers and social workers. With time, the corn chips were replaced by other meals. After two months of daily work, the boy accepted the dog as a therapist.

As mentioned above, before taking the classes, it is important to recognize children's health situation. Most often, a therapy with the participation of a dog takes the form of group work. However, sometimes there are situations that require special care when performing tasks. Then the therapy should be of individual character. One should also remember that not all children can perform certain exercises. Therefore, the selection of children and therapeutic tasks and matching the right tasks with child's abilities are important.

During the classes a child should notice the friendly nature of therapy and become convinced that its problems are taken seriously, and that the therapy's participants are willing and able to help him. Actions taken should be conducive to its conviction that "everything that happens around him," results from an authentic, sincere and friendly interest in its problem, and not from necessity or obligation of "solving the problem.

When introducing a child into the world of dog the therapists, one need to proceed carefully, gently, with tact, in order to encourage the child to work. One should also obtain the approval of parents towards this form of treatment, through a detailed explanation of their purpose and therapeutic tools.

Masgutowa (2004), when quoting the opinion of another author (Slavin, 1950), stresses that in the case of children with developmental difficulties a phenomenon of "semantic barrier" occurs. It consists of not adopting the requirements and persistently not performing the tasks. "Semantic barrier" may manifest itself as a rejection of a man (a particular teacher, therapist) or the requirement posed to a child (a difficult exercise).

A child's situation is particularly difficult when it has no psychological support from loved ones. Most of the children participating in activities with the dog were deprived of "warmth". Parents were often ashamed of having a "sick" child, often hiding its existence from others. Children born into the world of permanent disability are usually deprived of natural contacts with peers. The situation is particularly dangerous when such a child is an only child. It is then left at the contact with a parent. The child feels lonely. As well as, parents of disabled children feel alone. They repeatedly exclude themselves from various social groups, since they lost the belief that their presence can be enriching and "significant" for others.

Disabled children reluctantly join in various therapeutic projects. Rehabilitation and compensatory-developing classes can be sometimes treated by some children as a source of pain, causing negativism, and even active resistance. The child's resistance can take a rather dramatic form, which favors the two types of destructive adults' behavior: the first behavior is associated with an attitude of submission to the child. It involves the withdrawal of the adult with from the taken decision (i.e. withdrawing from the selected type of therapy). The second behavior is antagonistic and consists of persistent "forcing", the continuation of treatment against the child's will. Both the surrender attitude and the "excessive consequences" attitude generate the negative effects in child's development: in both situations, the child actually does not participate in therapy, because passive participation (under pressure) does not favor progress and positive developmental changes. A story of a nine-year old boy suffering from autism that was signed up by parents for a behavioral therapy was an example of the destructive therapy. During the therapeutic training, encouragement in the form of counters, which appeared on every proper, (according to a program of treatment), reaction of the boy, was used. Unfortunately, the penalty consisting in "snapping" with the rubber band tied to the wrist of the child, when the designated task was performed unsatisfactorily, was applied. It is not difficult to foresee what has happened with the child after a few sessions: his resistance became active. He tossed about on the corridor's floor, and the therapists forced the boy to go into the room, which was a real "torture room" to him. During each session, he feared it and not controlling the physiological responses he defecated himself.

Children characterized by normal mental and physical development, who participated in the activities with a dog in Gdansk's kindergartens, were reluctant to take part in rhythmic activities with elements of educational kinesiology, because these tasks required a high attention and effort. A boy singing to himself during rehabilitation and music exercises, "Kasia goes, Stas goes, what do I care" was a humorous example of a "rebellious child".

THE MOTIVATIONAL ASPECT OF THERAPY WITH A DOG

Pedagogues, therapists and physiotherapists often emphasize the shortcomings in the motivational sphere, which make the proper performance of the enhancing exercises more difficult. Motivation is a set of forces that make people behave in certain ways (Moorhead & Griffin, 1998). In the process of motivation, three types of measures: compulsion, encouragement and persuasion can be distinguished. Compulsion consists in the subordination of a motivated individual by the motivating one, regardless of the interests and needs of the motivated. Encouragement includes an award, which is a consequence of the implementation of the expected behavior. Persuasion consists in an invasion of the emotional and rational sphere of a man, causing a certain behavior. Supporting the disturbed development should not, in any way, be based on a strategy of compulsion. Participation in the classes should be a consequence of the appropriate use of encouragements and gentle persuasion.

Problems in the child's active participation in a therapeutic program are conditioned by different causes (Wardaszko-Łysakowska, 1980). Deficits in the child's motivation are a major obstacle in taking up the therapy. Many children perceive the participation in therapy in terms of constraint – namely, against their will. The task of parents, guardians of the child, teacher or psychologist is to create or strengthen the child's motivation to work on their own problems or limitations. The second important reason is that, especially children with general developmental disabilities, show poor ability of expressing and verbalizing their mental states, emotions, anxieties or moods. In this case, the task of those involved in supporting child development is to identify causes of child behavior and mitigate the discomfort. A third factor complicating an active part in the rehabilitation of the child relates to reduced opportunities of obtaining insight into their own problems. Children do not have a well-developed capacity for self-observation and self-diagnosis. In difficult situations they apply defense mechanisms: projection, denial, avoidance, aggression, regression, or isolation. The task of the person conducting the therapy is to involve dialogue with the child, explaining the cause and effect relationships of their own health status and behavior. Fourth demotivator means limited children's ability (especially the youngest ones) in the reading of spoken messages but also those non-verbal (facial expression, mimicry, posture), originating from persons that conduct classes. An additional difficulty in awakening the excitation of being involved in therapeutic activities, derives from the unfavorable attitude of parents, who either do not know about the effects of therapeutic intervention or have lost hope for any improvement.

In psychology and other related disciplines one can find different approaches and models for the incitement of the motivation. The Experience gained while working with children suggests that effective motivational tools result from the theory based on the concept of reinforcement. The concept of reinforcement uses the concept of the causative behavior. There's a variety of measures serving to consolidate the causative behaviour: reward, punishment, avoidance and elimination. The strongest motivational tool is a positive reinforcement or reward. Strengthening behavior occurs as a consequence of the application of prizes immediately after performing the expected behavior. The award promotes establishing the behavior in the long term perspective, as well as builds a good atmosphere, favors mutual trust and starts the self-evaluation mechanism.

The use of negative reinforcement requires knowledge and pedagogical skills. Punishment, as a negative feedback of their own behavior, weakens this behavior, but it can also "lock" the child towards the therapeutic contact. Avoidance, consisting of reinforcing behavior by allowing the avoidance of undesirable consequences, requires a certain maturity and a good understanding of the social situation. This tool is difficult to apply to children, especially the children with intellectual disabilities. Elimination consists in the weakening of behavior by preventing the desired consequences (weakening of their undesirable behavior by not recognizing it or denial). The effectiveness of the last medium largely depends on the patience and diplomacy of the teacher and therapist. Therefore, in working with children one should focus on two motivational factors: reward and elimination, keeping in mind that their effectiveness largely depends on the adopted schedules of providing reinforcements. Studies on the conditions of effective motivation through reinforcement stress the importance and the role of reinforcement based on the procedure of variable frequency and variable relation, which make the subject operate in the area of motivational conditions, all the time.

Working with children, as well as opinions of other therapists engaged in activities involving dogs, demonstrated that a dog, in itself, is a motivation, of extraordinary attractiveness, in itself. Traditional motivational stimuli (praise, encouragement expressed by the word, granting the child "points" in the form of a counter, sun, etc.) are routine and are monotonous. Children have become accustomed to this type of reinforcements, and they cause no increase in activity aimed at accomplishing a specific task. The attractiveness of the motivational stimulus is conditioned by its uniqueness, which attracts, and by the fact that the stimulus is a source of pleasure. These criteria are met both by a dog and by the curriculum with its participation. Dog the therapist is reinforcement in itself (no need to acquire a number of "points" in order to get the prize). This award is alive and also carries the values of "advance-ment", for example, it gives a positive feedback to a child: through emotional contact indicated by licking, acceptance of a mutual hugging and petting. A dog is a reinforcing multi-sensory stimulus, influencing all the child's senses, which also affects the mental processes, especially the emotional and motivational ones. The dog is a particular reward, not requiring any "data processing" in the specialized areas of the cognitive system. Even the profoundly handicapped children understand the messages of dog the therapist that encode and reinterpret at the emotional level. The dog as a motivational stimulus can establish deep emotional contact, which contributes to the state of muscle relaxation, allowing the performance of the motivational rehabilitation activities. Another important feature of this type of reward is that the reinforcement happens not so much after a job, but often already during the course (e.g., under the influence of touching the dog's body, the muscles are relaxed and the child notices the improvement of its own functioning). Contact with a dog fulfills a rewarding role also regarding the theory of human needs. Sometimes, a disabled child suffers from a lack of friends and close emotional relationships – it simply suffers from loneliness and lack of love. In this sense, contact with a dog also acts as a motivational, namely, the dog-therapist allows the child to meet almost all the needs of creating a hierarchical system: the need for love, security, belonging, status (speaking of an impressive in terms of dog breeds and skills dog), and even self-realization: thanks to therapy, a child learns the principles of social influence and reaches designated by the program activities, tasks).

The motivational nature is also present in the curriculum of the activities involving dog the therapist. As mentioned in the first part, the therapy involving a dog can be realized in the form of "therapeutic play" or "effective cooperation". The first form is simply learning through play, focused primarily on the development of the child's social skills. Playing with the dog in the treatment group consists of, among others, to play hide and seek (the child is hidden e.g. under a therapeutic scarf) and the dog is looking for it, or walking the dog on a leash, on giving dog treats, throwing the ball to a dog, which it fetches. Particular games are performed in a certain order, which teaches children the principle of order and the principle of fair share in the fun. Participation in the game becomes an unintentional process of learning social rules. Children participate in such learning very willingly, and learn much faster than during the traditional classes.

"Effective cooperation" is associated with the performance of difficult exercises ranging from the locomotion and motorics to speech disorders area. Some exercises are really annoying and are associated with the child's great effort. For the physically disabled children, the tasks connected with the necessity of movement are not easy, because trying to creep or crawl causes enormous physical strain and weariness. Despite of the limitations, children eagerly make an effort, if the destination is a finishing line, at which there is a dog that they can annex for themselves for a moment. Motoric exercises require concentration and patience. Children work the rehabilitation devices with resistance; on the other hand, they gladly open the pockets on dog's clothes and take the treats out of it. As well as, they happily take part in learning how to put on a leash, tie a bow on the dog's neck, to feed the dog with "small treats" or to brush dog's hair. All these tasks are supposed to improve skills related to the so-called small motorics. During the therapy with a dog, children have the opportunity to exercise the speech therapy tasks. Such exercises are a serious problem, particularly for children with profound developmental disabilities. When accompanied by a dog, the job is done much more efficiently, because many tasks are fun, such as exercise of prolonged vowels which becomes an imitation of a dog howling or yawning. Repeating the difficult sound "R" is simply an imitation of growling.

Playing with the dog, especially walking the dog on a leash and giving simple commands, gives the child an opportunity to "have a control over events," which has a positive impact on the development of its personality and social skills.

A dog and therapy with a dog fulfill the motivational role also due to the fact that contact with dog the therapist is a natural phenomenon, characteristic for the childhood needs, and what is more, playing with the dog are often compatible with the children's interest in the animal world.

Proper conditions of therapy serve to shape the motivation to work, in order to improve the life's quality of a sick child– the care recipient. Before starting it, one must take care of hygiene and aesthetics of the dog, as well as the friendly character of the room in which the course is planned to take place. Even the most "taught" dog that looks messy will not evoke an adequate psychological response conducive to carrying out exercises. As mentioned above, external conditions like clean, bright, spacious room, with soft lining, having a place to sit and spatial conditions in which the child can practice, and in which a dog or a group of dogs can move freely.

Here are few cases, illustrating the influence of dog the therapist on behaviour of children included in therapy.

Krysia (9 years old). The girl was diagnosed with cerebral palsy and mental retardation of a high degree. Before the classes with the dog, Krysia presented herself as a sad child, prone to go into her shell. In Krysia's case, it is visible that she has serious problems with the regulation of muscle tone making the movement impossible. Krysia, most willingly, spent her time sitting, supported by a pedagogue or in a wheelchair strapped with additional belts. Classes with a dog were an important element of her experience. In the beginning, Krysia was very afraid of a dog and reacted to him with scream. After few sessions Krysia not only tamed the dog (Trapper), but continually wanted to stay in its company. In order to meet her need, she had to learn to crawl towards Trapper and to follow him on the floor. In this way, she practiced locomotion and strengthening the arms which is necessary in the future controlling of the wheelchair. As a reward, she could cuddle Trapper and lie down on it.

Daniel (9 years old). With no definitive medical diagnosis (autism?); a boy severely impaired, poorly developed speech - both parents are deaf-and-dumb; he gives an impression that he lives in his own world, shows anxiety – when seeing Trapper he ran away and hid behind the wardrobe. After few classes with the dog, Daniel underwent a visible transformation. Not only did he greet and play with the dog, but also, most of all, he began to participate in the classes. It was amazing that one day he began to sing a song about a dog: " I found him in the garden when he was a puppy; he looked as forty nine sorrows and kind of scruffy. So tiny and so thin, he had nobody to let him in. So I took him, gave him home and now I've got a mongrel of my own".

Pawel (14 years old). A boy with autism and mental retardation of a high degree has difficulty with controlling emotions, violent, lives in his own world. Pawel's first meeting with Trapper caused a panic attack. After a few weeks the situation has dramatically changed. Initially, Paul's contact with the dog consisted in Pawel stroking the outline of a dog in the air, then in stroking it with therapist's hand, and then... Then he rested his forehead on the forehead of the lying dog, and lay together on the floor, breathing evenly, for almost an hour. Pawel opened up a lot and began to speak of himself in first person. So far, Pawel's participation in therapeutic activities, such as behavioral therapy, was associated with the boy's strong resistance, who would, upon hearing that classes begin, lay down on the floor and defecate. Therapy with a dog was unintentionally changing the boy, and the changes were visible and permanent.

Rafal (14 years old). With a Down syndrome, a moderate handicap; a very introverted boy, when he was a small child, his dog died and since then he spent his days under the table, being very lonely. He would isolate himself and would not undertake any activity at school. When we met Rafal, the boy did not speak at all, and due to his age, he was not receiving any help in the form of speech therapy. From the first meeting it was known that "things will be happening". When he saw Trapper he walked towards him and suddenly he spoke. In a short time he sent simple commands to the dog: "sit", "hill", and „paw". After one year, Rafal went to an individual sessions with a speech therapist.

Mariusz (10 years old). A boy, who was modestly handicapped, very tense and aggressive towards others, seemed deeply wounded and unhappy; the school pedagogue suspected sexual abuse of the boy. Mariusz could not work in a group. He showed selfishness and antisocial behavior. For the teachers, working with him was ungrateful and unpleasant. However, activities with the dog resulted in Mariusz learning to accept the group norms and waiting patiently for his turn to play with the dog.

Darek (17 years old). With a high degree of handicap, he hardly understood human speech, he did not speak himself, and he would sit in a chair and howl. One day the dog could not stand it so he sat down in front of Darek and barked. It sounded like: "Enough is enough, shut up, okay?" Since then, Darek stayed calm in the presence of the dog.

Alicja (5 years old). A girl of a proper general development, but very loud and excitable. Teachers suspected that she has hypoacusia. The medical examination did not confirm the conjecture. During the session Alicja was becoming quieter. One day, she took Trapper aside and whispered something in his ear. Then she told about this secret to a therapist, who was the dog's guide. It turned out that Alicja feels unhappy because of difficult domestic situation. Activities involving the dog allowed the whole family to work with a psychologist.

The above mentioned stories illustrate the motivational aspect of the dog's presence during exercises. Therapy involving a dog consists primarily in the involvement of children in taking the following: locomotive, motoric, cognitive-educational and socio-emotional tough challenges. Presence of the dog as a therapist, as such, awakes an increased need for activity in a child. In the presented form of work with a child, all the positive child's behaviours (not just correctly completed tasks). A dog's guide and supervising pedagogue reward a child for making an attempt towards the given exercise. Having personal contact with a dog the therapist is a reward.

CONCLUSION

The paper provided a discussion on the three aspects of a method supporting the disturbed development, namely, a therapy involving a dog.

The first theme is an attempt to classify the methods of cooperation with the child to the "official" currents of contemporary psychology. The author of this article argues that the principles of working with a disabled child that is accompanied by dog the therapist and human the therapist are consistent with a holistic approach to individual's problem, which is characteristic of psychologists representing humanistic orientation in the way of understanding human problems and the way of working with a human. In therapy, working tools, consisting in the use of positive reinforcement, are "borrowed" from the theory of learning. Therapeutic relationship between a child and dog the therapist and a professional dog's guide – a therapist – resembles the "Me – You" relationship in Gestalt therapy. However, trying to recognize child's problems, both in terms of psyche and somatics, resembles biosynthesis, aimed to achieve integration between body and psyche. Therapy with a dog is a method of treatment which is oriented so that the child experiences somatic health symptoms, such as: regular, rhythmic breathing and proper muscle tone. This form of working with a child also provides the regulation of basic psychological processes, which include: developing the skill of making and maintaining contact with another human being, improving the abilities of expressing positive feelings. Furthermore, contact with dog the therapist helps to get rid of anxiety, by experiencing the state of security "on the biological level"

What follows is that, treatment with a dog is "rooted" in the various schools of psychology; however, the humanistic orientation states the "key root" of this form of working with the sick man.

Another important topic is the situation of a physically and intellectually disabled child, who is the most frequent recipient of this form of supporting the abnormal development. Children, who for various reasons are developing less, very often find themselves in a very difficult emotional and social situation. As children of a 'worse god' have no peer-environment. Another source of a sick child's suffering derives from taking part in various forms of rehabilitative and therapeutic activities that require strength, commitment and character to fight the physically experienced pain.

It also happens that parents show the attitude of rejection or being tired of having a sick family member. The sick child's lot is often characterized by a sense of alienation and loneliness. As well as, parents of the sick children (these are usually single mothers), are experiencing a deep loneliness, due to which they make self-exclusion from the family and other social groups, in which they were raised, because of lack of support and lack of understanding for their situation.

The third subject undertaken in this paper is the motivational aspect of therapy with a dog. Participation of the dog in classes causes an increase of the exercises' attractiveness, so that children, perceive difficult and monotonous tasks as fun.

Both the dog as a therapeutic stimulus and the curriculum are stimulating and motivating children to work. The dog's participation makes the arduous training fun, and the tasks undertaken are rewarded not only by strengthening the behaviour in accordance with the "after" procedure, but already in the performance of tasks, which in itself becomes a pleasure.

Reinforcement is coded here in a multisensory way, because contact with dog the therapist is realized in all senses and at all levels of the child's psyche.

Therapeutic relationships with a dog are also motivating because the dog expends the children's interest of a world, and frolics with a dog are characteristic of the childhood age.

Therapy with the dog, including the integration of family environment around a sick child, also serves a motivational role for parents, inviting them to change their own attitudes and programs of their behaviors in the face of the chronic illness of the child. Parents' participation in the activities at the rehabilitation center and organization of integration camps, thanks to which they get to know the problems of their children better, not only reinforce new attitudes but also valuable behaviors. Through joint meetings, parents have a chance to create specific groups of support - not only the one of a psychological nature, but most importantly, the one consisting in providing assistance in specific life-situations.

Despite of the numerous benefits of the activities with a dog, there are few centers in Poland, "allowing" dogs to work with children. It is particularly difficult to carry out such activities in hospital wards, where young patients are being treated. Dogs are perceived and treated there as an epidemiological "threat", and yet, contact with a friendly pet motivates a child to a faster recovery.

When making a summary of the presented study, it is worth noting that children, regardless of age, health status, level of intellectual development and social origin, very easily tame animals, especially dogs. In contact with dogs, they find primal ways of communication that open different developmental blockades. It is worth to mention an about a few years old girl, a Romany, who was found abandoned on one of the Polish railway stations. After completion of legal procedures, she found refuge in the care center. Contact with her was extremely difficult, because she was showing features of mutism. One day she was invited to join activities involving dogs. When she saw a flock of friendly dogs, she clung to one of them, and suddenly, began to speak. It appeared that she knew Polish language, but it took - a "professional" - unusual - therapist, for the child to open up.

Long-term practice with children proves that therapy involving a dog is a valuable method for stimulating the child's overall development, especially by method which favors progress in the emotional and social development, as well as, the development of personality.

REFERENCES

Allen, R. M. (1972). Children's cerebral palsy. J.F. Garret & E.S. Levine (eds.). *Psychological Practice in rehabilitation of disabled [Dziecięce porażenie mózgowe. Praktyka psychologiczna w rehabilitacji inwalidów]*. Warszawa: PZWL.

Bugental, J. F. T. (1978). In search of authenticity [W poszukiwaniu autentyczności]. K. Jankowski (ed.). *Break-through in Psychology. (Przełom w psychologii)* Warszawa: Czytelnik.

Feldman, R. S. (1985). *Social Psychology. Theories, Research, and Applications.* Mc Graw-Hill Publisher.

Horney, K. (1982). *The Neurotic Personality of our Time. [Neurotyczna osobowość naszych czasów]* Warszawa: PWN.

Kaja, B. (2002). The role of philosophy in supporting human development, the conditions necessary and possible sphere of realization of functions to support the development. [Role filozofii we wspomaganiu rozwoju człowieka-warunki konieczne i możliwe sfery realizacji funkcji wspierania rozwoju]. *Psychologia rozwojowa, VII, 1.*

Kępiński, A. (1985). *Melancholia [Melancholia].* Warszawa: PZWL.

Knabit, L. (2005). *Do animals have souls?* Kraków: Wydawnictwo Nemrod.

Kulisiewicz, B. (2009). *Pet Therapy in supporting the improvement of science and technology reading [Dogoterapia we wspomaganiu nauki I usprawnianiu techniki czytania].* Kraków: Impuls.

Kulisiewicz, B. (2011). *Hello darling [Witaj piesku].* Kraków: Impuls.

Kratochvil, S. (1988). *Issues of group psychotherapy [Zagadnienia grupowej psychoterapii]* Warszawa: PWN.

Levinson, B. M & Mallon, G. P. (1996). *Pet-Oriented Child Psychotherapy.* Springfield: Charles C Thomas Publisher LTD.

Masgutova, S. (2004). Role of pet therapy in the emotional rehabilitation of children with developmental diffi-culties. [Rola dogoterapii w emocjonalnej rehabilitacji dzieci z trudnościami w rozwoju] *CZE-NE-KA*, 4.

Masgutova, S. (2004). *Brain Exercise – an easy and enjoyable method of learning. [Gimnastyka mózgu - metoda łatwego i radosnego uczenia się]* Warszawa: Oficyna Wydawniczo-Poligraficzna-„Adam".

Moorhead, G. & Griffin, R. W. (1998). *Organizational behaviour: Managing people and organizations.* Boston: Houghton Miffin.

Szuman, S. (1955). The *role of action in the development of a small child [Rola działania w rozwoju małego dziecka]* Warszawa: Ossolineum.

Śpiewakowska, B. (2009). *Now I'm on the rainbow bridge. [Teraz jestem na tęczowym moście]* Kraków: Zysk i S-ka Wydawnictwo.

Tyszkowa, M. (1988). *Human psychological development throughout life. Theoretical and methodological issues. [Rozwój psychiczny człowieka w ciągu życia. Zagadnienia teoretyczne i metodologiczne].* Warszawa: PWN.

Wardaszko-Łysakwoska, H. (1980). *Group therapy in psychiatry. [Terapia grupowa w psychiatrii].* Warszawa: PZWL.

SUMMARY

The article presents the therapy with the dog in terms of motivational theory of reinforcement. The first part of the work is the characteristic of this form of supporting the child's development. The second part presents the issues of motivation of intellectually and physically disabled children in the context of necessity of realizing the rehabilitation activities. Attention was drawn to the plight of the child as the rehabilitation services' receiver. This section presents the motivational nature of classes with a dog. Another part of the paper contains a description of the selected cases of this form of working with children in Poland.

STRESZCZENIE

Artykuł prezentuje ujęcie metody terapii z wykorzystaniem psów, w ramach motywacyjnej teorii wzmocnienia. Pierwsza część pracy jest ogólną charakterystyką tego rodzaju wspierania rozwoju dziecka. Druga część prezentuje aspekty motywacji dzieci z intelektualnymi i fizycznymi niepełnosprawnościami, w kontekście konieczności rehabilitacji. Tu autor podkreśla ważność chęci dziecka do współpracy jako odbiorcy usługi rehabilitacji. Rozdział ten pokazuje motywacyjną naturę zajęć terapeutycznych z wykorzystaniem psów. W ostatniej części autor opisuje wybrane przypadki terapii dzieci z udziałem psów na terenie Polski.

SAMMENDRAG

Artikkelen tar for seg bruk av hund i terapi med begreper fra forsterkende motivasjonsteori. Den første delen er en beskrivelse av hvordan denne metoden kan være til hjelp i barnets utvikling. Den andre delen presenterer spørsmålet om motivasjon av psykisk og fysisk funksjonshemmede barn i sammenheng med nødvendige rehabiliterende aktiviteter. Oppmerksomheten var rettet mot barnet som mottaker av rehabilitering, og presenterer grupper av barn i motivasjonelt miljø med hund. Artikkelens andre del inneholder beskrivelser av utvalgte *eksempel* på hvordan man arbeider med barn på denne måten i Polen.

NOTES ABOUT THE AUTHORS

ALEKSANDROVICH, Maria – PhD, Doctor of Psychology, speciality Correctional Psychology (2004), winner of the National Academy of Sciences of Republic of Belarus Award (1997), holder of the Queen Jadwiga Scholarship, Jagiellonian University, Krakow, Poland (2001 and 2003), holder of the scholarship of Government of Poland for Young Scientists, Gdansk University, Gdansk, Poland (2003-2004), winner of the honourable scholarship of University of Genoa, Genoa, Italy (2005), holder of the Advanced Practitioner III level of Veronica Sherborne Developmental Movement, Gdansk, Poland (2006) participant of the Program of Academic Exchanges of LLP-Erasmus, Finnmark University College, Alta, Norway (2010 and 2012), member of the International Society of Studying of Behavioral Development (ISSBD), member of the European Council of High Abilities (ECHA), member of the American Psychological Association (APA). Now she is Associate Professor and the Head of the Department of Psychology at Pomeranian University, Slupsk, Poland and the Guest Professor at the Finnmark University College, Alta, Norway. Author of 3 books and over 50 scientific articles.

BAUGER, Lars – Master of Psychology from the University of Tromsø (2011). He has worked as a research assistant and lecturer at the University of Tromsø and Finnmark University College between 2011 and 2012. Since 2013 been he is employed as a PhD student at Telemark University College, where his research project investigates good mental health among senior citizens.

DAHL, Dagmar – PhD and M.A., Doctor of Sport Sciences from the Norwegian School of Sport Sciences, Scholarship from the Norwegian Research Council. Educated in Sport Sciences, Biology, Nordic Studies, Pedagogic, Psychology and Philosophy from Universities in Berlin, Kiel and Hagen/Germany. Main fields of research are "Sports, Ethics and Religion" and "Swimming in pedagogical and philosophical perspective". International research cooperations and presentations including several publications. Member of the IAPS (International Association for the Philosophy of Sports) and the DVS (German Association for Sports Sciences). Member of the Editorial Board of the International Journal of Religion and Sport. Since 2010 Associate Professor for Sports at Finnmark University College, cooperated with Tromsø University/ Norway.

KARDAŚ-GRODZICKA, Emilia – Master of Psychology; Graduate in Social Science Faculty at the University of Gdańsk; Nowadays she is working as an Assistant at the Department of Psychology at Pomeranian University, Slupsk, Poland. Her research interests involve psychological aspects of senility, question about quality of life and family psychology.

MURAWSKA, Ewa – PhD, Doctor of Pedagogic. Her main scientific interests are forming of adolescents' identity, identity of the teacher, as well as the phenomenon of power and resistance in educational relations. Nowadays she is working as Assistant Professor at the Department of General Pedagogic and Basics of Education at Psychology at Pomeranian University, Slupsk, Poland.

PASIKOWSKI, Sławomir – PhD, Doctor of Pedagogic, Master of Psychology. His main scientific interests are Methodology of Social Science as well as the phenomenon of power and resistance in educational relations. Nowadays he is working as Assistant Professor at the Department of Psychology at Pomeranian University, Slupsk, Poland.

PAWLIK, Beata – PhD, Doctor of Psychology, Assistant Professor at the University of Gdansk. Author of the first book dedicated to the therapy with dog in Poland. Member of the Scientific Council of the Association CZE-NE-KA, which deals with the promotion of the development of dog therapist. Her research interests related not only to clinical psychology, but also with the problems of social exclusion, economic psychology and cultural anthropology. The author of three books about homelessness and violence among women. Vice-President PANACEA Society which is providing assistance to the homeless.

PENSGAARD, Anne Marte – Professor in sport at The Norwegian University of Sport in Oslo. She has a joint position at the Norwegian School of Sport Sciences, department of Coaching and Psychology and head of Sport Psychology Services at the Norwegian Olympic Training Center. Her main research focuses are motivation and coping with stress at the elite level, and later also research involving Mindfulness and mental training among extreme performance participants. She has been working as applied sport psychologist for nearly two decades and been accredited sport psychologist at five Olympic Games and numerous World Cups and European Championships. She has more than 40 international publications and also produced several mental training audio programs (the latest together with world known jazz musician Bugge Wesseltoft), a mental training DVD and authored several books.

PRÓCHNIAK, Piotr – PhD, Doctor of Psychology, Senior Lecturer at the Department of Psychology at Pomeranian University, Slupsk, Poland. His primary interest is risk taking behavior. He is author of four books on this subject: *Risk taking behavior and sense of life, Teleological-temporal extension of risk activity, Psychological aspects of functioning policemen preparing to the peace mission in Kosovo, Adventure seekers in extreme weather* as well as numerous articles in this field. His current research interests include coping with wilderness.

SURINA, Iryna – Professor, the Dean of the Faculty of the Education and Filosophy and the Head of the Department of Sociology at Pomeranian University, Slupsk, Poland. Her scientific interests concentrate around questions of sociology of young people, sociology of education, ethno-sociology and ethno and social pedagogic. Author of three monographs, seven textbooks and scripts and co-author of six monograph in Russian language, editor of several scientific books concerning the questions of social pedagogics, as well as the author of numerouse articles in Polish, Russian and Ukrainian languages. She also worked as scientific supervisor for two doctoral students, who have been successfully defender (Russia, 2003; Poland, 2009) and as a reviewer of seven doctoral theses (Russia, 1998-2002).

THOMASSEN, Tor Oskar – Associate Professor at Finnmark University College (from1994), institute of sport, associate professor 2 at the University of Nordland, Sport Department 2006-2010, associate professor at The Regional Competence Center for Sport and Health North, 2011-2013, winner of the scientific price at Finnmark University College in 2005, head coach in ski jumping and combined skiers in Finnmark 1981-1994, head coach of Alta men Soccer Team 1. div, 2001-2003, head coach of elite cross country Team Finnmark, 2007-2011, member of the North-Norwegian Olympic Training Center with specialized area in mental training and physical training and testing, research area since 1992 on motivation, physical and mental training, testing and performance.

WAALER, Rune – Associate Professor in friluftsliv (Sports and Outdoorlife), Department of Sports and Science at the Finnmark University College, Alta, Norway. He worked 15 years as a teacher in friluftsliv in the primary and secondary school, in the Norwegian folk high school and in the adult education. Speciality in research and teaching is Self-Determination Theory, public use of common land in Finnmark and Norway, dog mushing and mountaineering. Experience with friluftsliv in Europe and the Arctic, did an early crossing of Norway by skies from south to north (1982). Author of four chapters in three books, two scientific articles and over 10 scientific reports.

ZOGLOWEK, Herbert – PhD, Doctor of Philosophy, Master of Pedagogic. Teacher training education at the Pedagogical University of Hagen and University of Dortmund, Germany; thereafter two years work teacher in primary school. 1981-1992 research fellow at the sports institute of the University of Dortmund. 1985 masterdegree in pedagogics, 1993 doctordegree in sports pedagogic at the University of Dortmund. Since 1992 associated professor at the Finnmark University College in Alta, Norway. 2004/05 research fellow at the University of Education in Weingarten, Germany; 2007 Guestlecturer at Riga Teacher Training Academy in Riga, Latvia. Since 2007 guestlecturer at the University of Education in Ludwigsburg, Germany and in the academic year 2009/10 substitution professor at the University of Education in Ludwigsburg. Since 2010 professor II at the Pomeranian University in Slupsk, Polen. His main teaching and research fields are professionalism of P.E. teacher, didactics of ball games and experiental education. In these subjects he is author of three books and a plenty of articles and chapters in books.

Erziehungswissenschaft

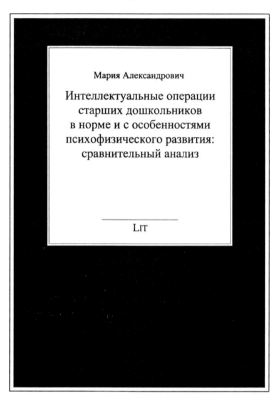

Мария Александрович

Интеллектуальные операции старших дошкольников в норме и с особенностями психофизического развития: сравнительный анализ

LIT

Maria Aleksandrovich
Intellektualnye operacii starshih doshkolnikov v normie i s osobennostyami psihofizicheskogo razvitiya: sravnitelnyi analiz
Bd. 66, 2012, 136 S., 39,90 €, br., ISBN 978-3-643-90248-1

LIT Verlag Berlin – Münster – Wien – Zürich – London
Auslieferung Deutschland / Österreich / Schweiz: siehe Impressumsseite